THE COUNCIL OF CHALCEDON AND

THE ARMENIAN CHURCH

By the Same Author

A Brief Introduction to Armenian Christian Literature
The Witness of the Oriental Orthodox Churches
The Armenian Church in Contemporary Times
The Armenian Christian Tradition in Iran

THE COUNCIL OF CHALCEDON AND THE ARMENIAN CHURCH

KAREKIN SARKISSIAN

*Prelate, Armenian Apostolic Church
of America*

A PUBLICATION OF
The Armenian Church Prelacy
NEW YORK

Library of Congress Cataloging in Publication Data

Sarkissian, Karekin, Bp.
    The Council of Chalcedon and the Armenian Church.

    Bibliography: p.
    Includes indexes.
      1. Armenian Church.   2. Chalcedon, Council of,
451.   I. Title.
BX126.2.S25 1975   281'.62   75-28381

To the
beloved memory of His Holiness
ZAREH I
Catholicos of the Great House of Cilicia
(1915–1963)
In humble recognition of his sacrifice for the
Armenian Church and Nation

CONTENTS

PREFACE TO THE SECOND EDITION

The Prelacy of the Armenian Apostolic Church of America, Eastern Diocese, considers it important to publish a second edition of the scholarly work *The Council of Chalcedon and the Armenian Church*, by Archbishop Karekin Sarkissian, Prelate of our Church.

The book, originally published in London in 1965 by the Society for Promoting Christian Knowledge (SPCK), has been out of print for the last four years. We are very grateful to the SPCK for assigning the publication rights to us.

The Council of Chalcedon and the Armenian Church is widely known in British theological circles and in Europe. It has been reviewed in many scholarly periodicals in more than eight languages and is included in bibliographies of reference works on Armenia, on the Council of Chalcedon, and on Christology.

Here in the United States, it deserves to be more widely circulated, for it has much to contribute, not only in Armenological circles but also in theological seminaries and universities, to a better understanding of the historical and doctrinal place of the Armenian Church in Christendom. For a variety of reasons, theological and historical, the Armenian Church took the position of rejecting the Council of Chalcedon. What were the significant stages in the process of that rejection? Where can one find accurate documentation of the issues? Archbishop Sarkissian deals with these questions ably and with scholarly thoroughness. His Grace also states very clearly the present-day relevance of the theme of his study, both in his own Foreword and in the Epilogue, "Looking Forward: Some Conclusions and Considerations."

We would like to draw the reader's attention to two other articles which His Grace has published on the same issue: "The Ecumenical Problem in Eastern Christendom" (*Ecumenical Review*, the official quarterly of the World Council of Churches,

Geneva, Switzerland, Vol. XII, No. 4, July 1960, pp. 436-454); and "The Doctrine of the Person of Christ in the Armenian Church" (*Greek Orthodox Theological Review,* published by the Holy Cross Theological Seminary, Brookline, Massachusetts, Vol. X, No. 2, Winter 1964-65, pp. 108-121).

We recommend this volume and the articles just mentioned to everyone concerned with ecumenism, with Christianity, with the Armenian Church, and Armenian studies in general, in the sincere hope that this publication will serve the ecumenical cause and provide a better understanding of the Armenian Church.

Executive Council
Armenian Apostolic Church of America,
Eastern Diocese

New York, New York
August 27, 1975

FOREWORD

This book was written five years ago as a thesis for the degree of B. Litt. in the University of Oxford.

The text has undergone no substantial change since then. The only addition has been the last chapter, in which I have tried to draw up certain conclusions with an ecumenical perspective and I have indicated some general lines for future studies concerning the historical and theological situations subsequent to and closely related to the period and the problems under study in this treatise.

I need not emphasize the importance of a study treating the early christological controversies which have had a permanent effect on the Christian Churches, particularly in the East. In fact, the clash between the two main traditions of christological thinking in the early Church, usually described as the "Alexandrian and Antiochene Schools", interwoven as it was with other factors of personal, ecclesiastical, and political nature, finally resulted after the Council of Chalcedon (A.D. 451) and particularly in the first half of the sixth century in the formation of two distinct, separate groups of Churches within the fold of Eastern Christendom: the *Chalcedonian Churches* under the protection of the Byzantine Empire, and the *anti-Chalcedonian Churches* within or outside the Byzantine Empire with a strong tendency towards an independent status of life. The latter group of Churches, mistakenly and misleadingly often depicted as "Monophysite Churches"—i.e. the Syrian, Coptic, Ethiopian, and Armenian Churches—have continuously maintained firm their doctrinal position throughout their history. The Churches of Byzantine tradition and origin have recognized them for many centuries as heretical or schismatic Churches. But thanks to sincere and serious attempts made in mutual understanding and in an atmosphere free from polemical heat and historical prejudices many of the misunderstand-

ings have fallen away. Owing to the present ecumenical spirit
that breathes in the Christian Churches all over the world, these
two groups of Churches have come to recognize their unity in
faith in the very depth of their christological confession. Fears of
heresy or alienation from Christian truth that lay behind the
minds of the leading theological figures of these Churches have
disappeared in the course of their long experience of Christian
faith and life in history. Political and other related factors have
disappeared equally. Recently, some positive signs are emerging
with regard to the possibility of mutual understanding and recovery of the lost sense and state of unity or communion. Thus,
the study of the Council of Chalcedon has become an item of
genuine interest at the present time. My sincere belief is that any
objective and deep-searching inquiry into the history and theology
of Chalcedon and post-Chalcedon may be a help towards a
deeper understanding of the most essential area of our common
heritage of Christian faith: christology.

It is with this desire in heart and with this view in mind that I
present this work to its readers, who will find a fuller presentation
of the nature and the scope of this study in the Introduction that
follows.

Before concluding this brief word of opening, I should like to
express my feelings of joy and gratitude in thanking many of my
friends who in one way or another have helped towards the pre-
paration and publication of this book. First of all, I should say a
special word of thankful recognition in memory of my Super-
visor, the Reverend C. S. C. Williams, the late Chaplain of Mer-
ton College, Oxford, whose constant support and help have meant
so much to me and have contributed so greatly to the improvement
of my work. My hearty thanks are due also to the Right Reverend F. J. Taylor, Principal of Wycliffe Hall (now the Lord
Bishop of Sheffield), who provided me with all the facilities for
quiet study in Wycliffe Hall where I had the pleasure of sharing
in the life of Anglican theological students for two years. I take
much pleasure in thanking my examiners, the Reverend Dr H.
Chadwick, Regius Professor of Divinity in Oxford University

and Dr C. J. F. Dowsett, Lecturer in Armenian in the School of Oriental and African Studies of London University, who carefully read the text and made valuable suggestions at the same time encouraging me to publish the work. Finally, it is with deep satisfaction and appreciation that I should like to express my thanks to the Calouste Gulbenkian Foundation as well as to the Harold Buxton Trust for their generous financial contribution towards the publication of the book.

KAREKIN SARKISSIAN

Antelias, Lebanon,
25 November 1964.

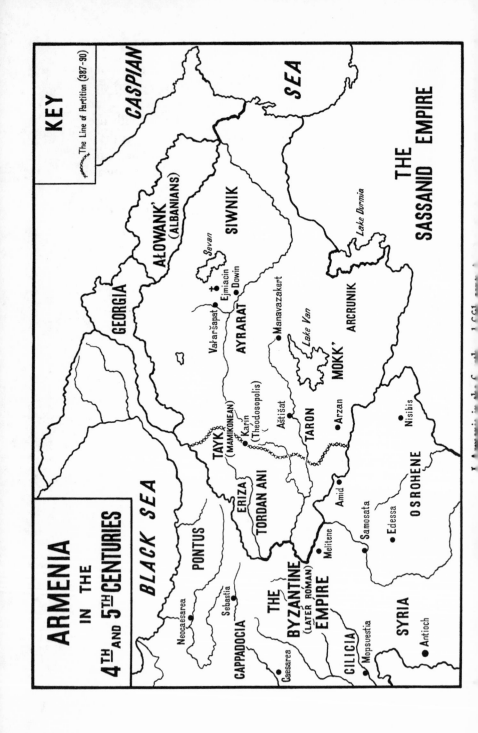

ARMENIA
IN THE
4TH AND 5TH CENTURIES

KEY

~~~~ The Line of Partition (387-90)

BLACK SEA

CASPIAN SEA

CAPPADOCIA

Caesarea •
Sebastia •
Neocaesarea •

PONTUS

THE
BYZANTINE
(LATER ROMAN)
EMPIRE

CILICIA

Mopsuestia •

SYRIA

Antioch •

Melitene •

ERIZA

TORDAN ANI

TAYK'
(MAMIKONEAN)

Karin
(Theodosopolis) •

Aštišat •

TARON

Amid •

Samosata •

OSROHENE

• Edessa

GEORGIA

ALOWANK'
(ALBANIANS)

Sevan

Valaršapat •
† Ejmiacin
• Dowin

AYRARAT

SIWNIK'

Manavazakert •

Lake Van

MOKK'

Arzan •

Nisibis •

ARCRUNIK'

Lake Durmia

THE
SASSANID EMPIRE

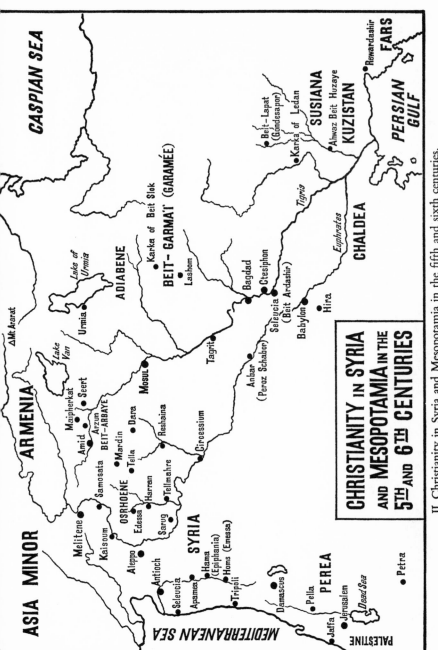

II Christianity in Syria and Mesopotamia in the fifth and sixth centuries.

EXPLANATORY NOTES

1. I have attempted to give a fairly literal translation of the Armenian texts, particularly the theological texts. Round brackets ( ) are added to words or expressions either to give an explanation or to make the meaning of the word more explicit. Square brackets [ ] contain words which are not found in the text but are added by myself to complete the form of the phrase in English translation or to make it clearer and more expressive.

2. In translating Armenian words I have followed the Hubschmann-Meillet system. The list of Armenian letters with their Roman equivalents is given at the end of the Additional Notes and before the Bibliographical Abbreviations (p. 237).

3. The Bibliography is arranged in alphabetical order. In the text and footnotes I have usually given the references by citing the name of the author and an abbreviation of the title. The full name and title as well as other necessary details are given in the list of Bibliographical Abbreviations.

4. Two maps are given on pp. xii and xiii to illustrate the historical situation of the Armenian Church in the fourth and fifth centuries and the geographical position of the Syro-Persian Church in the fifth and sixth centuries. The first is reproduced from the *Historical Atlas of Armenia* (2nd edition, Beirut, 1956), and the second from R. Duval's *La Littérature Syriaque*. Some details are not included in the reproduction.

THE COUNCIL OF CHALCEDON AND
THE ARMENIAN CHURCH

INTRODUCTION

I. THE PROBLEM AND ITS SIGNIFICANCE

There is no doubt that the Council of Chalcedon is of crucial importance in the history of the Armenian Church. It is now generally recognized that the attitude of the Armenian Church to the Council of Chalcedon determined not only its doctrinal position within the whole Christian world, but also, and at the same time, immensely affected the political life of the Armenian people. It is equally true that it played a prominent part in the shaping of the character and orientation of Armenian theological literature. In fact, the whole course of Armenian Church history, particularly the period between the fifth and twelfth centuries, is deeply affected by the position of the Armenian Church in relation to the Council of Chalcedon.

The extent to which it affected the life of the Armenian people may be understood from the expression of H. Grégoire, the famous byzantinist: in his own words, "la querelle des deux natures en Jésus-Christ [Chalcedon] fut sa tragédie".[1] Looked at from the political angle, the history of Armenia itself has been a tragedy all through the centuries. Every aspect of her life, the geographical situation of the country, her cultural tradition, and then, from the beginning of the fourth century, her adherence as a nation to Christianity—all these go to make up the tragic story of Armenia. It is a commonplace now to use the image of a ship tossed by the waves of the Assyrian, Persian, Greek, Roman, Byzantine, Arab, Seljūk, Tatar, and Turkish invasions.[2] In this wider context,

---

[1] Der-Nersessian, *Arm. Byz. Emp.*, preface, p. xix.

[2] The words of Gibbon are as true to-day as ever: "From the earliest period to the present hour, Armenia has been the theatre of perpetual war" (*Roman Empire*, vol. v, p. 169).

then, the expression of H. Grégoire seems exaggerated; yet there is some truth in it worthy of serious historical consideration for the Byzantine emperors regarded the rejection by the Armenians of the Council of Chalcedon as a sign, if not of hostility, at least of a diminishing loyalty to the imperial throne.[1] Because, on the one hand, of the close association of Armenian history with the Byzantine Empire for so many centuries, and because, on the other, of the great influence of religion on the politics of the time, the doctrinal attitude of the Armenian Church had immeasurable consequences not only for the Armenian people, but for the whole Byzantine empire as well.

On the other side, in the sphere of ecclesiastical history, it determined the subsequent relations of the Armenian Church with the Syrian, Byzantine, Georgian, and, to some extent, even the Roman Churches.[2] An adequate understanding of the historical and doctrinal position of the Armenian Church with regard to the Council of Chalcedon is therefore of the utmost importance for a study of the ecumenical aspect of Armenian Church history.

Again, an understanding of this position is essential if we are to appreciate the theological literature of the Armenian Church, particularly in the period of seven centuries referred to; for this doctrinal position made a decisive impact on the character of Armenian literature, which has been primarily concerned with the doctrine of Christ's Person and with all that that involves; Armenian theologians have been mainly occupied with criticizing the Chalcedonian christology, significantly stressing the real unity

---

[1] This may easily be seen in their many attempts made between the sixth and twelfth centuries to make Chalcedon accepted by the Armenians. (See Der-Nersessian, *Arm. Byz. Emp.*, chs. 1 and 2; Laurent, *Arm. Byz. Isl.*; Goubert, *Byzance*, ch. 7, pp. 191 ff; for a brief survey see Pargoire, *Église Byzantine*, pp. 182–5; cf Neale, *Eastern Church*, pp. 1080–3.

[2] For the relationship with the Syrian Churches see Tēr-Minaseanç, *Arm. Kirche*; for the Byzantine Church Tēr-Mik'ēlean, *Arm. Kirche*; Tekeyan, *Controverses christologiques* (only for the twelfth century); for the Georgian Church, Akinean, *Kiwrion*; Tamarati, *Église Géorgienne*, pp. 228–48; for the Roman Church Galanus, *Conciliationis* (entirely biased and uncritical).

of Christ's natures, and, at the same time, strenuously avoiding any idea of confusion or incompleteness therein.¹

¹ The theological literature in its present state, as explored and made available to us through modern scientific research, can testify to this effect in many ways. Thus, the *Book of Letters*—*Girk' T'lt'oc*—and the Patristic *florilegium* known and characterized as the *Seal of Faith*—*Knik' Havatoy*—both of them compiled and used in these centuries, are of supreme importance for the study of Armenian theological literature and for the understanding of the doctrinal position of the Armenian Church.

The *Book of Letters* contains official letters and short treatises on the christological problem; most of these bear the signatures of Armenian Catholicoi and theologians of high standing; some are documents of ecclesiastical councils. Scholars have shown a very keen interest in them. A positive sign of that interest is seen in the remarkable study and translation of the first six documents of the collection by M. Tallon; see his *Livre des Lettres*.

The *Seal of Faith* is a collection of fragments of Church Fathers—including the Armenian divines—having as their central theme the doctrine of Christ's person. It was compiled in the seventh century and used in the course of the controversy with the Chalcedonians. It was discovered and published by K. Tēr-Mkrtč'ean with a most valuable Introduction in Ejmiacin, 1914. See for its importance and for the identification of the Greek Patristic fragments, Lebon, *Citations Patristiques*.

Secondly, the Armenian literary and religious history of the sixth, seventh, and eighth centuries, is, to a large extent, a history of doctrinal controversies, dissensions, conflicts, negotiations, all of them being centred mainly on the Council of Chalcedon. Names as *Petros Siwneçi, Vrt'anēs K'ert'ol, Yovhan Mayragomeçi, T'ēodoros K'ṙt'enavor, Komitas Kat'olikos, Xosrovik T'argmanič', Step'anos Siwneçi, Yovhan Ojneçi*—to mention only the important authors and theologians of these three centuries—can be studied and set in their right places in the doctrinal history of the Armenian Church only when they are seen in the context of the Chalcedonian problem and understood accordingly.

Many articles by N. Akinean in *Handēs Amsorya*, by Galust Tēr-Mkrtč'ean and Karapet Tēr-Mkrtč'ean in *Ararat* have revealed the great importance of the religious literature of these centuries which had been overlooked for so long as being to some extent the "dark ages" of Armenian literature.

It is worth noting also that a great many theologians of later centuries, such as *Xosrov Anjevaçi* (10th cent.), *Anania Narekaçi* (10th cent.), *Polos Taroneçi* (12th cent.), the most distinguished of all, *Nersēs Šnorhali* (12th cent.), *Nersēs Lambronaçi* (12th cent.), *Step'anos Orbelean* (14th cent.), *Grigor Tat'evaçi* (15th cent.), and many others, would have been involved in the same problem as if it had been a permanent one in Armenian Church history and theology.

See a *compendium* of this post-Chalcedonian Armenian theological literature in Jugie, *Theologia Monophysitarum*, vol. v, pp. 480–8. Jugie in his exposition of the Monophysite christology has given a large place to the Armenian theologians, using the Latin translations made by the Mekhitarist Fathers. See pp. 500–42.

There can be not the least doubt, then, that this problem is crucial in Armenian Church history; and an attempt to understand it may shed light on other matters also—problems concerning the personalities and literature of later periods.

Furthermore, the question receives a higher importance from the fact that the Armenian Church had never been directly involved in the Chalcedonian controversies, either in their previous, Nestorian, phase, or in their subsequent, Monophysite, phase.[1] The fifth century was a fortunate period for the Armenian Church and nation, the "Golden Age", as it is usually called, of Armenian history: to this period belongs the downfall of the Arsacid Kingdom (428), a political crisis which followed another important event—the partition of Armenia between Persia and Byzantium[2] (387/390?); then there were grave threats to the Christian faith—the persecution by the Mazdaean Persians which was strongly resisted by the Armenians in the battle of Awarayr[3] (451); these and other new challenges were the crucial problems of this time for the Armenians. It was indeed, a time of great tension and culminated in great achievements in the literary, religious, missionary, and educational spheres, namely the preservation of Christianity, the invention of the Armenian alphabet, the translation of the Holy Scriptures, the liturgical literature and the Church Fathers, the remarkable flowering of Armenian literature, and the creation of national solidarity.[4]

[1] The only instance of any relation with the theological discussions taking place in the outside world is the correspondence between (a) Acacius of Melitene and Sahak, Catholicos of the Armenians—three letters—and (b) Proclus of Constantinople and Sahak Catholicos—two letters. (See them in *Book of Letters*, pp. 1–21; cf Tallon, *Livre des Lettres*, pp. 21–77.)

[2] See Aslan, *Études Historiques*, p. 207; Grousset, *Histoire d'Arménie*, pp. 163–84; Manandean, *Critical History*, pp. 232–43; Bury, *Later Roman Empire*, vol. i, p. 94; Demougeot, *Empire Romain*, pp. 112–13; Christensen, *Iran Sassanide*, p. 253–4; Baynes, *Rome and Armenia*, pp. 642–3; Goubert, *Géorgie*, pp. 119–27.

[3] The whole story is related by a fifth century historian, *Eliše*. See *Hist. of Vardan*; cf Grousset, *Histoire d'Armenie*, pp. 187–213; Christensen, *Iran Sassanide*, pp. 282–8.

[4] For a brief account of the fifth-century situation of the Armenian people and Church see below, pp. 68–72.

No wonder at all, then, that the Armenians did not participate in the life of the Church outside the boundaries of their country! They had no representative in the Council of Chalcedon itself. There is no evidence either for any invitation to them from the emperor or the bishop of Constantinople.[1]

Here we have a situation where the well-known personal feelings, ecclesiastical rivalries, political orientation, competition for supremacy, resentment, with all the heat of controversy that goes with them—all these did not affect the doctrinal position reached. And, if it is assumed that these factors played a considerable part in the Chalcedonian and Monophysite controversies and had an important effect on the attitude of both sides, here we have, then, a world quite free from such confusing factors, a world in which, therefore, we can find a different standpoint—perhaps a better one—from which to view the Chalcedonian question more closely. This different angle may help us to understand the historical and doctrinal place of Chalcedon in the life of the Eastern Church.

This is the reason why so often so many church historians have been at a loss to find any real theological justification for the position of the Armenian Church; not being able to find any serious reason for the Armenian rejection of the Council of Chalcedon, they have let their imagination run riot, and have offered, albeit quite sincerely, endless explanations for it.

What was and still is needed is a realization of the particular situation of the Armenian Church in the period in which the Chalcedonian problem arose for the Armenian Church authorities and theologians. We shall not be able to understand the position of the Armenian Church if we always think in terms of what happened and what was thought in Constantinople, Alexandria, Antioch, or Jerusalem! We have to realize, first of all, by a careful

[1] This, however, does not mean to us as it has meant to many others, that they were unaware of what was happening in the outside world, or that they were completely cut off from the life of the Church in the Byzantine empire, and, therefore, could not see clearly the doctrinal problems of the fifth century which came to their consideration later. This interpretation is contrary to the evidence at hand, as it will be shown later.

reading of the history and literature of the Armenian Church prior to the rejection of the Council of Chalcedon, what kind of situation existed in Armenia, particularly in the theological sphere.

This seems to be the proper standpoint from which to tackle the question, which may now be formulated as follows: *How, when, and why did the Armenian Church, formally and officially, for the first time in history, reject the Council of Chalcedon?*

Thus, having put the question directly, if briefly, and having hinted at its high importance in Armenian church history and, to some extent, in the history of the Chalcedonian problem as a whole, we turn now to the existing literature on the subject to see what we can find there which may help towards an understanding of the position of the Armenian Church.[1]

II. THE TRADITIONAL VIEW

In an attempt to present, in a very general survey and in chronological terms, the various views that were taken of the problem, especially in the Western world before the twentieth century, the most important work to start with is undoubtedly the famous and voluminous work of a well-known Roman Catholic missionary, orientalist, and theologian, Clement Galanus: *Conciliationis Ecclesiae Armeniae cum Romana*. In the historical part of his work, volume i, Galanus refers to the rejection of the Council of Chalcedon several times, but his essential point may be found in chapter 10:

> Nierses Ascdarachensis, primus patriarcha fuit, qui sanctam Synodum Chalcedonensem detestatus, inter Armenam et Universalem Ecclesiam apartum schisma molitus sit, etenim post annum Christianum 500 Conciliabulo Thevinensi decem Episcoporum in Armenia Persarum Regis, qui Christianorum divisionem, ad Armeniam sibi omnimode subiciendam, vehementer exoptabat, unam in Christo natura, pleresque eidem sacre Synodo Chalcedonensi repugnantes constitutiones stabiluit.[2]

---

[1] We shall give preference to the literature in foreign languages at the same time taking into account that part of the Armenian literature which has influenced the former in one way or another.

[2] Galanus, *Conciliationis*, vol. i, p. 86.

A little further on he continues:

Pervaserat itaque in Armeniam temporibus istis nefandissima Acephalorum[1] haeresis, belua inquam illa sine capite; quae pluribus tamen in Oriente prodierat armata capitibus, inter se quidem pugnantibus, sed in suscipiendis sacrilegi Dioscori partibus post infelicem eius interitum, atque in Chalcedonensi sacra Synodo oppugnanda, iniquissime foederatis.[2]

Le Quien, who has been recognized as a great expert on the history of the Eastern Churches for his imposing work, *Oriens Christianus*, is inclined to put the date of the rejection as late as 554, i.e. 103 years after the Council of Chalcedon. Having asserted that the Armenians maintained the orthodox faith in communion with the Universal Church before and during the fifth century, he says:

Verum insequente saeculo a Catholica fide et communione Armeni defecerunt, pro summo quod erga Nestorianam impietatem conceperant odio, atque Eutychianum errorem amplexi Chalcedonensem synodum abjecerunt.[3]

Then follows an account of the Chalcedonian problem in Armenian Church history as given by an anonymous author of the eighth century;[4] in this, the possibility of an earlier rejection is excluded. Then he concludes:

At vero ex his quae leguntur ad calcem Narrationis, Armenorum haeresis initium ardessendum omnino est ab anno Christi 554. Ibi

---

[1] The Armenian text has "Eutyches and Dioscorus" (*Ewtik'eay ew Dēoskorosin*) for this word. Apparently this is a false identification in the author's mind. But it is clear that for Galanus those who came to Armenia at this time were followers of Eutyches and Dioscorus, representatives of the extreme monophysite branch.

[2] Galanus, *Conciliationis*, vol. i, p. 87; cf pp. 92–3.

[3] Le Quien, *Oriens Christianus*, vol. i, col. 1357–8.

[4] The author of the pro-Chalcedonian work known as *Narratio de Rebus Armeniae* or simply Διήγησις. See it in Migne, P.G. t. 127, col. 885–900 and t. 132, col. 1237–53—two separate editions. A critical edition followed by a masterly commentary was recently made by Prof. Gérard Garitte. See Garitte, *Narratio*.

namque fertur Armenos, etsi a S. Gregori Doctoris sui aliorumque Patrum traditionibus utcumque desciverant, de Chalcedonensis tamen synodi Fide nihil quidquam, imo nec de duabus Christi naturis, in dubium revocasse usque ad annum 103 ... quo Tibenensem suam synodum celebrarunt. Qui certe annus 103 a synodo Chalcedonensi, seu Christi 451 ipsissimus est Christi 554.[1]

Č'amč'ean, who, with his massive work, *History of the Armenians* —for so many years regarded as the standard history of Armenia —exerted such a great influence on Armenian historians in the nineteenth century and also not an unimportant one on foreign historians, has provided a general pattern of interpretation often shared in their own ways and sometimes with slight variations by Armenian scholars and foreign historians on Eastern Christianity. He says that until the year 490,

> the news of the confusing reports of the opponents of the holy Council of Chalcedon had not yet reached Armenia; and even if some rumours had come, and a letter from the Dioscorians, they could not have any effect, because the whole nation was suffering tribulation on account of the great persecutions at the hand of the fire-worshippers (i.e. the Mazdaean Persians); they did not have time to give heed to such rumours or to take action accordingly. But when those persecutions ceased for a while in Armenia, confusing news was spread about the holy Council of Chalcedon in the times of the reign of Emperor Zeno and in the days of the Catholicate of Babgēn, some forty years after that Council.[2]

Like the Dioscorians or Eutychians, the Nestorians also came to spread their own ideas about the Council of Chalcedon, seeing in it the vindication of the doctrine of Nestorius. So, both Eutychians and Nestorians were claiming, though for different and opposite reasons, that the Council of Chalcedon had reaffirmed the Nestorian christology.

> And when all these allegations reached Armenia, the Armenian bishops not knowing the truth in what had happened, were perplexed, because they did not hear good things from either side about

---

[1] Le Quien, *Oriens Christianus*, vol. i, col. 1360.
[2] Č'amč'ean, *History*, vol. ii, bk. iii, p. 223.

the holy Council of Chalcedon; but what they were told was bad; and because the bishops of Armenia Major were not present at the Council itself, they could not be aware of what was meant in the decrees of that Council. In those days some brought to Armenia the copy of the edict of Zeno. Catholicos Babgēn, having read it and seen that many bishops had signed it, he also consented to it as representing the sound doctrine of faith; because, in fact, the doctrine of that letter, taken in itself, was orthodox and in conformity with the doctrine of Chalcedon.

... And, therefore, as Babgēn, Catholicos of the Armenians, had heard many calumnies against the holy Council of Chalcedon, when he saw that the edict with the signatures of many, supposedly rejected that Council, he also wished to reject it. But he did not dare to do that alone. So he convened a synod of bishops in the cathedral in the new city, which is Eǰmiacin in Vałaršapat, a city in the plain.[1]

He also invited the Catholicos of the Georgians, Gabriēl, with his bishops, and the Catholicos of Ałowank,[2] and some from parts of Byzantine Armenia. This was in 491.

In this assembly, first, they anathematized the Nestorians, Barsauma and Akak the Persian, with their adherents, and their false teaching; in addition, they anathematized the false teaching of the Eutychians. And, then, having read the copy of Zeno's edict which is called Henoticon (ἑνωτικόν) or Henaticon, they consented to it, and in accordance with the mind of that edict also explicitly rejected the holy Council of Chalcedon supposing that, first, according to the calumnies of the Nestorians and Eutychians, that Council had accepted the writings of Theodore of Mopsuestia and his supporters, and, secondly, that it had divided Christ into two persons (dēms= πρόσωπον) and two sons according to the conception of Nestorius.

... In the same year that the council of Vałaršapat was held, Anastasius became emperor; and seeing that there was great confusion in the East over the Council of Chalcedon prohibited all discussion of the matter, either for or against it. This being heard by the Armenians, they put aside altogether that holy council, saying: if the

[1] Ibid., pp. 224–5.
[2] The Caucasian Albanians in the north-east of Armenia.

Greeks themselves do not accept that Council which they convened, why should we accept it?

This, then, was the first time that the Armenians rejected the holy Council of Chalcedon; and they did it not because they knew what that Council involved, but because they had no accurate information about it.[1]

J. M. Neale, the widely recognized English authority on the Eastern Churches, has made some important remarks concerning the christological position of the Armenian Church. Thus, after a careful scrutiny of the doctrinal documents of the Armenian literature, he fully recognizes the orthodoxy of the Armenian formulation of the doctrine of the Person of Christ, based, as it is, on the famous μία φύσις formula; but he blames them only "for obstinacy and schismatical perverseness in retaining their term when they were, or might have been, convinced that Chalcedon was a Catholic Synod, and that its meaning agreed with their own".[2] But his account of the rejection of the Council of Chalcedon by the Armenian Church does not take us very far beyond what we have seen above. He says:

The troubles of the times (i.e. the Mazdaean persecutions) prevented the Armenians from taking any part in the fourth Oecumenical Council. Surrounded as they were on all sides by Nestorian heretics, it was natural that they should regard with the greatest jealousy any teaching which seemed to condemn those who contended for the One Person of our Lord. Their nearest neighbours, the Syrian Bishops, misrepresented the Council; and unhappily, the Armenian language facilitated the misapprehension; one word only being employed to express the two senses of Nature and Person.
... The Armenians, then, learnt that at Chalcedon Two Persons had been recognized in our Lord, and they soon heard that the succeeding Emperors, Zeno and Anastasius, rejected the Council. What wonder

---

[1] Č'amč'ean, *History*, vol. ii, bk. iii, pp. 225–6. It must be said that Issaverdens, although he offered no contribution of his own to the understanding of the problem, nevertheless became very influential to Western scholars through his *Armenia and the Armenians*. In fact, it was he who made available to others Č'amč'ean's views which he, in fact, summarized. (See *Armenia*, pp. 90–7.)

[2] Neale, *Eastern Church*, p. 1090.

1 (a). That the Council of Chalcedon was rejected in the synod held by Catholicos Nersēs after the first quarter of the sixth century.[1]

 (b). That the Council of Chalcedon was rejected in the synod held by Catholicos Babgēn in the last quarter of the fifth century.[2]

2 (a). That they accepted the doctrine of Dioscorus, and specially of Eutyches.[3]

 (b). That they have always condemned the christology of Eutyches by anathematizing him as a heretic.[4]

3 (a). That not being themselves present at the Council, they were deceived and misled by others.[5]

 (b). That they were represented in the Council and accepted its decisions immediately after the Council, but later shifted from their position and moved over to the opposite side.[6]

4 (a). That it was under the pressure of the Persians that they were brought to reject the Council, this being a means to

[1] A. Fortescue, *Eastern Churches*, p. 413; Tournebize, *Arménie*, col. 303; Malan, *St Gregory*, pp. 29–32; Balgy, *Doctr. Cath. inter Arm.*, pp. 18–19; Vailhé, *Église Arménienne*, p. 209; Hefele, *Conciles*, t. ii, part 2, pp. 1077–8.

[2] Duchesne, *Church History*, vol. iii. p. 391; Kidd, *Church History*, vol. iii, pp. 424–5; Kidd, *Eastern Christendom*, p. 428; Hore, *Orthodox Church*, p. 273; Adeney, *Eastern Churches*, p. 544; Appleyard, *Eastern Churches*, p. 33; Dyer, *Armenian Church*, p. 1899; Williams, *Armenians*, p. 164b; Macler, *Armenia*, p. 804a; Petit, *Arménie*, col. 1896; cf col. 1928; King, *Rites Eastern Christendom*, pp. 530–1; Janin, *Églises Orientales*, p. 335; Bardy, *Églises de Perse et d'Arménie*, p. 336; cf p. 511.

[3] Rycaut, *Gr. Arm. Churches*, pp. 411–14; Riley (see Dowling, *Armenian Church*, pp. 43–4); Gibbon, *Roman Empire*, vol. v, p. 168.

[4] A. Fortescue, *Eastern Churches*, p. 411; Adeney, *Eastern Churches*, p. 546; Dyer, *Armenian Church*, p. 1899; Brightman (See Dowling, *Armenian Church*, p. 44); Malan, *St. Gregory*, pp. 31–2; Tchéraz, *L'Église Arménienne*, p. 327; Simon, *Chrétiens Orientaux*, pp. 139–40, where he calls the "Eutychianism" of the Armenian Church "*imaginaire*".

[5] K. Fortescue, *Armenian Church*, p. 21; Stanley, *Eastern Church*, Lect. i, p. 7; Adeney, *Eastern Churches*, pp. 543–4; Williams, *Armenians*, p. 164b.

[6] Balgy, *Doctr. Cath. inter Arm.*, ch. 3; A. Fortescue, *Eastern Churches*, p. 411; King, *Rites Eastern Christendom*, p. 530.

make them stand in opposition to the Byzantine empire, the rival of the Persian Kingdom.[1]

(b). That they rejected the Council in order to conform their attitude to the ecclesiastical policy of the Byzantine emperors of the time.[2]

5. That they were not able to understand the true meaning of the formulas used in the Tome of Leo and the Chalcedonian Definition; for linguistic reasons it was not possible to produce an accurate Armenian translation.[3]

6. Finally, that they confused the Chalcedonian doctrine with Nestorian christology, and, therefore, became opposed to it through their struggle with Nestorianism.[4]

III. RECENT CRITICAL APPROACH

This situation at the end of the nineteenth century can only be described as unsatisfactory, confusing, and misleading. Obviously it could not long remain acceptable to modern historians and theologians with their new methods of scientific research.

The publication of the *Book of Letters* (*Girk' T'łt'oç*) in the first year of this century was the start of a new approach and provided the basis of a new interpretation, which became almost the established one, although scholars differed in their attitude to the documents concerned.

This collection of letters made available to scholars, among

---

[1] Kidd, *Eastern Christendom*, pp. 431–2; Greenslade, *Schism*, pp. 68–9.

[2] K. Fortescue, *Armenian Church*, p. 27; Petit, *Arménie*, col. 1896; Duchesne, *Separated Churches*, p. 36; Bardy, *Églises de Perse et d'Arménie*, p. 336. Another interpretation closely linked with this is that they rejected the Council of Chalcedon because of the rising nationalism in Armenia. (See A. Fortescue, *Eastern Churches*, p. 412; Laurent, *Arm. Byz. Isl.*, pp. 137–9; Tchéraz, *Église Arménienne*, pp. 327–8; Der-Nersessian, *Arm. Byz. Emp.*, p. 32; Greenslade, *Schism*, pp. 68–9.)

[3] K. Fortescue, *Armenian Church*, p. 21; Dyer, *Armenian Church*, p. 1899; Nève, *Arménie Chrétienne*, pp. 26–7; Dowling, *Armenian Church*, pp. 61–2; Tournebize, *Arménie*, col. 302–3; A. Fortescue, *Eastern Churches*, p. 412; Hore, *Orthodox Church*, p. 273; Kidd, *Church History*, vol. iii, p. 425; Kidd, *Eastern Christendom*, p. 431.

[4] Dyer, *Armenian Church*, p. 1899.

many other most valuable texts, a group of documents entirely concerned with the relationship of the Armenian Church with the Syrian Churches.[1]

These documents could not escape the attention of Armenian scholars, not only because of their extreme importance for the history of the Armenian Church's relations with the neighbouring Syrian Churches, but also, and in particular, because they were of immense significance for the understanding of the doctrinal position of the Armenian Church.

Thus, E. Tēr-Minaseanç, taking advantage of this publication, made a stimulating study of the documents referred to in his well-known book.[2] His views are quite familiar, because Western scholars have had direct access to his book, and we need not present them here.[3]

But it must be said that even before Tēr-Minaseanç, K. Tēr-Mkrtč'ean, a pioneer in the scientific investigation of the Armenian patristic literature, had already challenged the traditional view and opened the way for a new interpretation. Therefore it would be valuable to present his views, especially as these latter have not yet found expression in any foreign language.

From 1896 onwards he was engaged in the study of the Armenian christological literature, and, in the beginning, he had accepted the traditional view, i.e. that the Armenian Church made its first decision on the Council of Chalcedon

> not in 491 in the synod of Vałaršapat held by Babgēn, as it is accepted among us following Č'amČ'ean, but in the middle of the sixth century in the synod held in Dowin by Nersēs II Aštarakeçi.[4]

Two years later, in an article with the characteristic title: "Babgēn Catholicos and the First Participation of the Armenian Church in the Doctrinal Controversies", in which the documents

---

[1] See B.L., pp. 41–75.
[2] See Tēr-Minaseanç, *Arm. Kirche.*
[3] Op. cit., ch. 2, pp. 29–36 (Arm. ed., pp. 63–83).
[4] Tēr-Mkrtč'ean, *Christ's Nature*, p. 157; cf his *Paulikianer*, pp. 55–6 (Arm. ed., pp. 83–4).

above-mentioned were used,[1] he radically changed his opinion. Here, after examining the historical circumstances and the evidence provided by the documents, and having established the date of the Council of Babgēn as 506, not 491, he says:

> Our final conclusion from all these inquiries is that the doctrinal controversies raised in the General Church became a vital problem for the Armenian Church for the first time when Nestorianism was recognized as the true faith by the State of Persia, and its adherents began to try to convert all the christians subject to the Persian Kingdom to this faith; at this point, a great council was held in Dowin, in 506, under the presidency of Catholicos Babgēn and with the participation of the Georgians, Albanians, and Orthodox Persian christians, where Nestorianism, which was accepted by the Persians, was condemned with its principal representatives, Acacius, Barsauma, Babai, etc.; the *Henoticon* of the emperor Zeno was recognized as the orthodox faith, and, therefore, the Council of Chalcedon was not officially condemned, but tacitly considered as an outcome of a veiled Nestorianism, and consequently was to be despised by the orthodox christians.[2]

Later researches and discoveries in the tradition of the Armenian patristic literature meant a considerable revision of his approach to the problem. Thus, when dealing with the works ascribed to Yovhan Mandakuni, a fifth-century author, he touches the same problem of the rejection of the Council of Chalcedon, and, basing his arguments mainly on a christological treatise of Yovhan Mandakuni, he maintains that even before the council of 506, i.e. earlier than the decision of Catholicos Babgēn, in fact, immediately after 484, Mandakuni had already opposed the Council of Chalcedon.[3]

Finally, in his most valuable introduction of the edition of the *Seal of Faith*, he reaffirms this last view. He says, again, that

---

[1] Before the publication of the *Book of Letters* in 1901, he had received the copies of the two documents in which the attitude of the Armenian Church to the Council of Chalcedon was discussed. He published them in *Ararat* and wrote an introduction to them. (See *First Participation*, pp. 431–6.)

[2] Tēr-Mkrtč'ean, *First Participation*, p. 436; cf his *Misunderstandings*, p. 832.

[3] See Tēr-Mkrtč'ean, *Mandakuni*, pp. 89–94.

Mandakuni must be regarded as the first churchman in authority to have rejected the Council of Chalcedon. The occasion which caused that rejection was most probably the promulgation of Zeno's *Henoticon*.[1]

This line was taken by many Armenian scholars later, and it soon became the predominant view. Ormanean, in his widely consulted *History of the Armenian Nation* (*Azgapatum*) combined this view with his own conclusions and made it a widespread and generally accepted interpretation of the problem. It is stated briefly in his popular book, *The Church of Armenia:*

> The synod of Armenian, Georgian, and Caspio-Albanian bishops, which assembled at Dwin (506) under the presidency of Babgēn, officially proclaimed the profession of faith of the Council of Ephesus and rejected everything that was Nestorian or savoured of Nestorianism, including the acts of the Council of Chalcedon. Far, indeed, from adopting the doctrine of Eutyches, his name, together with those of Arius, of Macedon, and of Nestorius, was officially condemned. Such was the first declaration of the Armenian Church with regard to the Council of Chalcedon.[2]

This view was challenged very categorically by V. Haçuni who, anxious to see the Armenian Church in communion with the Roman Church, went as far as to say that the Council of Chalcedon was condemned neither in the fifth century nor in the middle of the sixth. Opposition to it started in the last quarter of the sixth century and the condemnation took place at the beginning of the seventh. He declared that the documents of the sixth century which mentioned the condemnation of the Council of Chalcedon were either forged or altered in the later centuries.[3] However, there remained in Armenia a group of people who were faithful to the "Catholic Faith". Those who separated themselves off acted in ignorance. They were incapable of understanding the depth of the Chalcedonian doctrine.[4]

---

[1] See Tēr-Mkrtč'ean, *Seal of Faith*, Intr., pp. lix–lxii.

[2] Ormanean, *Armenian Church*, p. 27. See also Nersoyan, *Doctrinal Position*, p. 6.

[3] Haçuni, *Important Problems*, see pp. 358–63, 369–70, 376–8, 386, 389–416.

[4] We must note that this way of interpreting the problem, i.e. by dating the rejection of the Council of Chalcedon as late as possible, is a common tendency

Finally, we have to mention the article of V. Inglizean in *Das Konzil von Chalkedon* in which he maintains that the first condemnation of the Council of Chalcedon was instigated by the Syrian Monophysites and is recorded in the second letter of Babgēn, written soon after the council of 506. The Armenians acted under the directives of Simon Beth-Aršam, the leader of the Monophysite Syrians. And, secondly, they were influenced by the *Henoticon* of Zeno:

> Die feindselige Einstellung zu Chalkedon, die in diesem zweiten Briefe Babgens zum Ausdruck kommt, beruht also keineswegs etwa auf der Kenntnis der Konzilsbeschlusse, sondern lediglich auf den durch Simeon von Beth-Arsham vermittelten monophysitischen Schriften und dem Henotikon. Dadurch wurde in Armenien der Boden bereitet für jene erneute Verwerfung des Konzils von Chalkedon, die nach 50 Jahren auf Betreiben wiederum eines monophysitischen Syrers stattfinden sollte.[1]

This is the situation to-day. Let us, again, resume the main points of these recent studies:

1. There was no participation of the Armenian Church in the Council of Chalcedon.

2. In the first decade of the sixth century the Armenian Church came officially to face Chalcedon as a problem and to deal with it officially.

---

among the Armenian Uniate and some Roman Catholic scholars. It is inspired by their general assumption that the Armenians remained in communion with the "Catholic Faith" for long centuries. In order to strengthen their argument that the Armenian Uniate Church is the true descendant of the "Ancient Orthodox and Catholic" Armenian Church, they try to show that even after the "schism" there remained a "Catholic" element in the Armenian Church. That element is found expressed in the works of several Armenian Church Fathers and theologians as understood and expounded by them. (Some examples of this approach can be found in Balgy, *Doctr. Cath. inter Arm.*; A. Fortescue, *Eastern Churches*; Weber, *Kath. Kirche*; Tournebize, *Histoire*; and the prototype of all, Galanus, *Conciliationis*.)

[1] Inglizean, *Arm. Kirche*, p. 370. See on the same problem also Ananean, *Dowin Document*, pp. 68–9; cf Garitte, *Narratio*, pp. 152–3.

3. The same problem was dealt with again in the middle of the sixth century.

4. The *Henoticon* of Zeno was an important factor in the shaping of the Armenian attitude.

5. The impact of Nestorianism was of decisive importance for the Armenian position.

In spite of all these basic facts on which the great majority of scholars would agree to-day, the problem is still open to discussion, not only because the scholars do not agree on every point,[1] but also, and especially, because there are aspects of it still to be studied and investigated more fully. As may be seen from the literature which we have just reviewed, the problem has not been studied as a whole. What is said about it, is said in the wider context of other themes of study. Thus, it has been studied (*a*) in connection with the problem of the Armenian Church's relationship with other Churches (Galanus, Tēr-Mik‘ēlean, Tēr-Minaseanç), (*b*) in the context of the history of the Eastern Churches (Le Quien, J. M. Neale, Fortescue), (*c*) in relation with the general history of the Armenian Church and people (Č‘amč‘ean, Issaverdens, Dulaurier, Ormanean), (*d*) in connection with other particular studies (Tēr-Mkrtč‘ean, Akinean, Ananean), or (*e*) in the context of the Chalcedonian problem throughout the whole course of Armenian Church history (Haçuni, Inglizean).

Now the problem must be studied as a whole so that it may be understood more clearly and completely. This is what we propose to do in the following pages. Here we have the problem of the Council of Chalcedon at the very centre of our investigation and not on its fringes or in one of its phases.

This means that we have to concentrate on the study of that period of Armenian Church history and theological literature, which precedes the rejection of the Council of Chalcedon, because it seems to us that the rejection is not a clear-cut act of one

[1] Indeed, they display a large variety of views when they come to interpret the cause, the nature, and the significance of the rejection of the Council of Chalcedon, as will be shown in the course of our study.

moment, but rather the outcome of a process of theological thinking and orientation, and the early stages therefore have to be studied as much as the rejection itself. To understand the Armenian position involves, first of all, an appreciation of the historical situation of the Armenian Church and, particularly, its theological *milieu*, both in the period before the rejection of the Council of Chalcedon and at the time when the rejection was formally made. Therefore, the main part of our research will be devoted to the study of the background—historical and doctrinal—of the rejection of the Council of Chalcedon.

In the same way, we must try to understand what Chalcedon really meant to Christians in the eastern parts of the Byzantine Empire. In other words: what was the picture of Chalcedon in its historical and doctrinal setting of the fifth and the earliest years of the sixth centuries? Because this question has generally been overlooked, a great deal of confusion has arisen from the fact that many of those who have dealt with the position of the Armenian Church in relation to Chalcedon have had in mind the Chalcedonian doctrine as understood to-day and the Council of Chalcedon as accepted at present by the greater part of Christendom. We must find, then, the Chalcedon of the period in which it was faced and dealt with by the Armenian Church.

Finally, we must try to see the act of rejection through a careful scrutiny of the documents in the light of our study of the background and the historical circumstances of the time.

Then, we think, it will not be difficult to conclude that if the Armenians rejected the Council of Chalcedon it was not because:

(*a*) They were deceived or misled.

(*b*) They were unable to understand the doctrine of Chalcedon.

(*c*) They were compelled by the Persians.

(*d*) Their language was inadequate for an accurate rendering of the intricate meaning of the formularies.

(*e*) They were victims of a false and unfortunate identification of the Chalcedonian doctrine with Nestorianism.

Rather:

(*a*) Their attitude was primarily religious and theological, not political.

(*b*) The rejection of the Council of Chalcedon did not happen suddenly or accidentally. There was a struggle within the Church before it took place.

(*c*) The Armenians did not confound Nestorianism with Chalcedon; but the two only became closely associated and Chalcedon only became of vital importance for the Armenian Church when the Nestorians themselves took it as a source of strength and as a vindication of the orthodoxy of their doctrinal position.

(*d*) The rejection was a very natural and reasonable act, closely consistent with their doctrinal position, when seen in the context of their historical and theological tradition.

These are the main points which will come up in the course of the present study and which we will try to substantiate by the existing historical and theological evidence.

1

CHALCEDON AFTER CHALCEDON

The Council of Chalcedon has been described as "le plus œcuménique de tous ceux qui furent jamais".[1] This is true in so far as it refers to the extent of its attendance,[2] yet, at the same time, Chalcedon has been, and still is, the most controversial council in the tradition of Eastern Christendom. The rôle it played in the history of the Eastern Church at the end resulted in the unhappy schism of the Church: its division into "Orthodox" and "Monophysite" sections.

It is not therefore surprising that there is such an immense quantity of literature on the Council of Chalcedon. Its fifteenth centenary, celebrated in 1951, provided a new stimulus for further research and deeper study, which culminated in a reaffirmation by both the Roman Catholic and Eastern Orthodox Churches of its great importance and the value of its orthodox formulations.[3]

[1] Devreesse, *Antioche*, préface, p. xii.

[2] The number of the ecclesiastics—bishops and their representatives—who attended the Council varies between 500 and 636 in different documents and with different historians. See Hefele, *Councils*, vol. iii, pp. 297–8; cf Sellers, *Chalcedon*, p. 104, n. 1. E. Honigmann's new research into the original lists of the members of the Council makes it clear that 521 is the most probable number. (See Honigmann, *Original Lists*, pp. 41–64, particularly pp. 45–7, 62.) "In any case," as Hefele puts it, "none of the previous synods had been nearly so numerous, and even among all that were subsequently held, but very few can in this respect be placed beside the Council of Chalcedon" (*Councils*, vol. iii, p. 298). The presence of the imperial commissioners, eighteen in number, and then the appearance of the emperor Marcian and the empress Pulcheria in the sixth session, with all the attention and importance they attached to it, gave a singular significance to the Council.

[3] The imposing work which marked the significance of the Council in terms of new scientific research and theological reassertion was the *Das Konzil von*

23

Obviously our investigation is not concerned primarily with the study of the Council of Chalcedon as such. Yet it cannot be pursued properly and studied adequately without a clear understanding of the Council of Chalcedon as it was seen and understood at the time of its convention and in the immediately subsequent period of ecclesiastical life and theological thinking. In other words, it seems to us impossible to make any valuable statement about the relation of the Armenian Church to the Council of Chalcedon unless we have understood the latter in the particular conditions of the period with which we are dealing. And this means that we must start with the Council of Chalcedon.

But it must be added that our work does not amount to a thoroughgoing study of the Council. We do not propose to attempt such a vast task here. We shall look again at its proceedings in order to find there what we think to be the causes of the later troubles and the christological controversies which emerged from the Council of Chalcedon. For it seems to us that they have played a considerable part in the formation of the attitudes of so many Eastern provinces of Christianity, including the Armenian Church. Therefore, far from saying anything new about the Council of Chalcedon, we intend in this chapter only to describe the background of the later "Chalcedonian Question", which was faced by the Armenian Church and which can be understood only through a direct inquiry into the origins of the problem, i.e. the Council itself.

Chalkedon: Geschichte und Gegenwart—three large volumes edited by A. Grillmeier and H. Bacht with contributions from a host of distinguished scholars and theologians of the Roman Catholic Church. Several other articles and books also appeared in various theological reviews on the same occasion, each making in its own way new attempts for a fuller understanding of the Council and of the theological issues and attitudes in the fourth and fifth centuries. See among others Chadwick, *Eucharist and Christology*; De Juaye, *XVe. centenaire*; Diepen, *Troischapitres*; Idem, *Assumptus Homo*; Nicolas, *Christologie St. Leon*; Murphy, *Peter speaks through Leo*; Dombalis, *Symposium* (articles by G. Florovsky and A. Schmemann); Camelot, *Théologies*.

I. SOME SIGNIFICANT ASPECTS OF THE COUNCIL OF CHALCEDON

The death of the emperor Theodosius II (28 July 450) and the coming to power of Marcian (25 August 450) involved an important change, "aussi rapide que complet",[1] in the ecclesiastical policy of the Byzantine Empire. The religious sympathies of the new emperor shifted to the opposite side from those of his predecessor. If the former policy was fostered and dominated by Chrysaphios the eunuch, the new policy marked the victory of Pulcheria, Chrysaphios' victim.[2] "It is worthy to notice", says Bury, "that Chrysaphios had favoured the Green faction of the Circus and that Marcian patronized the Blues."[3]

In this new climate of policy Marcian, deeply concerned with the ecclesiastical unity of the Empire, as any other emperor would be if he was aware of the power and influence of the Church in the Empire, invited the bishops to a council

> that they might reach agreement in their discussions and the whole truth be investigated; that the passions which some on earlier occasions have displayed and so made havoc of one holy orthodox worship, might be excluded; that our true faith might be more clearly understood for all time; and thus there could be in the future no doubt or difference of opinion.[4]

In this hope the Council was opened on 8 October 451. It covered the whole month. The closing session was held on 1 November.

The Council thus concluded, Marcian now felt that his wish

---

[1] Lebon, *Monophysisme Sévérien*, p. 8; cf 10–11.

[2] See Goubert, *Pulchérie et Chrysaphios*; see also an interesting remark in Michael Syrus, *Chronicle*, bk. viii, ch. 10 (Chabot, *Michel le Syrien*, vol. ii, p. 38).

[3] Bury, *Later Rom. Emp.*, vol. i, p. 236; cf Wigram, *Separation*, p. 13. For the "*Blues*" and the "*Greens*" see Grégoire, *Peuple de CP*. Sellers characterizes this change in the sphere of ecclesiastical life in the following statement: "But when, upon the death of Theodosius (450), Pulcheria and Marcian came to the throne, the tables were turned. The new rulers would not tolerate the Alexandrian supremacy: in future it was from Constantinople that, like the State, the Church was to be governed" (*Chalcedon*, p. xii).

[4] *A.C.O.*, t. ii, vol. i, pt. 1, p. 27.

was accomplished. Unity would be restored and maintained.[1] Every obstacle in the way of the unity and orthodoxy of the Church seemed to have been removed. So, with a quiet mind and an assured heart he could give his imperial confirmation to the decisions of the Council, at the same time ordering the people to obey and follow them:

> At last what we wished, with earnest desire, has come to pass. Controversy about the Orthodox religion of christians has been put away; remedies have been found for culpable error; and diversity of opinion among the peoples has issued in common consent and concord. All, therefore, shall be bound to hold to the decisions of the sacred Council of Chalcedon and to indulge no further doubts.[2]

No one can miss the firmness of the emperor's conviction and the force of the command. And yet "on n'obéissait guère aux décrets impériaux".[3] This soon became evident. To put it again in the words of the same writer:

> Lorsque le concile de Chalcédoine fut achevé, lorsque les évêques qui y avaient prit part furent rentrés dans leurs diocèses, on put apprécier à sa véritable valeur l'œuvre qui venait d'être accomplie, et bien vite il apparut que cette œuvre était loin d'être parfaite.[4]
> ... Il était réservé à l'avenir de montrer à quel point leur œuvre était fragile.[5]

For, to use another expression borrowed from Devreesse: "Des points névralgiques ont été touchés".[6]

But before we proceed to that later period we must try here to examine the proceedings of the Council itself and to find there the "fragility" or the "points névralgiques" referred to. These

---

[1] He already had expressed his full satisfaction with the work of the Council even before the conclusion of it. He did this when he addressed the sixth session by congratulating the Council for its great achievement in restoring the unity of faith. (See *A.C.O.*, t. ii, vol. i, pt. 2, pp. 139–40[335–6].)

[2] Kidd, *Documents*, vol. ii, p. 301; cf *A.C.O.*, t. ii, vol. i, pt. 3, pp. 120–1 [479–80].

[3] Bardy, *Chalcédoine*, p. 276.

[4] Ibid., pp. 271–2.

[5] Bardy, *Brigandage*, p. 240.

[6] Devreesse, *Antioche*, p. 63.

were proved later to have been present, though they could not easily be recognized or clearly appreciated in the enthusiastic atmosphere of the assembly.

A. *A New Language*

The first characteristic feature of the Council of Chalcedon, as it emerges from a reading of its Acts, is the prominent part played by the Roman legates with their insistence that the Tome of Leo should be accepted unconditionally and *in toto*.

In fact, throughout the Council, the Roman delegation was in control. Thus, the very beginning of the first session was not only marked by a hostile, and even aggressive, attitude towards the person of Dioscorus, and through him towards the See of Alexandria,[1] but also by the striking initiative of the Roman legates in taking control of the Council.[2]

[1] It must be remembered that Alexandria had taken the lead in Eastern Christendom in the sphere of Christian thought. It reached the peak of its strength and influence with Cyril in the Council of Ephesus. From that moment onwards its ever-increasing prestige and doctrinal authority began to overshadow the influence of the other Eastern christological tradition, i.e. the Antiochene school, and to reduce the significance of the Patriarchate of the imperial city.

[2] This aspect of the Council is very well expressed by Hefele in the following comment: "In what relation the legates stood to the Synod and to the imperial commissioners may be ascertained with sufficient certainty from the detailed history of the Council. We shall see that the official arrangements of the business were managed by the Commissioners. . . . As, however, the business was managed by the imperial commissioners, the papal legates appeared in the transactions rather as the first voters than as the presidents, but with an unmistakable superiority over all the other voters, as representatives of the head of the whole church, as they expressly said, and firm in the conviction that every resolution of the Synod to which they did not assent was null and void" (*Councils*, vol. iii, pp. 296–7).

This was later said more clearly by the great expert of the historical study of the Roman Church's authority, Mgr Batiffol: the Council of Chalcedon "sera l'apogée en Orient du principatus du siège apostolique" (*Siège Apostolique* p. 534). Again and more explicitly: "Il est incontestable, en effet, que le concile de Chalcédoine est le moment où l'Orient reconnaît le plus explicitement le droit du siège apostolique à ce principatus que Rome revendique en matière de foi et d'ordre comme la condition de la communion de l'Église universelle" (*Siège Apostolique*, p. 618. See the whole ch. 8; *La Papauté à Chalcédoine*, pp. 493–589).

The subsequent unswerving support of the Council of Chalcedon by the Roman Church will be taken into account later in this chapter.

They manifested an authority in the Council unequalled in any former Council or in any previous ecclesiastical affairs in the East. The words uttered by Paschasinus, the head of the delegation, at the opening session were strong enough to impress the members of the Council with the firmness of their conviction and sense of authority:

> We have a commission from the most holy and most apostolic Bishop of Rome, who is the head of all the Churches, to see that Dioscorus shall have no seat (or vote) in the Council, and if he shall venture upon this, that he be expelled. This commission we must fulfill. If it seems well to your highnesses (the imperial commissioners), either he must retire or we depart.[1]

We have to note carefully that the authority they claimed was not simply of a disciplinary nature. Neither was it intended for mere disciplinary measures or purposes. The papal legates were not there to settle a problem of Church order or administration. Theirs was an authority also in a doctrinal sense. In simple terms, they were not there merely for the purpose of deposing Dioscorus, who had gone so far in the exercise of his authority; their commission extended further and deeper: to secure the acceptance of the christological doctrine as set forth in the Letter of Leo to Flavian, known as the "Tome of Leo". The condemnation of Dioscorus was not, then, the final aim. It only removed the most difficult obstacle to victory. This would be achieved by a general assent to and acceptance of the Tome as *Regula Fidei*.

The Letter of Leo was read in the second session of the Council. Roman influence, supported as it was by imperial authority, was predominant. In this atmosphere many bishops hailed the Tome with acclamation. Yet there were others, namely those from Palestine and Illyricum, who found it, mainly on three points,[2] ambiguous and its language unfamiliar. Its doctrine seemed at first sight unsound, or at least not in harmony with what they were

---

[1] *A.C.O.*, t. ii, vol. i, pt. i, p. 65. Particularly revealing in this respect is the final session, in which the famous twenty-eighth canon was strongly opposed by the papal legates.

[2] See Additional Note i.

used to. They showed enough courage, even in the absence of Dioscorus and other leading figures of their group, to protest and raise objections.[1]

The explanations given at the moment did not satisfy them,[2] so they asked time to consider the passages in question more carefully and to scrutinize them in detail. They were given five days to study the Tome to see whether it corresponded to the true faith, which was, in their minds, as in many others', the Cyrilline Christology.

In the fourth session, Paschasinus declared once more that the "true faith" was the faith as expounded in the Tome of Leo and that faith the Synod held, and allowed nothing to be added to it or taken from it.[3] On this declaration, which came again as a warning, the bishops of Illyricum and Palestine finally gave approval to the Tome, having been already assured of its orthodoxy during previous consultations with the Roman legates and the other bishops.[4]

Their change of attitude, however, did not solve the problem, which had been raised by them when the Tome was first read. Now the Council faced the most unyielding opposition to the Tome by the bishops from Egypt, the stronghold of Cyrilline christology. These, thirteen in number, said openly that they could not, as representatives of the Egyptian hierarchy, subscribe to the Tome. They had to wait until an archbishop was elected to the See of Alexandria in succession to Dioscorus, now condemned and deposed by the Synod. This objection was not a mere escape from responsibility, as it may appear at first sight. It was, indeed, basically the result of their realization that acceptance of the Tome of Leo and subscription to it would mean failure on their part to maintain their loyalty to the theology of Cyril. The language of the Tome was so hard to their ears and revealed such close associations with Antiochene christological terminology, that they simply could not consent to it. This is clearly shown in a rather dramatic and yet most revealing episode which followed their

---

[1] See *A.C.O.*, t. ii, vol. i, pt. 2, pp. 15–17 [211–13].   [2] See Additional Note 1.
[3] See *A.C.O.*, t. ii, vol. i, pt. 2, p. 105.   [4] See *A.C.O.*, t. ii, vol. i, pt. 2, p. 103.

first refusal in the Council. Thus, when they were urged insistently by the Synod to subscribe they simply answered all the more clearly because they could see the consequences of their actions: "We can no longer live at home if we do this." The pressure became stronger. The Roman legates were not the kind of men to give up easily. Their commission was strict. They had to carry it out to the end. But again the Egyptian bishops, now in a desperately critical and difficult situation, cried out: "We shall be killed, we shall be killed if we do it! We would rather be made away with here by you than there ... Have mercy upon us, show us kindness!"[1]

Now, these words may easily be taken as denoting a deplorable failure to face difficulties for the sake of the truth of God. They can equally be regarded as revealing a tactful way of exaggerating or intensifying the facts of the moment and the foreseeable events of the future. But these interpretations, however plausible they may seem for various reasons or from various standpoints, are far from explaining the real meaning of the Alexandrian bishops' move.[2]

In fact, the bishops knew more than anyone else what the theological situation was, or, to put it perhaps more accurately, what was the state of theological feeling in Alexandria in particular and in the provinces under its influence in general. No doubt,

[1] See the episode in A.C.O., t. ii, vol. i, pt. 2, pp. 112–13 [308–9].

[2] The opposition to the Tome of Leo was by no means confined to the thirteen bishops from Egypt. In an additional note to this passage in the French translation of Hefele's work, Dom H. Leclercq states that the opposition extended even outside the Council in the city of Constantinople: "Hors du concile ce document provoquait une attention et des controverses non moins vives par suite de l'obligation étendue aux monastères de Constantinople de souscrire cette lettre" (Conciles, vol. ii, pt. 2, pp. 705–7, n. 1). Jalland somehow minimizes the opposition to the Tome of Leo within the Council itself when he says: "Apart from a few dissentients the majority of those present loudly approved these statements" (Leo the Great, p. 292). He seems to have passed over the objections raised there; he does not give due consideration to them and treats them as if they were of secondary importance. Again, he does not make any attempt to realize the implications of those objections taken in the circumstances of the Eastern theological atmosphere. However, he does seem to have recognized the importance of this opposition in his The Church and the Papacy. (See pp. 307 ff.)

Alexandrian christology at this period and in the shape given to it by Cyril, the unrivalled theologian of the time, had been formed and strengthened through the struggle with the Antiochene School of theology, widely and commonly known as the Separatist or Dualistic christology. That christology was now condemned. The Council of Ephesus had pronounced its final word of judgement upon it. Its champion, Nestorius, had lived in exile for many years now. Of course it is true that the School had not yet died; but it is equally true that it had been confined mainly to the eastern borders of the Empire and was beginning to lose its hold on the provinces within the Empire. The struggle was still continuing; but it was a struggle which in the eyes of all those who welcomed the Council of Ephesus would end with the victory of the Church, as it had done with Arianism and the other heresies. At least, one thing was clear: Antiochene christology was discredited on a large scale because of the condemnation of Nestorius.[1]

And now to hear a new language from the West so consonant with the one condemned, and, in some places, even surpassing it in its separatist tone, was indeed distressing for the followers of the Ephesian tradition. This was the real motive of their action, which was far from being an act of sheer "stubbornness" as Sellers puts it.[2]

Furthermore, another instance in which the Tome of Leo had an unsympathetic reception was the discussion over the doctrinal formula drafted most probably by Anatolius, bishop of Constantinople, the aim of which was to meet the criticisms of those who were finding themselves embarrassed by the Tome of Leo. While the majority of the bishops in the fifth session acclaimed this new formula with enthusiastic approval, the Roman legates were suspicious, and, therefore, very reluctant to join the other bishops. They saw in this new formula a dangerous alternative to

[1] See below, pp. 35 ff.
[2] Sellers, *Chalcedon*, p. 116. (Nor was Harnack justified in characterizing these reluctant bishops as "der Koptische Fanatismus" (quoted by Lebon, *Monophysisme Sévérien*, pp. 14–15).

the Tome of Leo which compromised the absolute authority of the latter and might overshadow it. So the legates, having fully realized this, threatened to leave the Council and to return to Rome. In the same authoritative way they made their position clear in strict and unequivocal terms:

> If they do not agree with the letter of Leo the apostolic and most blessed archbishop, give orders that we be given our papers that we may return home and a synod be held there.[1]

This was a crucial moment for the imperial commissioners. They were "alarmed"[2] by the threat. They could not allow any clash or breach, because their only purpose in convening the Council was to settle the disputes in order to secure the unity and peace of the Empire. The departure of the Roman legates would complicate the matter and, consequently, the difficulties would become harder to cope with later. So they proposed the way of compromise by creating a commission to amend the proposed formula or to draw up a new definition of faith acceptable to all. They went as far as to order the synod to "receive into the creed the doctrine of Leo, which has been stated".[3]

At this juncture there is a break in the Acts. As Hefele says:

> Whether anything, and if so what, was here objected to by the majority we do not know. It is apparent that there is here a break in the minutes, since without anything more and without any indication of the reason for the alteration which was introduced, they go on to relate that the whole of the members of the Synod now asked for the meeting of the commission which they had previously opposed.[4]

Unfortunately the text of the formula drawn up by Anatolius is lost, as it is not included in the Acts of the Council. Therefore, it is difficult to say precisely what in it was objected to by the Roman legates, or in what kind of terminology it was shaped.

But what is important for us to note in this story is a very small change in the text of the previous formula; the significance of this change is out of all proportion to its textual or literal form. It

[1] A.C.O., t. ii, vol. i, pt. 2, p. 123 [319].   [2] Jalland, Leo the Great, p. 296.
[3] A.C.O., t. ii, vol. i, pt. 2, p. 125.   [4] Hefele, Councils, vol. iii, p. 345.

is tremendously important for both theological and historical reasons. There can be no doubt that what we have now in the so-called Chalcedonian Definition, the reconstructed form of Ana-tolius' formula, as ἐν δύο φύσεσι must have been ἐκ δύο φυσέων in the previous formula which was so categorically rejected by the Roman legates.[1]

This change reveals the true spirit of the Council. ἐκ δύο φυσέων was of course accepted by Dioscorus, as was stated in the Council itself, and, no doubt, would be acceptable to all the Alexandrians, as the post-Chalcedonian controversy showed. It was coherent with their christology. And when this was pointed out by the Roman legates as an objection to the orthodoxy of Anatolius' formula, the latter answered that Dioscorus was not condemned for doctrinal unorthodoxy but for disciplinary reasons.[2]

However, things did not go in the direction of Anatolius, but turned to the Roman side again, when in spite of the spontaneous opposition of the majority of the bishops[3] the ἐκ δύο φυσέων was changed into ἐν δύο φύσεσι. This happened most probably, as we saw above, during a break in the meeting when, under the pressure of the imperial commissioners and the insistence of the

[1] See for the arguments for the probability of this change Sellers, *Chalcedon*, pp. 116 ff; Galtier, *Cyrille et Léon*, pp. 358–62; Diepen, *Trois Chapitres*, pp. 71–2; Hefele, *Conciles*, vol. ii, pt. 2, p. 720 n. For the discussion of its original form in the text of the Definition see Hefele, *Councils*, p. 348, n. 1; Sellers, *Chalcedon*, p. 120.

[2] See *A.C.O.*, t. ii, vol. i, pt. 2, p. 124 [320]. One has to note also that not only Anatolius, but most of the Oriental bishops stood for the proposed formula, ἐκ δύο φυσέων. It is surprising to see among these bishops Eusebius of Dory-laeum, the staunch opponent of Eutyches and one of the ardent leaders of the anti-Dioscorian group. It must be accepted that in the Chalcedonian Definition—itself a "mosaic" form of doctrinal document exposing before us many similar-ities with other Eastern confessions of faith, namely the Formulary of Reunion of 433 and the Confession of Flavian (see Sellers, *Chalcedon*, pp. 207–8; cf Diepen, *Trois Chapitres*, pp. 107–15)—the change of ἐκ into ἐν was the heart of the theo-logical issue. Whatever significance we may give to it now in the general context of the Definition, there is no doubt that it was the centre of the discussion. In-deed, it denotes the victory of the separatist way of thinking and as such it was, as Diepen puts it, the "pivot de la Définition" (*Trois Chapitres*, p. 117).

[3] See *A.C.O.*, t. ii, vol. i, pt. 2, pp. 123–6 [319–22].

papal legates, the Orientals gave way. The tension came to an end, again with the victory of Rome, with the new language gaining status as part of the *Regula Fidei*.

Full agreement had now been reached within the Council. But although the Tome of Leo had secured its place of honour and its position of authority in the Council, it had still to be defended and firmly established. So, again, it is not unimportant to note that in the *Allocutio* sent to the Emperor Marcian the Council spoke of Leo as the champion against every error, and added:

> Let no one attack the contents of the Tome by alleging that it is somehow alien to the faith, saying that it is not allowed for the formulation of the faith to be at variance with the faith of the Nicene Fathers.[1]

They concluded the letter to the emperor with the same doubts and fears or anxieties in the background of their minds:

> Let them (i.e. the opponents of the Tome) not bring forward the Tome of the admirable bishop of the Roman See as being an innovation.[2]

What we learn from the tension, as revealed in the Acts and which we examined above, amounts briefly to these two points:

(*a*) The Roman legates had to make sure that the Tome was accepted *in toto* without any alteration or amendment being made to it and that its orthodoxy was never questioned or challenged.

That was the price paid for the Chalcedonian Definition.

(*b*) The holders of the Cyrilline christology or Ephesian tradition had to be assured that they were not following Leo, but Cyril; therefore no change had occurred in their traditional position.

That was the purpose aimed at by the Definition.

Did the price prove to be worth paying? Was the aim achieved? More explicitly, was there a real coming together, a finding of

---

[1] *A.C.O.*, t. ii, vol. i, pt. 3, p. 110 [469].   [2] *A.C.O.*, t. ii, vol. i, pt. 3, p. 113 [472].

common ground, a synthesis, in the true sense of the word, quite apart from what may be called a juxtaposition of views or attitudes? These are questions which must be answered in our account of the subsequent events of the Council of Chalcedon.

At this juncture one thing is clear enough to be stated straightforwardly: "Saint Léon a dominé (le concile) de Chalcédoine".[1] And Pope Leo was a new voice in the East speaking a new language.

What the bishops at the Council were afraid would happen, namely that this language would be interpreted as an innovation, was in fact what happened after the Council.

B. *The Taint of Nestorianism*

The Acts of the Council of Chalcedon reveal to us another aspect which is more closely linked with the principal theme of our study. Obviously, the Council accepted and affirmed once more the condemnation of Nestorius. Eutyches and Nestorius equally stood for two extremes which the Council formally anathematized. Its task, as it is understood by the great majority of the Church historians and theologians of to-day, was to find the *via media*, i.e. the solution of the conflict in terms of a compromise, or, to use a

---

[1] Galtier, *Cyrille et Léon*, p. 345. Diepen, in his turn, puts the question straightforwardly: "Synthèse de l'Occident et de l'Orient? Disons plutôt présidence de l'Occident sur toutes les églises. Les Pères de Chalcédoine référèrent le Tome de saint Léon aux écrits de saint Cyrille pour en constater l'orthodoxie: Λέων εἶπεν τὰ κυρίλλου Saint Léon, lui, s'affirme au contraire, comme le Docteur authentique, par sa charge, de l'Église universelle. C'est lui qui approuve la théologie cyrillienne, et désapprouve certaines tendances de l'épiscopat qui se réclame de saint Cyrille." Then, after saying how St. Leo avoided the Eutychianism, he returns to the problem of Anatolius' formula which was amended by the Roman legates and shows how Leo influenced the doctrine of the Council. "Le projet présumé d'Anatole ne semble pas avoir eu la même précision tandis qu'au contraire son exclusion du dualisme antiochien n'eut qu'à recueillir l'entière approbation de saint Léon. Sur ce dernier point il n'y eut ni compromis, ni synthèse, ni complément, mais convergence et unité. L'œuvre de saint Léon à Chalcédoine a été une œuvre de modération et de mesure.

"En tant qu'elle sera pour tous les siècles suivants le phare qui indique les deux écueils opposés du monophysisme et du nestorianisme, la Définition de Chalcédoine fut une œuvre romaine, l'œuvre de saint Léon le Grand" (*Trois Chapitres*, pp. 117–18).

happier term, a synthesis. But sometimes the attempt is one thing and the achievement another thing. And, as it seems to us, this is true of the Council of Chalcedon.

Let us, then, see how this happened in the case of the attitude which the Council took towards the burning issue of the time, i.e. Nestorianism. In order to understand this we must first be aware of the theological situation and the ecclesiastical affairs of the period which lies between Ephesus (431) and Chalcedon (451).

The struggle between the Orthodox and the Nestorians—in other words, between the Alexandrians and Antiochenes—was still going on. The condemnation of Nestorius at Ephesus and his exile in the desert had not resulted in the extinction of his doctrine, which was now being supported and strengthened by the students of the Antiochene School. These, in fact, deeply resented that condemnation, which they regarded as an act of injustice and which they interpreted as a hard blow at the roots of their own christological position. As they had not moved from their position, they could not bear this blow in a spirit of resignation.[1] That, indeed, would mean treason to their own cause.

The Reunion Act of 433 reached by Cyril and John of Antioch, the leaders of the two sides, was a momentary and very precarious one, and it did not achieve its desired object in the life of the Church. It was an *act*, it remained a *formulary*, but was never changed into an *event* in the full sense of this term, that is to say, with important and permanent consequences.[2] The high repu-

---

[1] See Devreesse, *Après Ephèse*; D'Alès, *Symbole de 433*; Diepen, *Trois Chapitres*, pp. 30–45; Doucin, *Hist. Nest.*, pp. 246–70; Vine, *Nestorian Churches*, pp. 33–4; Labourt, *Christ. Perse*, p. 253.

[2] For Cyril himself this was necessary for the peace of the Church. The Formulary of Reunion meant for him the acceptance of his christology by the Antiochenes. The "Theotokos" was included there. But what was more important was that the expression " the union of two natures" (δύο γὰρ φυσέων ἕνωσις γέγονε) was accepted. Therefore he could say, "Let the heavens rejoice and the earth be glad, for the middle wall of partition is broken down, exasperation is stilled, and all occasion for discussion utterly removed through the bestowal of peace upon his churches by Christ, the Saviour of us all" (Evagrius, *Eccl. Hist.* bk. i, ch. 6, Engl. tr. p. 10; Bidez, p. 11).

In a similar way, John of Antioch, the leader of the opposite side, also had the

tation of a Theodore of Mopsuestia[1] the skilful activities of a Theodoret of Cyrus,[2] with a group of ardent supporters behind them

---

same feeling. But many other influential figures on the Antiochene side, such as
Alexander of Hierapolis, Andrew of Samosata, or even Theodoret, either entirely
disagreed with or practically disregarded the Reunion Act. They persistently refused to accept the condemnation of Nestorius. (See their attitude, well presented
by Diepen, *Trois Chapitres*, pp. 30–45; Sellers, *Chalcedon*, p. 20 ff; Devreesse,
Essai, pp. 131–4.)

The reality of the tension, still strong, is reflected in a very characteristic way by
the words ascribed to Theodoret, who on the death of Cyril (440) wrote: "At
last with a final struggle the villain has passed away ... observing that his malice
increased daily and injured the body of the Church, the Governor of our souls
has lopped him off like a canker.... His departure delights the survivors, but
possibly disheartens the dead; there is some fear that under the provocation of his
company they may send him back again to us.... Care must therefore be taken
to order the guild of undertakers to place a very big and heavy stone on his grave
to stop him coming back here.... I am glad and rejoice to see the fellowship of
the Church delivered from such a contagion; but I am saddened and sorry as I
reflect that the wretched man never took rest from his misdeeds, but died de-
signing greater and worse" (Theodoret, *Ep.* 180, quoted by Prestige, *Fathers and
Heretics*, p. 15; cf Amann, *Trois Chapitres*, col. 1876–7).

As Theodoret's position is the most important of all, one must read also Bardy's
comment. (See Bardy, *Théodoret*, col. 300–1.)

[1] It is beyond doubt that Theodore held almost the same kind of position in the
Antiochene tradition as Cyril in the Alexandrian. His reputation was not touched
in any way by the Council of Chalcedon. The silence of the latter enhanced his
authority through the rehabilitation of his faithful followers, Theodoret and Ibas.
In the preface of his essay, Mgr Devreesse says: "Les contemporains de Théodore
l'ont regardé comme l'un des plus redoutables adversaires des hérésies qui s'étaient
implantés dans les églises orientales; ils l'ont défendu avec une ardeur et une
émotion dont les accents nous touchent aujourd'hui encore, car ils voyaient dans
l'attaque entreprise contre sa mémoire et son œuvre, se faire jour des préoccu-
pations qui n'étaient pas celle de l'orthodoxie traditionelle" (*Essai*, p. v). Ibas
admired him as the greatest authority in Christian doctrine. Writing to Mari the
Persian about the "wicked" attack of Rabbula on Theodore, he describes this
latter as "héraut de la vérité, docteur de l'Église, qui non seulement en sa vie
souffleta les hérétiques pour l'honneur de sa vraie foi, mais après la mort a laissé
dans ses écrits une arme spirituelle aux enfants de l'Église." (See d'Alès, *Lettre
d'Ibas*, p. 8; cf *A.C.O.*, t. ii, vol. i, pt. 3, p. 33.)

[2] Particularly important are his writings against Cyril and his theology. Apart
from his book against the *Twelve Anathematisms* which was written in the beginning of 431, he wrote two others after the Council of Ephesus, one against
Cyril and the Council of Ephesus and the other in defence of Diodore and Theodore. Unfortunately both of them are lost in their original text. Only a few fragments survive. (See Bardy, *Théodoret*, col. 304.)

were keeping the condemned doctrine alive. For that doctrine was not Nestorius' own; but as it belonged to a famous School, being attached to the memory of Diodore of Tarsus and Theodore of Mopsuestia—to mention the most important teachers—and having such a long history behind it, it could not be abandoned so easily and suddenly.[1]

Apart from the efforts of Theodoret and his close friends, there were the Syrian regions on the south-east borders of the Empire, where the teaching of Nestorius was gaining considerable ground and securing a firm stand.[2] The School of Edessa was the centre of such a widespread activity in both literary and "missionary" domains. From here, for example, came the translations of the works of the Antiochene theologians and especially those of Theodore of Mopsuestia, the great Master of Nestorianism as well as the "Interpreter" of the Scriptures,[3] "dont l'œil s'obscursit dans l'étude des Écritures sans arrêt et sans interruption".[4]

Being always under the hostile eyes of the Byzantine rulers and driven out of the Empire, the Nestorians became the doctrinal teachers of the Christians in the Persian Empire. The expansion of Nestorianism, in fact, was to gain such a firm hold there that the Church in the Persian Empire later accepted and proclaimed it as the official confession of faith.[5]

This was, then, the atmosphere in which the Council of Chalce-

[1] The later controversy over the *Three Chapters* is highly significant to this effect. The testimony of Innocentius Maroniae, followed by that of Liberatus, is most valuable, as we shall see later. However, it is worth noting, as Amann suggests, that Cyril himself had already changed his position. His former rather mild attitude towards the Reunion Act had already gone. He soon became anti-Diodorian and anti-Theodorian. (See Amann, *Trois Chapitres*, col. 1872–3.)

[2] The masters and the disciples of the school of Edessa "malgré la condemnation solennelle des erreurs de Nestorius au concile d'Ephèse en 431, avaient toujours continué à professer les doctrines de cet hérétique" (Chabot, *École de Nisibe*, p. 45).

[3] See Devreesse, *Essai*, pp. 5–42, 53–93; cf Doucin, *Hist. Nest.*, pp. 279–80.

[4] Narses, *Trois Docteurs*, p. 509.

[5] Later we shall present this situation in detail with its subsequent developments. Here we state the facts in broad terms only to bring out the main aspects of the general situation.

don met. A sensitive world, indeed, where terms and formulas were more than terms and formulas as we take them now.

With the full realization of this situation we now turn to look once more at the proceedings of the Council of Chalcedon.

The first thing to note is that Nestorius is openly and formally condemned, even, perhaps, with more firmness than at Ephesus. No one at all shows sympathy for him personally. He was justly condemned at Ephesus. There could be no going back on the attitude taken there. Many years now had already passed since his condemnation and his life-long exile had made his "cause"almost a dead one.

But more important than the fact of the condemnation is the significance of it in terms of the situation of the time. What did it really mean to condemn Nestorius, or more precisely, to reaffirm his condemnation? What impact could it have in the life of the Church?

It is clear from what we said earlier in this chapter that Nestorianism was by no means confined to the personal teaching of Nestorius; neither was he the builder of the christological system of which he later came to be the spokesman. He was only the man who brought it into open conflict with Alexandrian christology, a conflict in which he found himself finally on the defeated side. If we look beyond the actual terms, then, it is perfectly legitimate to say that Nestorius and Nestorianism were not identical. It was possible, therefore, to stand by the doctrine known as Nestorianism or, to use other terms, separatist or dualistic christology, without being necessarily a follower of Nestorius in the strict sense of the word.

In fact, this attitude came to be for the Antiochenes not only one possible way of saving their christological tradition, but at the same time the wisest way of preserving it. For many of them it became a clear conviction that what was condemned in Nestorius could be saved from destruction only by dissociating it from the name of Nestorius. And whatever they felt about him personally, they had to pronounce the formal condemnation or anathema on Nestorius when they were invited to do so to prove their orthodoxy. In any case, Nestorius had to be sacrificed for the survival of the doctrine condemned under his name. All those who at the bottom of their hearts could not or did not agree with his condemnation nevertheless had to accept it as a fact.[1]

It is obvious that with this important change in the position of the Antiochene side, the affirmation of Nestorius' condemnation in the Council of Chalcedon had no serious meaning, nor could it have any consequence of much importance to the "Nestorian" cause. Nestorius belonged to the past. It was to the future that they had to look.

There were other people, higher in authority than Nestorius, whose names could shelter the doctrine which was attacked and condemned in Nestorius. Thus, they had reasons also for accepting Nestorius' condemnation by the Council of Chalcedon, for two incidents which occurred in that Council could make them confident that their tradition would survive:

(a) The rehabilitation of their two leading theologians, Theodoret of Cyrus and Ibas of Edessa, in their episcopal functions.

(b) The recognition of the orthodoxy of their faith.

Thus, in the first session of the Council Theodoret of Cyrus was admitted to the meeting. This aroused vehement protests from among the bishops of Egypt, Palestine, and Illyricum, the supporters of Dioscorus. In fact, Theodoret had always obstinately refused to give assent to the condemnation of Nestorius. Well-known for his anti-Cyrilline writings, he was the highest authority now on the Antiochene side, and he openly declared his agreement with the teaching of Nestorius. It was this attitude of his that led to his condemnation and his subsequent deposition from the episcopal see of Cyrus in the second Council of Ephesus

---

[1] Lebon has well recognized this aspect of post-Ephesian history: "Nestorius avait seul était frappé par la sentence du concile d'Éphèse (431); ceux qui restaient en secret, les partisans de ses doctrines, se décidèrent enfin à le laisser dans l'ombre. Ils se mirent avec ardeur à traduire et à propager les écrits de Diodore de Tarse et de Théodore de Mopsueste. Cette tactique rusée, suivie surtout par Ibas d'Édesse et par ses collègues de l'école des Perses, ne servit qu'à exciter la résistance des adversaires du nestorianisme" (*Monophysisme Sévérien*, p. 2; cf Labourt, *Christ. Perse*, p. 252).

(449). It is, then, a matter of no surprise to see him inseparably associated with Nestorius. This explains why the bishops when they protested against his presence in the Council introduced the name of the empress Pulcheria who formerly had sympathized with the Cyrilline party against Nestorius: "The Empress drove out Nestorius—long live the orthodox empress—the Synod does not receive Theodoret."[1]

But Theodoret had already won the sympathy of Leo before the Council of Chalcedon met.[2] This sympathy made his way into the Council all too easy; as the imperial commissioners themselves said at his arrival in the session, he had been already reinstated in his episcopal function and he had been washed from all suspicion of heresy by Leo.[3] Meanwhile, notwithstanding all this opposition, he was accepted by the Council and began to take part in the deliberations. He asked that his deposition by Dioscorus be examined and judged. But his case did not come up for consideration until 26 October, in the eighth session of the assembly.[4]

Now, the criterion by which his orthodoxy had to be tested and proved was a formal anathema required of him against Nestorius. And that he was not prepared yet to do.

One of the most interesting and eloquent passages in the Acts

---

[1] A.C.O., t. ii, vol. i, pt. 1, p. 69.

[2] See for the evidence Diepen, Trois Chapitres, p. 85; also Zachariah, Chronicle, bk. iii, ch. 1, p. 42.

[3] See A.C.O., t. ii, vol. i, pt. 1, p. 69.

[4] Diepen, relating the story of Theodoret's introduction in the Synod, makes the following remark which is worth quoting: "L'incident se termina ainsi et Théodoret put prendre part aux délibérations sans être inquiété par personne. Mais il avait pu se rendre compte combien sa situation était précaire dans l'assemblée. Les exclamations en sa faveur semblaient plus inspirées par l'hostilité à l'égard de Dioscore que par l'unanimité avec lui, Théodoret. Et celles du parti contraire témoignaient d'une inimitié implacable. Il était toléré provisoirement comme accusateur, mais pour être mis bientôt en état d'accusation. Car le passage des Palestiniens et des Illyriens au parti des Orientaux, et l'exclusion des Egyptiens aura bien pour effet de rétablir l'unité dans le concile, mais non pas d'apaiser les ressentiments qui s'étaient fait jour dans l'épisode que nous venons de raconter. Le rôle d'accusateur que saint Léon lui avait destiné, ne serait pas pour l'évêque de Cyr de tout repos" (Trois Chapitres, p. 87).

of the Council is that one in which Theodoret and the bishops are engaged in a lively debate. Apparently the bishops[1] on the one hand are anxious to have the anathema in clear, unequivocal words, but, on the other hand, Theodoret makes several attempts and uses divers skilful means to escape doing what he has always refused to do. Finally, under the pressure of the unyielding demand of the assembly he is brought to pronounce the anathema. Curiously enough, as if to overshadow this anathema, he also declares his entire adherence to the Tome of Leo and to the Definition:

> Anathema to Nestorius and to every one who does not call the holy Virgin Mary Theotokos, and who divides the one Son, the only-begotten, into two Sons. Morover, I have subscribed the definition of faith by the Synod and the letter of the most holy archbishop Leo; and thus I think.[2]

And when his "orthodoxy" is thus established he is given back his bishopric.

A further example of pro-Antiochene sympathy in the Council of Chalcedon was the rehabilitation of Ibas of Edessa in his orthodoxy, as it is described in the ninth and tenth sessions of the Council, on 27 and 28 October.

Ibas had been the bishop of Edessa since 435. He had succeeded the famous Rabbula, whose pro-Cyrilline policy he had opposed. He was well known for his sympathies with Nestorianism. In particular, he was himself wholeheartedly devoted to the propagation of the works of Diodore of Tarsus, Theodore of Mopsuestia, Theodoret of Cyrus, and other Antiochenes; this was done by means of Syriac translations made by himself or by his supporters.[3] All these activities had aroused a strong opposition to

---

[1] No precise identification of the bishops is given. No evaluation of their tendencies is made either. With all probability, the whole assembly is understood without any distinction.

[2] *A.C.O.*, t. ii, vol. i, pt. 3, p. 9[368].

[3] "Les œuvres de Théodore ont été traduites en Syriaque, dans la première moitié du Ve. siècle peu de temps après la mort de leur auteur, à l'École d'Édesse, par Ibas et ses disciples Probus, Koumi, Mana" (Duval, *Litt. Syr.* p. 87; cf pp. 254, 316, 343–4; Idem, *Histoire d'Édesse*, pp. 174, 177–8; cf Venables, *Ibas*, p. 196; Doucin, *Hist. Nest.*, p. 286; Amann, *Trois Chapitres*, col. 1877).

him among the people and the monks of Edessa, who remained faithful to the memory of their former bishop, Rabbula, and continued the tradition of loyalty to Cyril's christology. After a stormy period of conflict[1] he had been condemned and deposed as a heretic by Dioscorus in the second Council of Ephesus (449).

Now, in the Council of Chalcedon when the tide had turned in the opposite direction, his case was brought up. Like Theodoret, he too complained of his condemnation and deposition. So the proceedings of the previous councils which had dealt with his case, i.e. Berytus and Tyr, were read. In conclusion he was recognized as orthodox on the basis of his famous letter to Mari,[2] which was read here and approved.[3] Again, the final approval of his orthodoxy was given when he pronounced a formal anathema against Nestorius.[4]

Now, it may seem that these events which occurred in the Council and these aspects revealed therein are really of minor importance, especially when compared with the generally assumed "great doctrinal achievement" of Chalcedon, in which

---

[1] He had been tried three times within two years, in Antioch (448), in Berytus (449), in Tyr (449).

[2] See d'Alès, *Lettre d'Ibas*; cf Labourt, *Christ. Perse*, pp. 133-4, n. 6.

[3] See *A.C.O.*, t. ii, vol. i, pt. 3, pp. 32-4 [391-3], 39-42 [398-401].

[4] See *A.C.O.*, t. ii, vol. i, pt. 3, p. 42 [401]. That Nestorianism had become a haunting idea in the minds of the bishops—those who were maintaining their loyalty to St Cyril—is evident from many other passages in the Acts of the Council. Without going into a detailed examination of them, we can point out the following instance as a mere example. When the formula proposed by Anatolius in the fifth session was opposed by John of Germanicia, this latter was immediately accused as Nestorian by the majority of the bishops who supported the formula, in which, as we already noted, the ἐκ δύο φύσεων was the central, essential statement. (See *A.C.O.*, t. ii, vol. i, pt. 2, p. 123 [319].) And a little later, the same charge is repeated by the bishops of Illyricum with an even stronger emphasis. In fact, they went as far as to say: "The opponents are Nestorians, let the opposers depart to Rome" (*A.C.O.*, t. ii, vol. i, pt. 2, p. 125 [321]). This identification of Nestorianism with Rome is most revealing in reflecting the mind of the bishops at Chalcedon on the relationship of Leo's christology with Nestorius' teaching. (See below, pp. 52 ff.) Particularly interesting is the account of the Council of Chalcedon given in the Chronicle of Zachariah, who reflects the mind of the anti-Chalcedonians concerning the Council. (See iii, 1, pp. 41-7.)

"the Church possesses a treasure of inestimable worth".[1] But if we try to see them in the proper context of the theological issues of the time, they are shown to be extremely important; and in fact they played a decisive rôle in the history of the Church and of doctrine in the second half of the fifth century and throughout the following century.

Again, in the limits we imposed on our study, we cannot go into the details of that subsequent history. Indeed, it is a very complicated story in itself, which should be a matter of special concern and investigation.[2] But we must try to trace its general lines and indicate its characteristic features.

This story may very easily be characterized as a history of sheer polemics. And sometimes, how disheartening and depressing these polemics are and how futile they seem to be! But apart from any judgement we may make about their significance or value, we have to see the events in their right historical perspective. In that perspective we observe a continuous struggle between two sections, both of them still remaining within the fold of the Church. In this struggle one cannot fail to see the increasing strength and the growing predominance of the anti-Chalcedonian section over the supporters of Chalcedon.

Let us illustrate this statement.

[1] Sellers, *Chalcedon*, p. 350. That great doctrinal achievement is usually thought of as being the combination in a synthesis of the different and, outwardly seen, contradictory ways in christology. Sellers sees in Chalcedon the real meeting point. (See the views of G. Florovsky and A. Schmemann in Dombalis, *1500th Anniversary*; Kelly, *Doctrines*, p. 342.) Long ago Chalcedon had been considered as the "prudent measure" or the "middle way". As early as 1698 the Jesuit author and the historian of Nestorianism, Doucin, had said: "[the Decrees of Chalcedon] doivent être considérés comme le chef-d'œuvre de la prudence évangelique. Nestorius n'y fut pas plus épargné qu'Eutychès. Les deux erreurs furent également proscrites" (*Hist. Nest.*, p. 313).

[2] The importance of that period from historical, literary, philosophical, and theological points of view, has already been recognized and considerable attention given to it by some prominent scholars. To give some names: J. Lebon, *Monophysisme Sévérien*; *Monophysisme Syrien*; his Latin translations of Severus' works; Wigram, *Separation*; R. Draguet, *Julien d'Halicarnasse*; many articles in *Le Muséon*; Brooks with the edition of Severus' Letters in P.O.; C. Moeller, *Néo-Chalcédonisme*; and many others. (See for a short bibliography Lebon, *Monophysisme Syrien* p. 429.)

Soon after the conclusion of the Council, the clash between the Chalcedonians and anti-Chalcedonians became strikingly apparent. It was not now a mere theological dispute or a conflict between ecclesiastical authorities or patriarchal jurisdictions. In fact, it did amount to a larger conflict which involved the whole ecclesiastical policy of the Byzantine Empire. Nor was it confined to the city of Constantinople; it spread over the Empire from Constantinople to Edessa and eastwards, passing through Anatolia, and from Antioch through Palestine down to Egypt. It soon became a crucial problem, in fact, *the* problem of the time.[1]

All the successors of Marcian, Leo (457–74),[2] Basiliscus (475–6),[3] Zeno (476–91),[4], Anastasius (491–518),[5] Justin (518–27),[6] Justinian (527–65),[7] without exception were engaged in some way or another in the problem, which preoccupied Byzantine policy for more than a century.[8] The emperors were somehow compelled

---

[1] As Zachariah of Mitylene says, it "shook all the world; and added evil upon evil; and set the two heresies, one against the other, and filled the world with divisions; and confounded the faith delivered by the Apostles, and the good order of the Church; and tore into ten thousand rents the perfect Robe of Christ, woven from the top throughout" (*Chronicle*, bk. iii, ch. 1, p. 41).

[2] See Evagrius, *Eccl. Hist.*, bk. ii, ch. 9; Zachariah, *Chronicle*, bk. iv. ch. 5; Bury, *Later Roman Empire*, vol. i, p. 322; Lebon, *Monophysisme Sévérien*, pp. 21–5.

[3] Evagrius, bk. iii, chs. 3–7; Zachariah, bk. v, chs. 1–3. Lebon, *Monophysisme Sévérien*, pp. 25–9.

[4] Evagrius, bk. ii, ch. 17, bk. iii, chs. 1, 8–24. Zachariah, bks. v and vi; Lebon, *Monophysisme Sévérien*, pp. 29–39; Bury, *Later Roman Empire*, vol. i, pp. 402–4; Vasiliev, *Byzantine Empire*, vol. i, pp. 107–9; Stein, *Bas-Empire*, pp. 20–7, 31–8.

[5] Evagrius, bk. iii, chs. 29–30 ff; Zachariah, bk. vii; Lebon, *Monophysisme Sévérien*, pp. 39–66; Duchesne, *Église VIe. siècle*, pp. 1–42; Bréhier, *Anastase* col. 1453–7; Bury, *Later Roman Empire*, vol. i, pp. 111–12, 115; Stein, *Bas-Empire*, pp. 157–76; Charanis, *Anastasius*.

[6] Evagrius, bk. iv, chs. 1, 4, 6; Zachariah, bk. viii, chs. 1–3; Lebon, *Monophysisme Sévérien*, pp. 66–72; Duchesne, *Église VIe. siècle*, pp. 43–77; Stein, *Bas-Empire*, pp. 223–38; Vasiliev, *Justin I*, pp. 132–253.

[7] Evagrius, bk. iv, chs. 10–11, 38–41; Zachariah, bk. ix, chs. 15–16; Lebon, *Monophysisme Sévérien*, pp. 73–8 (only for the first part of Justinian's reign); Bury, *Later Roman Empire*, vol. ii, pp. 372–93; Stein, *Bas-Empire*, 376–95.

[8] It was not solved even in the days of Justinian. Later emperors also faced the same problem which had now lost its theological significance and become a problem of Church relationship on political grounds. (See Goubert, *Successeurs de Justinien*; Bréhier, *Successeurs de Justinien*, pp. 486–7.)

to try to solve the problem that disturbed the internal situation of the Empire and was even beginning to affect its foreign affairs.

The most remarkable aspect of all this story is that most of these emperors either favoured the anti-Chalcedonian movement (e.g. Basiliscus, Zeno, Anastasius) or directed their efforts to a compromise solution. Either way meant overlooking the Council of Chalcedon or reducing its importance, thus finally challenging its very ecumenicity and authority. Obviously, if they took this line of policy it was mainly because of the rising strength of the anti-Chalcedonians. This, in their view, could lead to a breach within the Empire itself, thus weakening its power of resistance to various invasions pressing in from so many sides, a fear, in fact, that was justified in the later history of the sixth and seventh centuries.

But if the emperors looked at this anti-Chalcedonian section from a purely political point of view that does not mean that the movement in itself was the expression of sheer political tendencies within the Empire. First of all and basically it was a positive view in christology; secondly, it was a movement opposing the Chalcedonian christology for doctrinal reasons. And, therefore, as we take it as a religious fact, without losing sight of its political aspects and implications, we do not need to go into the political consequences it had or into the political tendencies which were associated with it. If we referred to the political approach of the Byzantine rulers it was only to show that Monophysitism[1] soon

[1] Now we use this term for the anti-Chalcedonian movement simply because it has become the generally accepted term in the historical and theological literature. But we should like to remark that it is not the appropriate or adequate term to characterize the movement as a theological position or system, for it is, first of all, an ambiguous term which may very easily lead—as indeed it has led—to a false appreciation of the doctrinal attitude of the movement. G. Bardy is right when he says: "Rien n'est plus difficile ... que de définir le monophysisme" (*Chalcédoine*, p. 309, n. 1). Then, secondly, it implies a counter-term, "Dyophysitism", which in fact has no current use in characterizing the Chalcedonian position. Thus, without maintaining the right balance between the two opposite terms, the exclusive use of one of them can become misleading. It has already caused much confusion in understanding the doctrinal position of the so-called "Monophysite" Churches. But, as we said, it is difficult to avoid it as its use

became such a widespread, influential, and dominant movement in Eastern Christianity that it could cause anxiety to the emperors for so many years after the Council of Chalcedon.[1]

Having said this, let us turn now to our immediate purpose, i.e. to indicate some aspects of post-Chalcedonian ecclesiastical history which are closely linked with the characteristic features of the Council of Chalcedon itself as stated above.

II. SOME ASPECTS OF POST-CHALCEDONIAN HISTORY

Taking the same line of investigation as that adopted in the reading of the Acts of the Council, we find in this movement simply the continuation of the opposition which we discovered within the Council itself to its formularies and actions.

That opposition had two grounds:

A. *The Council of Chalcedon was not consonant with the predominant Christological tradition of the East*

The truth in this statement is clearly shown in the subsequent, ultimately unsolved, difficulties which were felt by all those who tried to reconcile the Monophysites and the Chalcedonians and to restore unity within Church and Empire.

We can see this in the following points:

1. One of the striking aspects in post-Chalcedonian history is

---

has become widespread now. (See, about its ambiguities and various meanings, Lebon, *Monophysisme Sévérien*, Intr., pp. xxii–xxiv; but particularly Jugie, *Eutyches*, col. 1595–1601; Idem, *Monophysisme*, col. 2216–19.)

[1] "In large districts", says Wigram, "the Council was rejected at once, and in none, save only in Rome, was there any enthusiasm for its doctrine" (*Separation*, p. 16). There were times when the Monophysites became "supreme and triumphant" (ibid., p. 63). They "were the winning party in the Church for a full generation after 451 (ibid., p. 147; cf Idem, *Assyr. Church*, pp. 144–7.)

the apparent readiness of the Eastern Christian leaders to come to terms with the Monophysites without making the acceptance of the Council of Chalcedon a necessary prerequisite.

When we read this history carefully it is not difficult at all to see how the Eastern bishops and theologians were often, if not always, prepared to reconsider the problem of Chalcedon and to find a way to reconciliation apart from the decisions of the Council of Chalcedon. Thus, they were always ready to welcome imperial decrees and encyclicals intended to break down the deadlock between the two sides. One may easily argue that if they did agree to those decrees or encyclicals it was because they wished, sometimes in a servile manner, to show themselves loyal to the imperial will either for fear of deposition or for expected favours or benefits. It is obvious that erastianism played an important part in the ecclesiastical history of the fourth and fifth centuries. But it was not the most important factor in determining the decisions of the bishops of the post-Chalcedonian period. We think that there were other and more important reasons for this willingness of the Eastern bishops to welcome imperial moves aimed at reunion. First of all, we have to remember that they were living in the midst of the troubles. Chalcedon had generated a crisis which now was creating situations in Church life which were difficult to face and control. Everywhere, in the East, opposition was being organized which often got bishops appointed to the ecclesiastical sees, sometimes with the support of the imperial authorities. In short, for them Chalcedon had become a tormenting issue through its consequences in the practical life of their own Churches. This may explain why they were so eager to see the problem solved and the troubles settled for more than purely theological reasons.

But there is another reason for this their willingness, the most important of all, to which we must give serious attention: they were not happy themselves with the Chalcedonian terminology. We saw what reaction was made to the reading of the Tome of Leo in the Council itself.[1] We remember how uneasy the Eastern

[1] See above, pp. 27 ff.

bishops were over the changing of some crucial terms in the formulary of faith which later became the Chalcedonian Definition. What was there felt generally and sometimes said openly proved to be true in this post-Chalcedonian period.[1]

Thus, when the bishops who had attended the Council of Chalcedon returned to their sees, they found themselves strongly opposed by their clergy, monks, and faithful laity. They were regarded as "traitors" to the Orthodox or traditional faith. They had to be protected by the Government or yield to the opposition by joining it, thus returning to their traditional positions. For example, Juvenal, bishop of Jerusalem, on his return from Chalcedon found his flock against him. So he came back to Constantinople to seek help from the Emperor.[2] In Syria the opposition grew rapidly and rather surprisingly, because Antioch had been the stronghold of the Dyophysite School of christology apparently favoured now at Chalcedon. This opposition grew to such an extent that later, in the next century, Antioch became one of the most important centres of the opposite, Monophysite, movement.[3] The Egyptian bishops had rightly cried out at the Council of Chalcedon: "We shall be killed!" The bloody scenes in Alexandria which followed the Council of Chalcedon proved this to be true.[4] Here imperial decrees and the military support provided by the Government could not keep in office for long any Patriarch of Chalcedonian inclination.[5] In Mesopotamia even

[1] "Les craintes qu'ils [the Egyptian bishops] manifestaient au sujet de l'attitude des populations de leurs diocèses n'étaient que trop fondées; la suite se chargea de le montrer à l'évidence" (Lebon, *Monophysisme Sévérien*, pp. 14–15).

[2] See Evagrius, bk. ii, ch. 5; Zachariah, bk. iii, chs. 3–9. "Soon he realized that his conduct at Chalcedon had leached unexpected fury in Palestine. The majority of his flock considered him an apostate who had betrayed his former faith" (Honigmann, *Juvenal*, p. 247; see the whole passage: pp. 247–57).

[3] See Devreesse, *Antioche*, pp. 63–76; cf Bardy, *Chalcédoine*, p. 287.

[4] To these bloody scenes the following words in the *Henoticon* refer: φόνους τε τολμηθῆναι μυρίους καὶ αἱμάτων πλήθει μολυνθῆναι μὴ μόνον τὴν γῆν ἀλλ᾿ ἤδη καὶ αὐτὸν τὸν ἀέρα. (See Evagrius, bk. iii, ch. 14; Bidez, p. 112.)

[5] The case of Proterius is quite eloquent in itself. (See Evagrius, bk. ii, ch. 8; cf Zachariah, bk. iii, ch. 2, bk. iv, ch. 2.) On the troubles in Alexandria see Zachariah, bk. iii, ch. 11, bk. iv, chs. 1–12, bk. v, chs. 1, 7, 9–12.

Monophysitism began to gain wide popularity in spite of the previous expansion of Nestorianism.[1]

All these events cannot be properly explained by reference to political tendencies, namely on the rising nationalist feeling among the peoples of the Patriarchates or provinces mentioned above, nor by the servile subjugation of the bishops to the imperial decrees. Of course these factors must be taken into account in any attempt to understand fully this growing strength of Monophysitism; but they must be seen in the right perspective in which the fundamental fact remains the theological dislike of and unfamiliarity with the new formulations of the Council of Chalcedon. To the ears of the Eastern bishops the Tome of Leo could never sound perfectly orthodox. The soil in the East, being already sown with Cyrilline thought, was not prepared to receive the foreign seeds of Western christology as found in the Tome. Or, more precisely, the theological *milieu* created by the dominance of Cyrilline over Nestorian thought could not accept the apparently "Nestorianizing" terminology of Leo. This seems to us the essential point which is sometimes overlooked when the opponents of the Council of Chalcedon are too easily described as men of "schismatical spirit", "champions of nationalism" with a character of typical "oriental stubborness", etc. G. Bardy is one of those rare people who have seen beyond the outward appearance of the things. Thus, speaking of the readiness of the Eastern bishops to conform to the official policy of the Empire, he says:

> Une telle unanimité de l'épiscopat oriental pour signer tout ce qu'on voulait n'avait evidemment rien de digne. De plus, elle pouvait donner à réflechir à des hommes doués de quelque sens politique. N'était-il pas évident que si l'on acceptait le Tome de Léon et le

[1] "Le mouvement monophysite gagna même la Syrie euphratésienne et l'Osrohène, autrefois le boulevard du dyophysisme. Quand Théodoret et Ibas disparurent (457), la cause antiochienne ne trouva plus de champion dans ces provinces" (Labourt, *Christ. Perse*, p. 260; cf pp. 133, 288). The sixth century marked the conquest of Edessa and the north-western regions of Mesopotamia by the Monophysite movement. As Duval puts it, "Le grand évènement religieux de ce siècle fut la conversion au monophysisme des chrétiens de la Syrie et de la Mésopotamie" (*Histoire d'Édesse*, p. 216).

concile de Chalcédoine, c'était pour plaire aux autorités, alors que, au fond du cœur, on était beaucoup plus attaché aux formules cyrilliennes? Tous les évènements qui, depuis 451, s'étaient passés en Orient ne démontraient-ils pas que le monophysisme attirait à lui les meilleurs esprits, les hommes les plus pieux, voire les théologiens les plus savants?[1]

An outstanding example of this tendency among the Eastern bishops is undoubtedly the attitude of Acacius, the Patriarch of Constantinople (471–89). This is clearly seen in the famous *Henoticon* (ἐνωτικόν) promulgated by emperor Zeno in 482, but inspired or designed by Acacius.[2] The important points for us to note here are the following features of the edict:

(*a*) It accepts the Nicene Faith, "the faith of the three hundred and eighteen bishops", as possessing the only binding authority for all the Churches.

(*b*) It stresses also the Council of Ephesus (431) as having followed faithfully those three hundred and eighteen holy Fathers.

(*c*) It gives Cyril his right place in the brief formulation of its doctrine, after having accepted and approved the orthodoxy of his *Twelve Chapters* (δεχόμενοι καὶ τὰ δώδεκα κεφάλαια) which were discarded at Chalcedon.

(*d*) Chalcedon is not rejected in a direct way, but regarded as something unnecessary for the maintenance of orthodoxy; it is even charged in an indirect way as heterodox. Thus, after the brief exposition of faith made in terms of Cyrilline christology it

---

[1] Bardy, *Chalcedoine*, pp. 289–90. Duchesne, a severe critic of Cyril, had already recognized the affinity of thought which these Eastern bishops showed with the Cyrilline christology. Speaking on the achievement of the Council of Chalcedon, he says "En somme les légats romains et l'empereur Marcien avaient remporté à Chalcédoine un succès contestable. Sans s'en douter aucunement ils avaient blessé vivement la plupart des théologiens grecs, et, avec eux, beaucoup d'âmes religieuses qui pensaient ou plutôt sentaient, en ce genre de choses, comme Cyrille et son groupe" (*Autonomies*, p. 38).

[2] See the text in Evagrius, bk. iii, ch. 14 (Bidez, pp. 111–14). *P.G.* t. 86, col. 2620–5 (reprinted in *D.T.C.*, t. iv, col. 2160–2); cf Zachariah, bk. v, ch. 8. See a thorough study from the Roman point of view by Salaville, *Hénotique*. (I have seen only the last part of the study.)

adds: πάντα δὲ τὸν ἕτερόν τι φρονήσαντα ἢ φρονοῦντα, ἢ νῦν ἢ πώποτε, ἢ ἐν καλχηδόνι ἢ οἵᾳ δή ποτε συνόδῳ, ἀναθεματίζομεν.

It is evident then, that even if this was not an anti-Chalcedonian measure, strictly speaking, it was certainly an act which compromised the authority of Chalcedon. Moreover, it was an act which revived the pre-Chalcedonian christology as set forth in Ephesus and spread mainly through the writings of Cyril and his school.

The *Henoticon* in later years, namely during the reign of Anastasius (491–518), became the recognized form of orthodoxy for the whole Empire, being supported by the imperial authority.

Thus, while the East enjoyed a relatively peaceful situation, the storm arose now from the West with the opposition to the *Henoticon* by Rome. Hence the well-known "Acacian Schism". And this brings us to our second point in this section.

2. In our examination of the Acts of the Council we had no difficulty in detecting the Roman influence during the whole course of the sessions. That influence culminated in two major successes: (a) It made the Tome of Leo accepted as *Regula Fidei*, a kind of criterion of orthodox faith by which the orthodoxy of any other statement on christology had to be judged, and (b) it brought the *Definitio* in line with the Leonine terminology. Leo now took the place of Cyril in the Council. So much was easy to achieve. But it was not easy to take the place of Cyril in Eastern Christianity, where Cyril had left deep and permanent influences not to be removed by a conciliar decision or imperial decree.

However, Rome regarded the Council of Chalcedon as the victory of its own christology and, at the same time, a vehicle for spreading its authority throughout the East. This only can explain the strenuous efforts and the use of all possible means of influence to preserve that victory throughout the course of the subsequent events. Thus the interventions of Leo, and later of his successors, in the troubles caused by Chalcedon in Palestine,[1] Egypt,[2] and Antioch[3] betray his fear of seeing his victory undermined by the opposition. No compromise could give assurance to Rome, which remained "staunchly Chalcedonian".[4]

The attitude of Rome was made very clear in two cases in particular in the post-Chalcedonian history:

(a) When the *Henoticon*, designed by Acacius, was promulgated by Zeno, Rome went as far as to condemn Acacius, thus causing a schism between itself and Constantinople which lasted for about forty years (482–519). Rome opposed the *Henoticon* not because the christology contained therein was heterodox but because it had ignored the Council of Chalcedon. That meant for Rome, compromising the authority of the Council and, therefore, undermining the Leonine victory.[5]

The Acacian Schism has a great significance for us not only as a mere phase in the growing tension between East and West or, more precisely, between Constantinople and Rome, but also as a sign of the fact that Rome regarded Chalcedon as a corner-stone in the structure of Christian orthodoxy which could not be removed or displaced, whereas, on the other hand, the same Chalcedon did not mean the same thing to Eastern Christianity in that period.

(b) The same insistence of Rome on the maintenance of the Council of Chalcedon is manifested more clearly perhaps in the next century at the time of the controversy on the *Three Chapters*.

Justinian, who played such a decisive rôle in the history of Eastern Christianity, especially in connection with the reconciliation of the Monophysites and Chalcedonians, became fully aware of the real difficulties, both doctrinal and practical, felt by

---

[1] Kidd, *Church History*, vol. iii, p. 401; Batiffol, *Siège Apostolique*, pp. 582–3.

[2] Kidd, *Church History*, vol. iii, p. 403; Batiffol, *Siège Apostolique*, pp. 583–4.

[3] Batiffol, *Siège Apostolique*, pp. 584–7. For the relationship with Constantinople see Batiffol, *Siège Apostolique*, pp. 568–81; cf Jalland, *Leo the Great*, pp. 321–49.

[4] Wigram, *Separation*, p. 19; cf Idem, *Assyrian Church*, p. 145.

[5] See Lebon, *Monophysisme Sévérien*, pp. 31 ff; Duchesne, *Church History*, vol. iii, pp. 348–9, 355–9; Bardy, *Chalcedoine*, p. 297.

the Monophysites.[1] He had behind him the experience of his predecessors. Neither Rome nor the Monophysites should be disregarded in any serious and hopeful attempt of reconciliation.
Therefore, the Nestorians or the "Nestorianizers" had to be sacrificed. Now, Nestorius had been equally condemned by the two
sides. But Chalcedon had been so favourable to the Nestorians or
"Nestorianizers" that the opposition of the Monophysites was
justified in that respect at least. So Justinian thought he had found
the real obstacle which had to be removed to smooth the way of
reconciliation for the Monophysites. That obstacle, i.e. Nestorianism, as we saw earlier, was shielded behind the names of ex-
ponents other than Nestorius, namely Theodore of Mopsuestia,
Theodoret of Cyrus, and Ibas of Edessa. The last two were
recognized and openly declared as orthodox at the Council of
Chalcedon. Theodore was already known as the great teacher
of Nestorianism. He had not been mentioned in the Council of
Chalcedon, but he had been refuted by Cyril.[2] Justinian was
determined that these three had to be condemned.[3] Hence the
problem of the *Three Chapters*.

Later, we shall consider the impact of Chalcedon on the Nestorian expansion in the East. Again, we are not concerned here
with the *Three Chapters* themselves, which were finally condemned by the Church in the second council of Constantinople
(553). What is essential to our purpose is to note Rome's continuous defence of the *Three Chapters* both during the controversy
and after their official condemnation. The problem of Pope
Vigil's attitude to the condemnation of the *Three Chapters* is in-

[1] The disposition of the monophysite bishops who wrote to Justinian
freely after their return from exile is clearly seen in a passage in the Chronicle
of Zachariah (see ix, 15). Justinian must have taken into account such dispositions.

[2] λογὸς κατὰ Διοδώρου ἐπισκόπου Ταρσων, πρὸς τὰ Θεοδωρου. See fragments in
Pusey's edition of Cyril's works, vol. iii, pp. 492–537.

[3] "Malgré l'échec complet de ses tentatives de conciliation Justinien ne renonça
jamais à l'espoir de ramener ses peuples à l'unité religieuse par l'extirpation des
anciennes hérésies, par la condamnation des écrits à tendances nestoriennes, dont
les auteurs avaient été réconciliés par le concile de Chalcédoine" (Bréhier, *Justinien*, p. 457).

deed a very long and complicated story.[1] But significant in this history is the widespread Western opposition to the second Council of Constantinople until the beginning of the seventh century.[2]

Obviously, there is a considerable variety of opinions about the significance of the condemnation of the *Three Chapters*, the attitude of Pope Vigil, and the second council of Constantinople.[3] But the fundamental reason for that opposition to the condemnation in the West was that to condemn the *Three Chapters* and especially the writings of Theodoret and Ibas would imply rejecting the decisions of the Council of Chalcedon;[4] and Chalcedon in Western eyes was untouchable, because it was the most solid bulwark of their christology and influence.

B. *The Council of Chalcedon revealed*
close associations with Nestorian Christology

This was the second major problem which the Monophysites faced in their attitude towards the Council of Chalcedon.

Hitherto we have tried to show how Chalcedon, being chiefly a triumph of Western, Latin, christology, sounded so unfamiliar and heterodox to the ears of the faithful holders of Eastern, Greek, christology. But our argument would indeed lose its power if it were left alone or taken in an absolute sense. In fact, the Council of Chalcedon was held in the East and attended by Easterns. The only non-Easterns were the four papal legates or representatives. Therefore it would not be fair to appropriate the term "Eastern" to the opponents of the Council. These latter did not represent all

[1] See the whole story with its many complications in Duchesne, *Église VIe. siècle*, pp. 156–218. Concise sketches are given in Bury, *Later Roman Empire*, vol. ii, pp. 383–91; Stein, *Bas-Empire*, pp. 632–75. Among more recent and detailed studies we must mention Devreesse, *Ve. Concile*; Idem, *Essai*, pp. 194–242; Moeller, *Ve. Concile*; Amann, *Trois Chapitres* col. 1868–1924, particularly col. 1888–1911.

[2] See Bréhier, *Successeurs de Justinien*, p. 494; Stein, *Bas-Empire*, pp. 676–83; Devreesse, *Essai*, pp. 259–72.

[3] The above mentioned articles can illustrate this point very clearly. See particularly Devreesse, *Ve. Concile*; Idem, *Essai*, pp. 194–242.

[4] Every, *Byzantine Patriarchate*, pp. 64, 66; Devreesse, *Essai*, p. 208.

of the Eastern bishops among whom were those who stood by the Council in one way or another.

Having made, then, this important point, we have to show the limits of our terms of reference in order to avoid confusion and misunderstanding. Thus, broadly speaking, those of the Eastern bishops who supported the Council of Chalcedon without any further restatement or reinterpretation of it were holders or inheritors of the Antiochene School of christology. Its opponents, on the other hand, were representatives of the Alexandrian School, which, as we saw, had taken the lead in Christian thought at the time and, since Ephesus, had become dominant in theology. And it is only in this sense that one can say that Eastern orthodox christology as a whole was predominantly Alexandrian.

Now, we noted and underlined the sympathetic attitude of the Council of Chalcedon towards theologians and Church leaders who were constantly supporting and trying to propagate the Antiochene tradition. That Chalcedon reaffirmed the position of the Antiochene School is also shown in the attitude of the Nestorians themselves. It would be very valuable to see what the Nestorians thought and felt about the Council of Chalcedon in this post-Chalcedonian period.

There are three points which can give us some idea on their attitude.

(*a*) Most significant is the attitude of Nestorius himself towards the Tome of Leo. In fact, during his exile he was kept in touch with the development of the theological controversies in the Capital.[1] He knew all about the conflict between Eutyches and Flavian, the condemnation of the latter, and the intervention of Leo.[2] He was even provided with a copy of the Tome, which he found perfectly orthodox:

> Pour moi, lorsque j'eus trouvé et lu cet écrit je rendis grâces à Dieu de ce que l'Église de Rome avait une confession de foi orthodoxe

[1] See Nau, *Héraclide*, Intr., p. ix.
[2] See his own account of the events in Nau, *Héraclide*, pp. 294–317.

et irréprochable, bien quelle eût été disposée (lit. "ils étaient disposés—les Romains") autrement à mon égard.[1]

In a further passage commenting again on the Tome of Leo, he states more explicitly the similarity or identity of Leo's doctrine with his own. He says:

> Comme ils avaient des préjugés contre moi et qu'ils ne croyaient pas ce que je disais, comme si je cachais la vérité et si j'en empêchais l'exacte expression, Dieu suscita un héraut qui était pur de ce préjugé—Léon—qui proclama la vérité sans crainte. Comme la prévention (créée par) le (nom de concile) en imposait à beaucoup, même à la personne (*prosôpon*) des Romains et (les empêchait) de croire ce que je disais et qui était resté sans examen, Dieu permit que le contraire arrivât, qu'il retirât (de ce monde) l'évêque de Rome (Célestin) lui qui avait eu le principal rôle contre moi au concile d'Ephèse et qu'il fît approuver et confirmer (par Léon) ce qui avait été dit par l'évêque de Constantinople.[2]

Another testimony to Nestorius' own attitude to Leonine christology comes from his letter to the monks of Senoun.[3] Here, again, he praises Leo and thanks God for the reaffirmation of his doctrine:

> Quant à ce qui a été fait maintenant par le fidèle Léon, chef des prêtres, qui a combattu pour la piété et s'est opposé à ce qu'on a appelé concile, j'en ai loué Dieu avec grande allégresse, et je passe tous les jours dans l'action de grâces. Sachez donc en vérité, vous aussi qui êtes instruits par Dieu, que mon enseignement—celui-même de la piété—est celui qui a été défini par les hommes vénérables dont je viens de parler, par Flavien et Léon. A cause de celà, puisque tout le monde tient mes doctrines et surtout les clercs, ce n'est que par envie que j'ai été jugé, anathématisé, et haï comme hérétique.[4]

Had he lived until the end of the Council of Chalcedon no doubt

---

[1] Nau, *Héraclide*, p. 298.   [2] Nau, *Héraclide*, p. 327.

[3] Translated from Syriac by Nau and published as an appendix to the French translation of the Book of Heraclides. (See pp. 373 ff.)

[4] Nau, *Héraclide*, pp. 373–4; cf Loofs, *Nestorius*, pp. 99–101; Bethune-Baker, *Nestorius*, pp. 189–96.

he would have hailed it as the official acceptance of his doctrine in spite of the condemnation of his person.[1]

(b) After the Council of Chalcedon the Nestorians themselves regarded its work as being the reassertion of their position. There is no record of any official or formal acceptance of the Council as such. In fact, they were not in a position to accept it officially. They had been cut off from the life of the Church in the Byzantine Empire. But it seems that they welcomed the Council as an official move by the "Western" Church to restore justice by rehabilitating bishops like Ibas and Theodoret. How could they be against such a Council? Ibas was one of their greatest and most efficient leaders and teachers. In fact, their sympathy with the Council of Chalcedon is reflected in their official collection of Synodical Acts and Canons. The Canons of the Council, the Definition, and even the Tome of Leo are found there.[2] The canons are classified together with those of Nicaea and Constantinople.[3] Then, we must remember that whenever the Byzantine emperors, such as Zeno and Anastasius, supported Monophysitism against Chalcedonism the Nestorians felt themselves involved in this policy by opposing it.[4]

[1] It is generally accepted now that his death falls between the convocation and the actual meeting of the Council of Chalcedon. There have been several legends invented by the Monophysites about his death. See the echoes as given by Timothy Aelurus and Philoxenos of Mabboug in Nau, *Héraclide*, Intr. pp. ix–xi; cf Zachariah, bk. iii, ch. 1. Of course, no one can take these legends seriously. On one point, however, they all agree and in that they are supported by a Nestorian source. (Brière, *Légende de Nestorius*, p. 24); namely, that Marcian had invited Nestorius to Chalcedon before his death. (Cf Jugie, *Nestorius*, pp. 60–2, 304–12.)

[2] See Chabot, *Synodicon Orientale*, p. 6.

[3] See Chabot, *Synodicon Orientale*, p. 611. The Council of Ephesus is excluded. (See Chabot's remark on p. 556, n. 1.)

[4] We shall see this in a more detailed form later when we come to study the Armenian Church's position. Here it seems worth quoting Duchesne and Labourt. The first says: "Sans doute le nom de Nestorius avait été associé à celui d'Eutychès dans la liste des personnes condamnées; mais la formule proclamée n'était pas pour déplaire à ses anciens alliés: ils se réservaient de l'exploiter; ils espéraient même le faire assez aisément" (*Autonomies*, pp. 37–8). The second confirms this: "Depuis l'avènement de Justin, la défaveur impériale était réservée aux monophysites et les chrétiens persans circulaient plus librement sur le territoire de l'empereur orthodoxe" (*Christ. Perse*, pp. 164–5).

(c) Thirdly, in the later years of the post-Chalcedonian period when the problem of the *Three Chapters* arose again and troubled the religious situation in the East, and when the second council of Constantinople was convened by Justinian, the Nestorians again felt that the tide was turning against Chalcedon and against themselves. What they had gained in the Council of Chalcedon they lost in the second council of Constantinople. The work of the former was destroyed in the latter. Their doctrinal teachers rehabilitated in Chalcedon were now condemned as heretics. So they resented the fifth "Ecumenical" Council as much as they were delighted by the fourth. Finally they came to reject it categorically, thus bringing their separation from the Church in the Byzantine Empire to completion. Now there was no way left open to reconciliation.[1]

Finally, we can see these two important features of the Council of Chalcedon clearly reflected in the post-Chalcedonian literature, especially in the writings of the Monophysite authors. The quickest glance at the existing literary data will immediately reveal them. But within the limits of our survey we cannot embark on a detailed examination of it. We take only as an example the *Refutation* of Timothy Aelurus, the complete text of which has been

---

[1] "Personne n'ignore quel tumulte suscitèrent en Afrique et en Italie l'édit de Justinien et sa confirmation par le concile œcuménique. Mais si l'émotion fut telle dans les contrées où les auteurs des Trois-Chapitres étaient personellement peu connus, on s'imaginera facilement quelle elle dut être dans la Syrie Orientale. C'était frapper au cœur l'Église persane que de dénoncer comme hérétique, les docteurs antiochiens, mais surtout l'illustre Théodore le Commentateur" (Labourt, *Christ. Perse*, p. 275; see also pp. 276–8. Cf Wigram, *Assyrian Church*, pp. 218 ff; Idem, *Doctrinal Position*, pp. 42–3; Every, *Byzantine Patriarchate*, p. 66; Devreesse, *Essai*, pp. 272–7.)

Wigram in another book says that the second council of Constantinople "estranged the almost reconciled Church of the Persian empire by its unjust condemnation of Theodore" (*Separation*, p. 131). He is definitely convinced that this council had erred by contradicting the earlier ones. And he makes his point in an interesting passage which I quote: "So, the council of Constantinople counts among the General Councils, and perhaps there is none of them concerning which the Anglican feels more grateful for the statement of Article XXI that General Councils may err, and sometimes have erred. It might be an interesting intellectual exercise to present a debating case against any of them, and in no case would it be so easy as in this" (*Separation*, p. 130).

preserved in an Armenian translation. Here, in this book, we have an attempt to demonstrate how the doctrine of the Tome of Leo and the Chalcedonian Definition were contrary to the orthodox faith. Timothy does this first by quoting passages from them, secondly, by collating parallel sayings taken from heretics such as Paul of Samosata and Diodore, but particularly Nestorius and Theodoret,[1] thirdly, by refuting the passage, and fourthly, by adducing passages from Orthodox Fathers in support of his own refutation. It is, indeed, very significant to note that against the fourteen chapters devoted to the refutation of the Tome of Leo, there are only four devoted to that of the Chalcedonian Definition. This in itself shows how the Tome incurred so strongly the stricture of the Monophysites, whereas the language of the Definition was not as foreign to them as that of the Tome.

[1] The absence of any mention of Theodore is a very curious fact, which, to my knowledge, has not attracted the attention of scholars.

2

THE HISTORICAL BACKGROUND (1)
The Political Situation

We have noticed already in the Introduction of our study what an important period the fifth century was for Armenian history in general and for Armenian Church history in particular.[1]

In order to understand the ecclesiastical situation and the theological *milieu* in which the Armenians came to reject the Council of Chalcedon we must bear in mind the political situation of the country. An adequate understanding of this political situation is necessary for two reasons: first, it provides us with the framework, as it were, of the ecclesiastical situation with which we are concerned here; secondly, it may clarify the political aspect of the rejection of the Council of Chalcedon. This is necessary because, as we tried to show in the Introduction, scholars and church historians have often tended to explain that rejection either purely or primarily on political grounds. This survey will necessarily include an account, however brief, of the political history of Armenia before the fifth century. Otherwise it would be difficult, if not impossible, to understand the situation of that century.

Mgr Duchesne has a very suggestive remark on the history of Eastern Christendom in his book *Churches Separated from Rome*, which can serve us as a sound starting-point. He says:

> In studying the origins of Christianity the Roman Empire alone is usually taken into consideration. It was on its eastern frontier that Christianity was born, and the light of the Gospel moved westward conquering those provinces subject to the Roman Empire. At all

[1] See above, pp. 4–5.

events, this is the principal feature of its progress dwelt upon by historians.

Nevertheless there were, outside the Roman Empire, important States bounding it on the east; first of all the Empire of Parthia, then the Kingdoms of Armenia and Ethiopia.[1]

Armenia was, in fact, an independent kingdom during the first four centuries of Christian history. It stood on the cross-roads between the Roman—later, the Byzantine—Empire, on the one side, and the Parthian—later, the Sassanid (Persian)—Empire, on the other. This was a critical position, indeed, which is undoubtedly the chief cause of the tragedy of Armenian history. More precisely, Armenia had been an independent, autonomous country from the second half of the first century to the very end of the first quarter of the fifth century. This whole period was occupied by the reign of the Arsacid dynasty, which lasted longer than the sister Parthian Arsacid kingdom in Persia.

The kingdom of the Arsacids [says Manandean, the greatest authority on Armenian political history] lasted for more than three centuries as an autonomous State in Armenia, until the partition of the latter between Persia and the Byzantine Empire (A.D. 66–384/87) ... Even after the partition of Armenia, the Arsacids ruled in the Persian section of Armenia for about half a century: 387–428. So the whole duration of this kingdom is counted as 362 years.[2]

Politically, during the whole course of this period, Armenia oscillated between the two sides. To put it in very general terms, the political situation was that of either (a) a protectorate from the Roman side or (b) a sort of overlordship from the Parthian side. But in both cases Armenia was an independent, autonomous country—at least, it was not an integral part of either side: it had its own place and its own identity; it moved to one side or the other according to its own interests; it fought this or that side for its own purposes and with its own forces; it was invaded by this or that side, and in case of defeat made its own pacts. In all these varying ways it expressed its self-determined, autonomous state of existence.

[1] *Separated Churches*, p. 13.   [2] *Critical History*, p. 6.

The situation in Armenia in the period between A.D. 63 and 223 is well pictured and genuinely characterized by René Grousset. He says:

> Du traité de Rahndéia[1] à la chute de l'empire parthe (63–224) l'Arménie avait maintenu son indépendance. Les cadets arsacides qui y régnaient sous le protectorat romain n'avaient certes échappé ni aux tentatives d'annexion romaine ni aux brusques interventions des Parthes eux-mêmes, toujours disposés à considérer leurs cadets d'Arménie comme de simples vice-rois; mais toujours aussi l'equi-libre oriental selon la formule du traité de Rhandéia avait fini par prévaloir, et de cet équilibre l'Arménie était l'heureuse bénéficiaire.[2]

In the cultural sphere, this situation resulted in a combination of elements from two distinct civilizations: Iranian and Roman. In fact, this situation provided a solid ground for "une double pénétration culturelle irano-romaine". More explicitly, "La formule du traité de Rhandéia—quand elle jouait correctement—avait fait de l'Arménie un terrain d'entente où les deux cultures se recontraient".[3] This twofold basis of Armenian culture is a very important fact which played a prominent part in the subsequent development of Armenian Christian culture.

In the third and fourth centuries there occurred some changes on the political scene which played a decisive rôle in the political history of Armenia. Moreover, all these changes carried with them religious and cultural consequences of great importance. Here, I take into account only the important ones.

1. In 226 the rule of the Parthian Arsacid dynasty in Persia was overthrown and replaced by the Persian Sassanid. Now the ruling

---

[1] By this treaty (A.D. 63) the Romans recognized the autonomy of Armenia, which would have its own king under the protection of the Roman empire. (See Grousset, *Histoire d'Arménie*, p. 108.)

[2] *Histoire d'Arménie*, p. 113.

[3] Ibid., p. 111. The influence of the Iranian language and culture on Armenian civilization is best studied by A. Meillet, largely quoted by Grousset. (See for the references *Histoire d'Arménie*, pp. 113–27.) Ačaṙean's *History of the Armenian Language* illustrates this point more thoroughly. However, the work has not been at my disposal to give the references. (See Łazarean, *Armenian Language*, p. 166.)

dynasty in Armenia was a branch of the same Arsacid dynasty. Therefore, as could be expected, this change on the Persian throne was echoed in Armenia by a hostility towards the new Eastern neighbour. That hostility was accompanied, for very natural reasons, by a closer association with the Western neighbour, the Roman Empire. The new master of the ancient Parthian Kingdom and the founder of the Sassanid Empire, Artašir I (224–41), was contemplating the restoration of the former Parthian Empire. He therefore planned to extend his rule over countries other than those inherited from the overthrown Kingdom. Naturally, Armenia was one of his first targets because of the kinship of the ruling power with the overthrown dynasty and also because of its independent status just on the western fringes of Persia, a situation which was dangerous, indeed, when looked at from the angle of Sassano-Roman conflict.[1] All along the years between 226 and 387 this hostility remained the basic factor in Armenian political history.

The first important result of this hostility was the gradual attraction of the Armenians to the West, that is, to the Roman and, later, the Byzantine Empire. In fact, after a very hard struggle of nearly twenty years of continuous war against the Sassanid invaders and after the final defeat of the Armenians,[2] the recovery of independence by Tiridates III was made possible only by the help of the Romans.[3] This was a second decisive step which drew

[1] See Manandean, *Critical History*, p. 76.

[2] This happened in 252/53. Shapuh, the successor of Artašir, became the conqueror of Armenia. (See for details Manandean, *Critical History*, pp. 84 ff; Grousset, *Histoire d'Arménie*, p. 115.)

[3] The date of this recovery has been a matter of dispute. We need not go into it, though it has a great importance in determining the date of the official conversion of Armenia to Christianity. However, the two main suggestions have been 287 and 298. It must be said that not only the chronology but the history of this period is somewhat confused. There had been more than one war between Rome and Persia during this period. Accordingly, the political situation in Armenia underwent changes which were the natural consequences of this fluid and unsettled situation. Therefore the recovery of independence itself cannot be understood as a single event, but as the result of a process of struggle, victories, and defeats. Thus, in 287 the Persians ceded Armenia to Diocletian. Armenia became

the Armenians nearer to the West and, consequently, took them further away from the East in their political orientation.

2. The national adherence of Armenia to Christianity[1] laid firmer and deeper foundations for that orientation. It is difficult to understand that adherence merely as the outcome of such a Western political orientation, as some scholars are inclined to do.[2] Of course the growth of Christianity within the Roman Empire, with all the impact that it had on the Empire itself, contributed to the shaping of a more sympathetic attitude towards Christianity by the Armenian King, Tiridates III. But the fact of the presence of Christianity in Armenia was the decisive factor in that official move. As we shall see, the propagation of the Christian faith was making such a rapid advance in Armenia that the Christian religion was becoming an important power in the country, and the ruler could not disregard it, because it was growing continuously.

Armenia, thus, turned once for all to the West. That orientation was now irrevocable after the acceptance of Christianity with all its cultural implications. However, we must note that the adherence of the country to Christianity did not coincide with an integration of the country into the world of the Roman Empire. Armenia continued to stand in its traditional position of independence between the Persian and, now, the Byzantine Empires.

All through the fourth century Armenia's oscillation between the Persian and Byzantine alliances constitutes the central aspect

---

once more independent under the protectorate of Rome. Later the wars were renewed. In 298 the Persians were once more compelled to cede Armenia to the Romans. Tiridates III now became the undisputed master of Armenia. (See for all the complicated issues involved in this story Manandean, *Critical History*, ch. 7, pp. 91–115; cf Grousset, *Histoire d'Arménie*, pp. 113–17.)

[1] Again, the date of the official acceptance of Christianity as State religion in Armenia has always been a matter of acute controversy. To put it in the widest possible expression it has been fixed somewhere between 276 and 313. It is a long and complicated story with much confusion and misunderstanding mixed up with it. The generally accepted date is 301. See for a fuller treatment of the problem, Tournebize, *Histoire*, pp. 428–44; cf Manandean, *Critical History*, pp. 124–5.

[2] See, for example, Manandean, op. cit., pp. 117–18.

of its history.[1] Thus it was overrun alternately by its two strong neighbours, the new representatives of the traditional permanent political competition in Eastern history; sometimes, with great skill, as well as perils, it divided its loyalty between both sides; sometimes it inclined to the one side and at other times to the other. But in all and any case it succeeded in its traditional rôle: to maintain its self-governing status or, perhaps more precisely, its internal freedom and autonomy.

Here, on this internal scene of its life, the political struggle was reflected and materialized in a conflict between two major forces: (a) the Kingdom—the State with its centralizing policy, and (b) the Feudal Principalities (*Naxararowt'iwnk'*) with their centrifugal tendencies.

In the religious sphere, this struggle was translated into a conflict between the old and yet persistent paganism and the new and triumphant Christianity. In fact, it had been impossible to eradicate altogether the dominant pagan religion with its centuries-old institutions and traditions by a royal decree of adherence to Christianity, or even by the strictest anti-pagan measures taken by the State on practical grounds. The fourth-century history of the Armenian Church is full of examples which illustrate this struggle. The slightest look at the book of P'awstos Biwzandaçi can make us understand fully the extent as well as the importance of this struggle.[2]

The struggle both on political and religious grounds was carried on by two distinct groups or factions. To put it in a most general form the Iranophiles followed the policy of Persian overlordship with the revival of the pagan religion or the acceptance of Mazdaism in Armenia as their line of political and religious activities. Whereas, the Romanophiles sympathized with Byzan-

[1] See a study of the fourth century Armenian history in its relations with Rome by Baynes, *Rome and Armenia*; he has used the data provided by P'awstos Biwzandaçi. A more thorough study is that of Asdourean, *Armenien und Rom*.

[2] See for example bk. iii, chs. 3, 14; bk. iv, chs. 13, 14, 23, 24, 59. In these and many other passages the political and religious factors seem to have been combined together to counter-balance the increasing tide of Christian influence in the country.

tium politically and became defenders of Christianity, though sometimes even fearing its strength and trying to reduce it or bring it under their influence and control.[1]

In the fourth century Armenia can be likened to a boat beaten by the huge waves of the Persian and Byzantine Empires. Apart from the perils of the waves themselves, the boat itself was not strong and safe, because the two main political orientations within it tried to navigate it in opposite directions. This internal opposition weakened immensely the power of resistance to the Arsacid Kingdom and therefore became a serious threat to the maintenance of the autonomous state of the country. The fall of the Arsacids was being prepared!

The Church could not stand apart from these changes and troubles. The official authority of the Church supported naturally the Romanophile side; but there were sections within it which sympathized with the Iranophiles. This situation was to play a not unimportant part in the coming doctrinal controversies and ecclesiastical dissensions, as we shall see in the next chapter.

3. A major change in this situation in the last years of the fourth century was the partition of Armenia between Persia and Byzantium (387/90). According to the treaty signed between Shapuh III and Theodosius I in Constantinople[2] Armenia was now divided into two sections: the eastern part of the country was left to the Persians and the western districts were annexed to the Byzantine Empire. However, both sections were governed by two kings of the same Arsacid dynasty (Xosrov IV for Persarmenia and Aršak III for the Byzantine Armenia, both of them being vassal-kings under the two great powers). The largest and the most important section of Armenia was that left to the Persians[3]—

---

[1] See Manandean, *Critical History*, pp. 224–6.

[2] See Manandean, *Critical History*, pp. 232–3; Asdourean, *Armenien und Rom.*, pp. 316–321. (For other references see above, p. 4, n. 2.)

[3] A fifth-century historian, Łazar P'arpeçi, speaks about this partition and describes the Persian section of Armenia, namely the province of Ayrarat in an elaborate and touching passage. (See bk. i, chs. 6–7; Langlois, *Historiens Arméniens*, vol. ii, pp. 262–3.)

actually four-fifths of the country, as Manandean says.[1] In this section, the Arsacid kingdom remained in power for about forty years, whereas in the Byzantine section after the death of Aršak III, a Byzantine military ruler was appointed by Byzantium.[2]

In the following years the weight of Armenian history fell upon the Persian side. The centre of the Church was now there, and the western regions were totally integrated into the Byzantine world. So, when now we speak of Armenia it is this Persian Armenia that we have in mind.

4. The partition, however, did not change the autonomous state of the country. On the contrary, the Armenians here tried to consolidate their independent situation by establishing their own national culture through a newly invented alphabet and the immediately subsequent flowering of a national literature. Later in this chapter we shall return to this important aspect of Armenian history and try to show its consequences for the Armenian Church and nation in the fifth and following centuries.

For forty years the Arsacid kingdom was maintained in Armenia (387/90–428). When, at the instigation of the Armenian rival feudal princes (*Naxarark‘*) it was abolished in 428 by the Persians, a new system of government was established in its place. The Persian King of Kings appointed a governor—*Marzban*—for Armenia, whose main function was to survey the situation and to keep it under tight control in order to avoid the possibility of any attempt at rebellion or communication with the Byzantine Empire.[3]

The abolition of the Armenian Arsacid kingdom was an important phase in the development of the Sassanid policy towards

[1] *Critical History*, pp. 239–40. (See Map 1.)

[2] The political significance of this change and its consequences for the history of Eastern Christendom are pointed out in an excellent passage by René Grousset; the whole problem is seen and judged here, in the context of the general history of the East, of which Grousset is undoubtedly one of the most competent experts. See the passage in *Histoire d'Arménie*, pp. 165–6.

[3] On the status and functions of the Marzban see Christensen, *Iran Sassanide*, pp. 136–7.

Armenia. That policy was aimed ultimately at the total integration of Armenia into the Sassanid world. This was only possible through a break-off or complete separation of Armenia from the Byzantine Empire. Isolation would be the first stage of the policy. That negative stage, however, would provide them with the possibility of an easier cultural and religious assimilation of the country by the Sassanid Mazdaean Empire, with all that that implied.[1] By the partition of Armenia the first stage of their policy had been achieved politically. The abolition of the Arsacid kingdom now gave them the opportunity of a wider and deeper penetration into the country through the establishment of the new government of Armenia ruled by a Persian Marzban.[2]

In order to achieve this assimilation the Persians had to use Iranophile elements in the country. These were mainly (a) Naxarars who sympathized with the Sassanid policy and culture, and (b) religious leaders who sympathized with the Syriac tradition now being favoured by the Persian Empire in order to oppose it to the Byzantine Church and to hinder any influence from the latter on the Christians under its rule.

It is relevant here to note how strong was the anti-Byzantine mood in Sassanid policy and what consequences it had for the Armenian Church. "The Persian rulers", says Xorenaçi, "did not permit any of the inhabitants in their territories to study Greek literature, but only the Syriac language".[3] But we shall speak of this later when we look into the ecclesiastical situation more closely.

[1] During the reign of Yazdgard II (438–57) this idea had become a definite conviction and culminated into a firm policy for the Sassanid Government. As Christensen says: "Le progrès du christianisme en Arménie était depuis longtemps une source d'inquiétude pour le gouvernement de l'Iran. On comprenait à Ctésiphon que la possession de l'Arménie resterait précaire, tant que les différences religieuses existaient, et l'idée d'employer des mesures de coërcition eut un avocat puissant dans la personne de Mihr-Narseh [i.e. the director of the Persian foreign policy of the time] (*Iran Sassanide*, p. 284; cf Hannestad, *Relations*, pp. 433–8).

[2] However, that government was only external and the Armenians still had a large measure of autonomy in their public life. This is very well illustrated by Manandean. (See *Critical History*, pp. 285–7.)

[3] Xorenaçi, bk. iii, ch. 54.

5. This policy could not remain unanswered by the Armenians now firmly established in their faith and, at the same time, in a strong consciousness of national identity fostered especially through the cultural achievements of the century. In fact, all the measures taken by the Persian Government with a view to achieving this assimilation met strong resistance on the part of the Armenians. After the fall of the Arsacid kingdom, the fifth-century political history of Armenia is the history of this resistance movement, now strengthened by religious, cultural, and national factors.

The first important outburst of that resistance was the battle of Avarayr, afterwards and even now known as one of the greatest moments of Armenian history and commemorated by the Armenian Church as a "holy war" fought in defence of the Christian faith in Armenia.[1]

It is worth noting that it occurred in May 451, in the very same year that the Council of Chalcedon was convened, preceding the latter by four months.

Actually, the Armenian forces were defeated by the huge elephant-built army of the Persian Empire. Although the battle did not stop the policy of dechristianization and assimilation carried on with such skill and firmness by the Persian rulers,[2] yet, at the

[1] Those who lost their lives in that battle, or in the course of the later resistance movement are venerated as martyrs and saints in the Armenian Church. They are called *Vardanank'* and *Levondeank'* after the names of the chief of the army, Vardan Mamikonean, and of the priest Levond who was the inspiring figure of the whole movement, the "Peter the Hermit" of Armenian history. The story of this battle is related by a contemporary historian, Eliše, *History of Vardan*. (See Bibliography for the English translation.) The second book of P'arpeçi also is devoted to the history of this battle. (See P'arpeçi, bk. ii, chs. 20–48; Langlois, *Historiens Arméniens*, vol. ii, pp. 183–251.) For a concise study of it in French see Mécérian, *Bilan*; cf Hannestad, *Relations*, pp. 437–8.

[2] Though it must be accepted that the policy of Persia underwent a considerable change, without losing sight of their chief aim they nevertheless changed their method in achieving it. Immediately after their military victory over the Armenian army, they were compelled to change tactics or strategy in view of the demonstration of the strong determination of the Armenians in standing firm to their faith and national consciousness. (See Christensen, *Iran Sassanide*, p. 288; cf Grousset, *Histoire d'Arménie*, p. 211.)

same time, their defeat was not the end of the resistance. This continued through isolated, individual attacks on the Persian forces stationed in Armenia for the establishment and consolidation of Persian rule. So a kind of guerilla warfare swayed over Armenia for about three decades after the battle of Avarayr. The famous Mamikonean House was the chief organizer or the pioneer of this resistance movement with the collaboration of other feudal princes of various Armenian provinces.

6. Finally, another great figure of the same House, Vahan Mamikonean, achieved the aim of the resistance when he compelled the Persians to recognize the full autonomy of Armenia.[1] He himself was nominated Marzban. Thus, he, in his turn, recognized once more the overlordship of Persia after having secured the freedom of the Armenian people in their faith and national culture. This happened in 485. The situation of Armenia during the reign of Vahan Mamikonean is very well pictured by Grousset:

> Le Marzbanat de Vahan Mamikonian dura de 20 à 25 ans (de 485 à 505 ou 510). Ce fut une véritable royauté sans le titre. On peut seulement regretter qu'il n'ait pu profiter des circonstances pour rétablir en sa faveur la monarchie haïkane. Il en fut évidemment empêché par la crainte d'une rupture avec la Perse, sans doute aussi par suite de la jalousie latente des autres familles féodales envers celle des Mamikoniens. Du moins, son long gouvernement présida-t-il dans tous les domaines à une véritable restoration nationale.[2]

With this period of complete autonomy and peace under the reign of Vahan Mamikonean we conclude our survey of the political situation of Armenia prior to the rejection of the Council of Chalcedon. This period was the decisive moment of Armenian Church history as regards its position *vis à vis* the Council of

---

[1] See the full story of the event and the three conditions put forward by the Armenians in P'arpeçi, bk. iii, ch. 89; Langlois, *Historiens Arméniens*, vol. ii, pp. 354–5). A French summary is in Mécérian, *Bilan*, pp. 96–7; cf Christensen, *Iran Sassanide*, p. 295; Labourt, *Christ. Perse*, p. 154.

[2] *Historie d'Arménie*, p. 230.

Chalcedon. In fact, it was during this period that the Chalcedonian problem came to the official consideration of the Armenian Church and the attitude towards it was already formed. During the reign of Catholicos Babgēn it was to be sanctioned through a conciliar act which was afterwards repeated and reaffirmed in all subsequent dealings with the Chalcedonian problem.

Now, as we come to conclude this chapter, we have to make the following point by way of summary and conclusion. The autonomous political and national situation of Armenia was maintained all through the first five centuries of Christian history. That autonomous situation was not the same at every stage in the course of these five centuries. It took different forms of self-government; it knew different degrees of freedom; and yet, there was something common in all of these various forms and varying degrees: the basic fact of being a distinct country with a special status of self-recognition and self-expression. Armenia never became an integral or constituent part of either the Roman or Byzantine Empires, nor of the Parthian or Sassanid Empires.

In order to show what this situation of Armenia could mean for the doctrinal orientation of the Armenian Church, I suggest the comparison of this state of autonomous, semi-independent existence with the political situation of the Christian Church within the Persian Empire. It is not difficult to appreciate that it was not at all easy for the Persian rulers to impose on the Armenians the anti-Byzantine attitude in their policy as they did upon the Persian Church politically integrated into the Persian Empire, which, because of that integration, followed strictly the Persian policy in its attitude to the Church within the Byzantine Empire. It must be noted with special attention that it was this autonomous situation which served as an important factor in the preservation of orthodoxy in the Armenian Church against the Nestorian advance in and around the Persian Empire; an expansion which, encouraged by the Persian rulers, was becoming alarmingly dangerous for the Armenian Church, as we shall see.

In the context of this survey one can see how misleading may be any interpretation of the rejection of the Council of Chalcedon by the Armenian Church based on purely political grounds. Indeed, without appreciating this particular political situation of Armenia it is all too easy to imagine that the Armenian Church took its decision with regard to the Council of Chalcedon on political lines as suggested or imposed by its Persian masters. More explicitly, at first sight, it would seem quite logical to say that if the Armenians pronounced against the Council of Chalcedon it was only because they had to show their political loyalty to their Persian rulers by a positive expression of an anti-Byzantine attitude. Or, in the opposite way, that they rejected the Council of Chalcedon because they wished to stand by the official Byzantine religious policy which, at the end of the fifth century, was marked by an anti-Chalcedonian colour.

What we may conclude from the political and national situation which we have just reviewed above, can be expressed as follows. The Armenian Church in the fifth century confronted a political dilemma which it had to solve in one way or another. The dilemma was this: on the one hand, the country in which it was situated was under the Persian overlordship which professed another religion to Christianity, and so it had to show its loyalty to the Empire in political matters and yet to resist its policy of integration and assimilation. On the other side of Persian Armenia there was the Byzantine Empire which had appropriated to itself parts of the Armenian territory and with which it had a close relation in terms of religious and cultural affinities. The dilemma was an acute one. The creation of a national literature was the natural way, perhaps, to face it. However, that new cultural movement did not estrange the Church from the Christian world in the West, because for a long time during and after the translation of the Holy Bible and the Church Fathers, the Armenians maintained their relations especially with the centres of Greek Christian culture, mainly with Constantinople and Alexandria. The communion of faith was never compromised or shaken between the two Churches, the Armenian and the Greek.

The Councils of Nicea, Constantinople, and Ephesus were accepted and held firmly as the basis of orthodoxy. On the other hand, that new cultural movement strengthened the Armenian Church in its firm stand against the Persian policy of integration.

Now, all these are expressions of an autonomous Church and people. They accepted the Council of Ephesus not because the Roman emperor imposed it on them, but because they made their own decision about it and judged it as orthodox. They rejected Nestorianism in spite of all the Persian influence and Syrian infiltration and propaganda in their country, because they had doctrinal objections to it. In the same way, when they faced the Council of Chalcedon they were able to take their stand in accordance with their doctrinal and ecclesiastical tradition.

In short, the political situation of their country provided them with the possibility of free action. In other words, the political conditions did not dictate their doctrinal attitude. They were able to avoid being mere victims of their political situation.

3

THE HISTORICAL BACKGROUND (2)
The Ecclesiastical Situation
Before the Council of Ephesus

Now let us turn to the religious aspects of the fifth-century history of Armenia and look at them more closely in order to appreciate the religious atmosphere of the time with which we are primarily concerned here.

We must again go quite a long way back to the origins and the early expansion of Christianity in Armenia, because many important aspects of its fifth-century history can be traced back to their origin and formation. We must therefore understand them in the light of the process of their formation.

This survey—very short, indeed, as we intend it to be—will first bring us to the end of the fourth century; more precisely, to the time of the partition of Armenia (387/90). Then we shall study the fifth century through a more detailed investigation by dividing it into three periods based on the doctrinal history of the century:

1. *Before* the Council of Ephesus. (The first three decades of the fourth century.)

2. *Between* the Council of Ephesus and the Council of Chalcedon (431–51).

3. *After* the Council of Chalcedon (451–508).

I. THE FIRST FOUR CENTURIES

It is always difficult to speak of the origins of Christianity in Armenia in clear terms, to give definite names and dates, or to show the various ways in which the Christian faith was spread there. Not only is authentic historical evidence weak and insufficient,[1] but also the traditions are mixed up in such a complicated way that it is difficult to distinguish clearly between fact and fantasy, between reality and imagination.

The traditional claim for the apostolic origins of Armenian Christianity has been questioned on historical grounds. The existing tradition concerning the preaching of the Apostles St Thaddeus (John 14. 22-4) and St Bartholomew (John 1. 43-51) in Armenia have come to our knowledge through written documents which are hagiographical pieces of literature compiled in later centuries.[2] Therefore it is not possible to rely on them as authentic historical documents. These arguments of course, form a quite strong challenge to the traditionally assumed historical apostolicity of the Armenian Church. Yet, on the other hand, it is equally difficult to reject altogether the tradition of the apostolic preaching in Armenia. It is, indeed, very difficult to discredit that tradition as completely void of any degree of historicity and to interpret it as pure invention.[3]

We think that the tradition deserves a higher degree of probability than that which some scholars are ready to give it. The limits of our study cannot permit us to embark here on the reasons for our assumption. But, besides the basic and most important fact

[1] It must be remembered that there was no Armenian literature in Armenian language during these first four centuries. It is not surprising therefore, that we have no contemporary written document in Armenian concerning the beginnings of Christianity in Armenia. All the Armenian writings on this subject date from the fifth century onwards.

[2] See Abełean, *Literature*, pp. 360-2. On the formation of the tradition of St Thaddeus' preaching in Armenia see Tournebize, *Histoire*, pp. 401-13 (in a special chapter on the conversion of Armenia). See also Ormanean, *Azgapatum*, col. 21-8 (on Bartholomew's tradition, col. 27-38); Haçuni, *Important Problems*, pp. 1-88; Kiwlēsērean, *Armenian Church*, pp. 171-248 (a thorough answer to Haçuni's criticisms).

[3] Cf Tēr-Minaseanç, *Arm. Kirche*, pp. 1-2.

that this tradition has in itself the character of being an echo of something already existing, there are two points which give weight, we think, to our assumption.

1. The neighbouring countries on the north-western frontiers of Armenia, Cappadocia and Pontus, had been evangelized by people of the first Christian generation. In fact, Asia Minor was, with Syria, the first place outside Palestine where the Christian faith was preached. Not only were its central and western parts soon conquered by Paul in the name of Christ, but its eastern regions were also touched. In 1 Peter (1. 1, 2) we read: "Peter, an apostle of Jesus Christ, to the exiles of the dispersion in Pontus, Galatia, Cappadocia, Asia and Bithynia, chosen and destined by God the Father and sanctified by the Spirit for obedience to Jesus Christ and for sprinkling with his blood, may grace and peace be multiplied to you."

The remarkable zeal for evangelism so characteristic of this first generation would naturally lead people towards the east, where the first country to be entered was Armenia. Moreover, Armenia had already had a long history of relationship with these two countries in the pre-Christian era, and many Armenians had settled in them and maintained steady and regular contacts with their own country.[1]

Secondly, it is highly probable that the eastern parts of Syria and the northern parts of Mesopotamia, i.e. the southern borders of Armenia, had been reached by the first apostolic missionaries. From the earliest times of Christian history, Christianity had gained a firm foothold in Edessa which, in its turn, became and remained for subsequent centuries a centre of Christian expansion towards the east.[2]

It is difficult, as Duval says,[3] to give a picture of the earliest situation of Christianity in Edessa. But it can be easily accepted

[1] The Roman road system was, indeed, so efficient that contacts between countries were easily and regularly made. (See Ramsay, *Asia Minor*, pp. 51–62, particularly pp. 55–6, 58; cf Idem, *Church Rom. Emp.*, pp. 11–12.)

[2] See Duval, *Histoire d'Édesse*, p. 81.

[3] Ibid., p. 107.

that second-century events and aspects of Christian life there, namely the emergence of various sects of gnostic character,[1] are of such importance that they can assure us of a beginning of Christianity in Edessa as early as the first century. If we put aside all the legendary story of King Abgar's correspondence with Christ, we cannot do the same with the tradition of the apostolic preaching in Edessa as such. The legendary character of Abgar's conversion is no reason for denying the existence of Christianity in Edessa in the first century.

All this can be said in terms of probability and not of historical certainty, which needs the affirmation of positive authentic evidence. We need not go into the complicated details of this story, which has already drawn attention from so many scholars.[2] What is relevant to our purpose and what we can accept with a certain degree of historical authenticity is the basic fact that Christianity existed in Edessa or in the Kingdom of Osrohene as early as the first century. "There can be no doubt", says Professor Vööbus, "that the Christian faith had been established before the end of the first century in Edessa and also in Osrohene."[3] And, as Tournebize says:

De L'Osrohène la foi avait sans doute rayonné assez tôt vers l'est; entre Édesse et l'Arménie la distance n'était pas grande. Bien longtemps avant Bar Hébraeus, les alliances et les compénétrations fréquentes entre Parthes, Perses, Édesséniens et les Arméniens avaient justifié la réflexion suivante du célèbre patriarche monophysite: "Parthes ou Perses, Parthes ou Édesséniens, Parthes ou Arméniens, c'est tout un." (Assemani: IV. *Dissert. de Syr. Nestor.*, p. 425.[4])

[1] "Vers le milieu du II siècle, les Maircionites et les Valentiniens, et peut-être encore d'autres sectes gnostiques, comptaient des adeptes à Édesse. Avec Bardésane surgit une nouvelle hérésie de même nature" (Duval, *Histoire d'Édesse*, p. 114; cf Vööbus, *Syrian Asceticism*, pp. 31–61).

[2] Besides Duval and among many others see Tixeront, *Église d'Édesse*; Martin, *Église d'Édesse*; Burkitt, *Eastern Christianity*; Hayes, *École d'Édesse*; Vööbus, *Syrian Asceticism*.

[3] *Syrian Asceticism*, p. 6; see pp. 3–10; cf Hayes, *École d'Édesse*, pp. 24–7; Burkitt, *Eastern Christianity*, pp. 33–5 (the traditional story, pp. 10–32).

[4] *Histoire*, p. 406.

2. The later rapid advance of the Christian faith in Armenia in the second and third centuries—the result of which was undoubtedly the national acceptance of Christianity as the official religion of the country at the end of the third or in the beginning of the fourth century—cannot be understood without postulating an early beginning. In fact, the adherence of Armenia to Christianity was not, strictly speaking, a single action, i.e. the result of the preaching of St Gregory the Illuminator. As Leon Arpee says, "The conversion of Armenia was not an event but a process."[1]

Here also, second-century events as echoed in the documents of later centuries assure us of an early expansion of Christianity in Armenia. Tournebize, who has used all the fragmentary and scattered information about the pre-Gregorian period of Armenian Church history, is quite convinced that in the second century Syrian and Greek missionaries had preached the Gospel in Armenia.[2] He concludes his investigation with the following statement:

En resumé, l'évangélisation de l'Arménie apparait comme une simple hypothèse pour le premier siècle; mais l'hypothèse devient de plus en plus probable à mesure qu'on avance dans le second; elle se pose à nos yeux comme un fait à peu près incontestable vers les années 190–195.[3]

Having thus hinted at the history of the beginnings of Armenian

[1] *Armenian Christianity*, p. 9.
[2] See *Histoire*, p. 416.
[3] *Histoire*, pp. 417–18. Cf Vailhé, *Église Arménienne*, p. 193. He has used exclusively the evidence provided by foreign sources—*Eusebius* ix, 8; *Athanasius*, De Incarn., P.G., t. xxv, col. 188; Sozomen, ii, 89. It is not, therefore, scientifically justifiable to treat the apostolic or early origins of Armenian Christianity as a pure legendary story. The statement of a scholar of such a high standing as H. Leclercq is more than ridiculous; he says: "On ignore tout, ou presque tout, des débuts du christianisme en Arménie; dès lors il faut s'attendre à y voir germer des légendes et des revendications sans aucun fondement historique. Puisqu'il y a quelques années seulement on revendiquait pour saint Thomas la prédication de l'Evangile en Amérique, on ne peut être surpris d'entendre certains anciens auteurs arméniens réclamer pour leur pays les apôtres Thaddé et Barthélémy". (*Litt. Arm.*, col. 1576.) What an ingenious association!

Christianity,[1] let us consider some important aspects of it and draw out their implications for our immediate purpose. The fundamental aspect to be taken into account is the twofold character of the early state of Christianity in Armenia: (a) "Greek-type" Christianity introduced from the north-western borders and (b) the "Syriac-type" Christianity introduced from the south-western sides. From all the evidence at hand it appears that up to the time of St Gregory the Illuminator the Syriac-type Christianity was more widespread and, therefore, more influential especially in the southern regions of Armenia than the Greek-type Christianity which existed most probably in the north-western provinces. These two streams of Christian penetration into Armenia could not remain separate from each other for long. They had to meet each other in their advance and ramification on Armenian soil. However, their encounter, of which we know very little, did not result in an amalgamation. In other words, they retained their distinctive characteristics in respect of language and worship, and presumably in that of doctrine.

Now, as we realize more and more clearly through the new studies on Syriac Christianity the differences between the Greek and Syriac interpretations of Christianity, we may conceive or imagine the consequences of these differences for the situation of Christianity in Armenia and for the later doctrinal controversies.

This twofold character of Armenian Christianity remains, then, the general background which we have to take into consideration in our study of the later doctrinal controversies which preceded the Council of Chalcedon and its rejection by the Armenian Church. Here, at this stage, we confine ourselves to asserting only that this early state of Christianity provided the grounds for the later doctrinal divergences in the Armenian Church which would reveal themselves to be deep-rooted in the Armenian soil, and,

[1] The problems involved in the history of this earliest situation of Christianity in Armenia are discussed extensively by Ormanean, *Azgapatum*, col. 37–70; Tēr-Minaseanç, *Arm. Kirche*, pp. 2–11 (Arm. ed. pp. 6–29); Tournebize, *Histoire* pp. 413–21. I believe a new investigation into Armenian sources, helped by recent studies on early Syrian Christianity, is necessary for a fuller understanding of the origins of Armenian Christianity and its character.

therefore, difficult to disregard or to uproot in a comparatively short space of time.

Let us now proceed to the study of the history of the Armenian Church in the fourth century and to see how this situation is reflected there more clearly and openly.

St Gregory Parthev, afterwards to be called *Lousaworič* ("the Illuminator") who opened this century and somehow dominated it, came from Cappadocia. He was educated as a Christian in Caesarea,[1] and both in answer to a missionary vocation and for patriotic reasons he came to Armenia to preach the Gospel and to serve his own people.

This was a very significant event not only in the general history of the Armenian Church and nation, but also, and especially, for the history of the two Christian traditions referred to in Armenia before the coming of St Gregory. In fact, he was the man who achieved the total and official conversion of Armenia. He soon became the most highly venerated figure for the Armenian people. Not only was he himself held in supreme honour, but also his descendants after him. Because of his former links with Cappadocia he went to Caesarea to be consecrated bishop. What was done by him afterwards became a custom which was followed more or less regularly by many of his successors. Thus, the relationship with Cappadocia was maintained for many years after his death. Agat'angełos tells us that St Gregory after his episcopal consecration in Caesarea, on his way back from Armenia stopped for a few days in Sebastia. "There he found a multitude of brethren (ascetics or monks) whom he persuaded to accompany him so that he could give them the charge of priesthood in his country. And many groups having assembled he took them with him."[2] In many chapters of the same book (e.g. 109 and 113), we see how the work of these missionaries is carried out with great success.

As we have already noted, the pro-Roman political orientation of Armenia and now this new wave of Greek or Hellenophile

---

[1] See Agat'angełos, ch. 3; Xorenaçi, bk. ii, ch. 80.
[2] Agat'angełos, ch. 113.

missionaries in Armenia increased the influence of Greek-type Christianity. But this new movement did not change altogether the existing *status quo*. It did not suppress the Syriac-type Christianity which had been rooted deeply, particularly in the southern regions of Armenia. On the contrary, the leaders of the Armenian people and Church, King Tiridates III and St Gregory the Illuminator, accepted the facts as they were and greeted the Syrian or Syrophile bishops and missionaries as collaborators instead of competitors or opponents.

This comprehensive attitude of theirs towards Syriac-type Christianity is clearly seen in the establishment of schools where both Greek and Syriac languages and cultures were taught for the instruction of the clergy, who were being recruited chiefly from among the families of the former pagan priests. This method was adopted because those who were intended to serve the newly established Church had to learn necessarily either Greek or Syriac; the Church services were said in one or the other of these two languages according to their influence in various provinces of Armenia. The Scriptures were read in these two languages and expounded in Armenian to the people.

Apparently, the two traditions continued to coexist all through the fourth century without any open or strong clash. Thus, half a century after St Gregory the Illuminator, St Nersēs the Great (353–73) followed his example by "establishing Greek and Syriac schools in all the provinces of Armenia".[1] In his gigantic work of restoring and strengthening Armenian Christianity, Nersēs also was convinced of the necessity of maintaining this peaceful coexistence of the two traditions, although one has to accept that the reign of Nersēs (353–73) marked a considerable increase of the influence of the "Greek-type" element, he himself having been educated in Caesarea.[2]

These two types of Christianity are reflected also in the monastic life of the Armenian Church in the fourth century. In all probability the earliest forms of the monastic life came from the

---

[1] P'awstos, bk. iv, ch. 4.
[2] See P'awstos, bk. iv, ch. 3.

Syrian Churches.[1] The famous figure of the Syrian group of missionaries and monks is Daniel, called "the Syrian", who not only was recognized as a most eminent and influential personality in the southern regions of Armenia, but also had been the pioneer, the leader, and the teacher of other missionaries and monks in the work of evangelizing Armenia.[2]

Besides this group of Syrian or Syrophile monks and missionaries, as we noted above, St Gregory the Illuminator had brought with him many Greek and Hellenophile monks from Cappadocia, particularly from Sebastia. He himself, as well as his son Aristakēs, spent some time of their life in ascetic withdrawal from the world.

During and after the second half of the fourth century, the Greek form of monasticism became more prevalent than the Syriac. Again St Nersēs the Great reorganized and improved Armenian monasticism along the lines of the ascetic rules of St Basil.[3] The peaceful coexistence of these two traditions, however, could not last very long. In a country like Armenia, torn by internal political factions and tossed to and fro by the waves of foreign influences and interventions, the differences in religious traditions soon would be affected by different political and cultural tendencies. Persian policy was definitely anti-Byzantine.

[1] See Vööbus, *Syrian Asceticism, Intr.* pp. vi–vii, but particularly pp. 155–6; cf Tēr-Minaseançç, *Arm. Kirche,* pp. 8–9.

[2] See about him and about his assistants P'awstos, bk. iii, ch. 14, bk. v, chs. 25–7, bk. vi, chs. 7, 16. This Daniel of whose identity we know so little, may perhaps be identified with the Daniel mentioned by Sozomen. Speaking of the great figures of Edessene Christianity, he says: "Besides the above, many other ecclesiastical philosophers flourished in the territories of Edessa and Amida, and about the mountain called Gaugalius; among these were Daniel and Simeon. But I shall now say nothing further of the Syrian monks" (iii, 14, p. 293b). Is he the same person as referred to in Vööbus, *Syrian Asceticism* (see pp. 215–17, 247, 274)? It is, indeed, very significant to know that Epiphanius, one of his pupils, was a Greek. This means that the two types of Christian tradition could coexist happily. The time of conflict had not yet arrived.

[3] See P'awstos, bk. iv, ch. 4, bk. v, ch. 31. There is a very interesting passage in Sozomen's *Ecclesiastical History* on the relation of Armenian monasticism with the Greek-type monastic orders. (See iii, 14.) On this early monasticism in Armenia see T'op'čean, *Arm. Monchtum;* cf Amadouni, *Hiéromoines Arméniens,* p. 282–5 (a very general survey).

When the Greek tradition gained a prominent place in Armenian Christianity in the second half of the fourth century, the Persians became worried about Armenia. They reacted to this advance of Christianity by using Iranophile elements in Armenia as their agents to establish the Mazdaean religion. Shapuh II (310–79) sent an Armenian prince, Meružan, with an army to conquer Armenia to Mazdaïsm and thus to put an end to the constant danger of Armenia's increasing association with Byzantium. Movsēs Xorenaci gives us a good account of this new policy. It is most interesting to note that all the measures taken to this effect were directed against the Greek tradition. There is no reference at all to the Syriac tradition. I translate the whole passage:

> After the death of Aršak, Shapuh gathered a huge army under the command of Meružan, and sent him to Armenia by entrusting him with the rule of the country. .... He promised to give him the kingdom of Armenia under the condition that he should convert the country to the Mazdaean religion by subduing the *Naxarars*. He (Meružan) consented and came and arrested many of the *Naxarars*' wives and kept them in custody in various castles hoping that their husbands would be converted. He endeavoured to abolish everything that was Christian. He sent the bishops and the priests to Persia under the pretext of their paying tribute; he issued orders not to study the Greek culture, but only the Persian; no one should dare to speak or translate Greek. [He did all these things] under the pretext of breaking off all contacts of information and communion of love between the Armenians and the Greeks. But, truly, he [intended] to abolish the preaching of the Christian faith. For, then the Armenians had no written language and the Church services were conducted in Greek.[1]

It is clearly seen here how strong was the Greek tradition; it presumably overshadowed the Syriac. Now, this anti-Greek movement was to contribute towards the restoration or restrengthening of the latter. Later the Persian rulers were to become aware of the impossibility of destroying Christianity altogether in the countries under their direct rule or under their sovereignty or overlord-

[1] Bk. iii, ch. 36; cf ibid., bk. iii, ch. 54.

ship. So they were to try to use the Syriac tradition as an alternative to the Greek influence and, therefore, to oppose it to the Byzantine Church.

But by this time we enter the fifth century.

II. THE FIRST THREE DECADES OF THE FOURTH CENTURY

The period which lies between the partition of Armenia (387/90) and the Council of Ephesus is a time of supreme importance alike for the political, cultural, and ecclesiastical history of Armenia.

The outstanding event in the period is the invention of the Armenian alphabet. It was at some time in this period that the alphabet was created by St Mesrop Maštoç, who later came to be known as the "Father of Armenian Literature". The story of this invention has rightly been considered as one of the most complicated problems in Armenian history. When one looks at the literature devoted to its study one is struck by its immense quantity as well as by the imposing names of famous scholars who have endeavoured so strenuously to uncover the nucleus of reality in the accounts of the event. And yet, with all these studies there remain, as these scholars themselves confess, a great number of open questions. To bring forward some of the testimonies of the most important ones, confining ourselves to the second quarter of this century alone: N. Adontz at the beginning of his masterly essay on Maštoç and his disciples says: "The lives of the founders of Armenian literature are not known as much as they deserve to be remembered for their great work."[1] Towards the end of his study, having offered quite important contributions to the understanding of their work, he still confesses that "The origins of [the invention of] the Armenian alphabet are obscure".[2]

P. Peeters, the late Bollandist scholar, has said this in a more explicit and striking way in his remarkable study on the origins of the Armenian alphabet rightly evaluated as "un des plus

[1] *Maštoç*, p. 1. [2] *Maštoç*, p. 43.

substantiels mémoires consacrés à cette matière".[1] Here are the opening words of his article:

> Si le lecteur sous les yeux duquel ce titre est tombé n'a pas déjà pris la fuite, qu'il veuille bien ne pas nous imputer le dessein de prolonger à plaisir un débat devenu lassant ni la prétention encore plus déraisonnable de le terminer. L'origine de l'alphabet arménien est un de ces thèmes litigieux que l'on ne parviendrait pas à supprimer, si même on pouvait se mettre d'accord pour les enterrer à frais communs. Eludé ou mis à l'écart, le problème reparait insidieusement dans d'autres questions dont il est indissociable et qui deviennent à leur tour insolubles, si on le laisse lui-même sans solution.[2]

H. Ačaṙean, who made the study of the origins of the Armenian alphabet a constant theme of his scholarly work throughout his life, and who summed up the results of his research as well as those of other scholars in his *Mesrop Maštoç*, shows very clearly how the issues involved in the history of the origins of the Armenian alphabet are still complicated. After offering his own contribution towards their solution he yet confesses that the most important problem, i.e. the date of the invention, remains unsolved: "Even the date of the invention of our alphabet is not yet completely fixed."[3] And as late as 1957, Manandean admits that the problems involved in this story are unsolved. He says: "It must be said that even many of the most essential problems concerning the invention of the Armenian alphabet are not yet solved and remain under dispute in spite of numerous studies written on them."[4]

Why, then, are we interested in this confused problem? What is its relation to the theme of our study?

As P. Peeters, whom we have just quoted, has remarked already, the invention of the Armenian alphabet is so closely linked with other problems that it becomes very important when we are

---

[1] Mécérian, *Bulletin Arménologique*, p. 254.

[2] Peeters, *Origines*, p. 203.

[3] Ačaṙean, *Mesrop*, p. 83.

[4] *Critical History*, pp. 246–7; cf ibid., pp. 243, 259; see also Idem., *Armenian Alphabet*, p. 42.

directly interested in one or the other of those problems. And our subject here is one of them, as we shall now see.

What are the original sources in which that history is recorded? They are to be found in three writers of the fifth century:

1. Koriwn, the biographer of Mesrop Maštoc, is the first to be taken into account, because his work, the *Life of Maštoc̣* (*Vark̒ Maštoc̣i*)[1] has served as the basis for other historical accounts of the same event.

2. Łazar P‘arpeçi is the second author who speaks of the invention of the Armenian alphabet. He refers to it more briefly than Koriwn and in quite a different manner, although somewhat surprisingly he mentions Koriwn as his source.[2]

3. Movsēs Xorenaçi is the third fifth-century author[3] to relate the

---

[1] There have been several editions of Koriwn's work. I have used the critical edition made by M. Abełean (see Bibliography). I have compared it at some places with a more recent edition made by Akinean (see Bibliography). The text has not reached us in the purity of its original form. It has suffered later alterations. (See Abełean, *Koriwn, Intr.*, p. 18.) Besides these changes in the manuscript, the text has gone through more than one recension, which resulted in various editions of the same work in quite different forms. But in spite of all these textual deficiencies Koriwn's work remains the basic source and the most important document for the study of the invention of the Armenian alphabet. (See Peeters, *Origines*, p. 204.)

[2] See P‘arpeçi, bk. i, chs. 9–11; French translation in Langlois, *Historiens Arméniens*, vol. ii, pp. 265–8. I have used the critical edition (see Bibliography).

[3] One of the permanent and most acute issues in Armenian scholarship, especially in the nineteenth century, has been the problem of Xorenaçi's date. When did this author live and write his famous *History*? Underlying all the various views are two main positions: (*a*) Some have held firm to the traditional view that Xorenaçi is a fifth-century author as he himself tells us; (*b*) others, questioning the traditional view and suspecting Xorenaçi of an intentional false representation of himself, have placed him in one or the other of the subsequent four or five centuries. At present, most Armenian scholars tend to side with the first position, at the same time recognizing in the *present* text of Xorenaçi's *History* the work of later compilers or editors. They maintain the view that Xorenaçi's work was regarded, so to speak, as the "Standard History" of Armenia and went through several recensions throughout the subsequent centuries. Therefore the passages in the present text which refer to later events must have been interpolated through these later recensions. I accept this view in its broad lines.

same story. His account has some divergences from both Koriwn and P'arpeçi.[1]

There have also been later historiographers who have spoken of the invention of the Armenian alphabet, but they all depend on Koriwn or Xorenaçi.[2]

The major fact in this story with which we are primarily concerned here is the journey of Mesrop Maštoç to the cities of Amida, Edessa, and Samosata, all of them situated in the southeast of Armenia. In order to understand the significance of that journey we have to recall the whole story in its general outline as related chiefly by Koriwn.

During his evangelistic mission to the north-eastern provinces of Armenia, where the old paganism still persisted in maintaining its existence, Mesrop Maštoç, a church divine (*Vardapet*) devoted to the christianization of his country, urgently felt the need of bringing the Word of God to the people in their own vernacular, the Armenian language.[3] He came to Vałaršapat, the capital of the country, and consulted Sahak, the learned Catholicos of the time. Together they first approached Vramshapouh, the King, who told them that he had heard of the existence of an Armenian alphabet in the possession of a Syrian bishop called Daniel. At the King's order this alphabet was brought to them. They put it into practice to see how successful it would prove, but soon realized that it was defective.[4] So Maštoç went to East Syria, most probably to make further investigation and to compose an adequate and complete alphabet. Let us now hear the story directly from the words of Koriwn:

---

[1] See Xorenaçi, bk. iii, chs. 47, 52-4, 57-8, 60, 62, 67. (The French translation in Langlois, *Historiens Arméniens*, vol. ii, pp. 161-3, 164-6, 167-9, 172-3.)

[2] We cannot mention them here. The minor differences from both Koriwn and Xorenaçi are studied thoroughly by Ačaŕean. See his *Mesrop*. However, we noted that many of them follow Xorenaçi's account rather than Koriwn's. This can be explained by the great influence that Xorenaçi had exerted on later Armenian historiographers.

[3] See Koriwn, p. 40; cf Xorenaçi, bk. iii, ch. 47; P'arpeçi, bk. i, ch. 10.

[4] Koriwn, pp. 42-6; Xorenaçi, bk. iii, ch. 52.

The blessed Maštoc̣ took with him a group of young people by the order of the King and with the consent of St Sahak, and departing from each other with the holy kiss, he journeyed in the fifth year of Vramshapouh, King of Armenia, and came to the land of Aram,[1] to two cities of Syria; the first of them was called Edessa, and the name of the second was Amid. He appeared before the holy bishops, the name of the first [being] Babilas and [that] of the second Acacius. [These] in company with the clerics and the princes of the cities met the arrivals and bestowed many honours upon them and received them with stewardship according to the rule of those who are named after Christ.

Then, the disciple-loving master, dividing those whom he had taken with him into two [groups], appointed some [to study] Syriac literature [in the city of Edessa],[2] and thence he sent some to the city of Samosata [to study] Greek literature.[3]

Maštoc̣ himself stayed in Edessa, where he worked hard to bring his task to completion. Finally, through the divine help of the "all-merciful God" he succeeded in shaping the Armenian alphabet.

Then he himself went to Samosata where a Greek calligrapher Rufinus (Hrowpʻanos) perfected the writing of the letters. There also he translated, with the help of two of his disciples, the Book of Proverbs. This translation was copied by the same calligrapher. Thus, with his mission achieved, he returned to Armenia, where he was given an overwhelmingly enthusastic and, at the same time, most solemn welcome.[4]

---

[1] See Gen. 10. 22, 23. Koriwn uses this term in the Biblical sense: "In the Old Testament Aram includes the northern part of Mesopotamia, Syria as far south as the borders of Palestine and the larger part of Arabia Petra" (Hastings, *D.B.* vol. i, p. 138a).

[2] "i kʻalakʻin edesaçwoç". Abełean in his edition of the text adds these words supposing that they existed in the original text and were lost in later recensions. The reason is that in the second part of the sentence the word *aťʻti* (= "thence") implies a former mention of the place which was Edessa. (See Abełean, *Koriwn*, p. 109, n. 64.)

[3] Koriwn, p. 46.

[4] Koriwn, pp. 48–56; Xorenaçi (bk. iii, ch. 53) relates the story somewhat differently, but on the main points his record coincides with Koriwn's.

This story, and particularly the passage just translated, has raised very important questions and has posed to scholars some most complicated problems which still have not found answers unanimously agreed upon or generally recognized as adequate and satisfactory. When did Maštoç go to Edessa? Who were the persons referred to? What did his work precisely consist of? When we take into account the information provided by Xorenaçi and P'arpeçi, both of whom differ on many points from Koriwn and in some places even contradict him, then these questions become thorny problems and are at first sight insoluble.

It is of course beyond the scope of our study to enter upon these complications.[1] For us, as we noted already, the important fact is the turning of Maštoç to the Syrian side for this most important work for the Armenian Church and culture. The basic question, then, is this: Why did Maštoç go to Syria to find help for the fulfilment of his purpose and not, for instance, to Caesarea or to Constantinople?

First of all, there are two obvious explanations we have to take into consideration.

1. The alphabet which was first brought to him came from Daniel, a Syrian bishop, and most probably from somewhere in the northern parts of Mesopotamia or the eastern borders of Syria. When he applied it and became aware of its inadequacy it was only natural that he should make further research and investigation in the area from which it was brought.[2] This was, then, a technical necessity which could not be avoided if the work started, as it did, from these Danielean letters.

2. The second reason is a more important one. After the partition of Armenia, Syrian culture came to be favoured by the Persians in the Persian section of Armenia for reasons that we have studied already. Sahak himself had experienced the perils involved in a relationship with Byzantium; he had been suspected already for his Byzantinophile inclinations. The Armenian king,

---

[1] Later, however, we shall be dealing with some of them.
[2] It is most significant to note that according to Xorenaçi's account, Maštoç went to see Daniel himself (bk. iii, ch. 53. See also Ačaṙean, *Mesrop*, pp. 60-1).

Xosrov (385–87/8), who appointed him as Catholicos had been trying to establish friendly relations with Byzantium; his ultimate purpose was the annexation of the Byzantine section of Armenia to his kingdom, which then covered only Persian Armenia. This policy led to his deposition by the Persian Government, followed immediately by his imprisonment. Sahak was associated with him, and it was therefore necessary for him to go to Ctesiphon and to show his loyalty to the Persian Government and win their sympathy and support.[1] In Ctesiphon of course he realized what an atmosphere of suspicion had surrounded the Persian Court. Only a supremely tactful policy could make Armenia live in peace, and he was the man for this task.

After the partition of Armenia the anti-Byzantine policy of Persia had become so much intensified that Syriac culture had gained predominance. Thus Xorenaçi tells us that when Maštoç returned from his mission to the Ałowans (i.e. the Caucasian Albanians), he found Sahak translating the Holy Scriptures "from Syriac for want of the Greek [text]. For the Greek books had previously been burnt by Merowžan throughout the country; again, when Armenia was divided the Persian rulers did not permit [the Armenians] to learn Greek in their section but only Syriac."[2]

This must have been the reason why the Armenian students were sent to centres of Syriac culture and the services in the Church were conducted in Syriac, as P'arpeçi, speaking of Maštoç's decision to create an Armenian alphabet, tells us in a sorrowful tone:

The blessed man, Maštoç, was constantly depressed in mind by seeing the great efforts and the exceeding expenses of Armenia's youth who for high fees and with distant journeys and long wanderings used to spend their days in the schools of Syriac culture. [This was because] the services of the Church and the lessons from the Scriptures were conducted in Syriac language in the monasteries and

[1] See the whole story as related by Xorenaçi, bk. iii, chs. 49–51; cf P'arpeçi, bk. i, ch. 9.
[2] Xorenaçi, bk. iii, ch. 54.

churches of the Armenian people. The people of such a big country as this[1] were not able to understand and benefit from this, and because of the incomprehensibility of the Syriac language there resulted [only] fatigue on the ministers' part without any profit on the part of the people.[2]

In such a political and cultural atmosphere it is understandable that Maštoç would turn to the Syrian side more readily than to any other centre.[3]

But there is a third reason, which is perhaps the most important one, because it seems to have a more direct relation on Maštoç's turning to East Syria.

We have already seen, in the first part of this chapter, what a great part the Syrian missionaries played in the country throughout the first three or four centuries of Armenian Christianity. That there was a close relationship between Armenian Christianity and the Syrian Christian tradition is beyond all doubt. Surely there must have been many Armenian students among those who used to go to the School of Edessa, the famous centre of theological teaching—undoubtedly rooted in the tradition of the Antiochene School—in the east.[4] It was basically this traditional familiarity with Syriac culture that made Maštoç's journey to Edessa so natural and so easy. Therefore, it must not be thought that his turning to Edessa was only the accidental result of the political circumstances and the cultural impact of the Syriac-type Christianity which was being so openly favoured and supported by the Persian Government. The ancient traditional familiarity

[1] He refers to Persian Armenia, which was the largest part of the country.

[2] Pʻarpeçi, bk. i, ch. 10.

[3] P. Peeters thinks that Sahak and Maštoç turned to the Syrians because they did not want to see their Church in a deeper dependence on the Byzantine Church; secondly, that they wanted to accomplish their work outside Armenia so that they could avoid Persian inspection of their work. (See *Origines*, p. 208.) It seems to us that there is too much speculation on Peeters' part. His view is not supported by any historical evidence.

[4] At the end of the fourth and in the beginning of the fifth century "l'École des Perses prospérait et attirait à Édesse des étudiants accourus des divers points de la Mésopotamie et principalement des provinces chrétiennes de la Perse en proie aux persécutions des Mages" (Duval, *Histoire D'Édesses*, p. 161).

of the Armenian Church with East Syria has a greater importance for the understanding of Maštoc̣'s turning to Syria.

Here we have an important point bearing on the immediate purpose of our investigation in this story: To what extent and in what way did that familiarity affect the doctrinal attitude of the Armenian Church in the fifth century, prior to the Council of Chalcedon? Of course it is easy to imagine that, since Syria and Mesopotamia were closely dependent on the Antiochene tradition, Armenian theological thought must have been deeply influenced by the latter. But this general and hypothetical conclusion cannot satisfy us. Let us, then, examine the problem more closely and on more solid grounds of evidence. Unfortunately, we have no written documents earlier than the fifth century which could provide us with some concrete evidence and illuminate our knowledge and understanding of the theological milieu of the time. The fifth-century Armenian documents in their present state, are, indeed, very restrained in their account of the relationship of Armenian theology with the Antiochene School before the Council of Ephesus. However, there are some indications, mainly in foreign sources, which throw some light on this very important point.

First of all, we have the testimony of Photius, the famous patriarch of Constantinople (810–95), who in his *Bibliotheca* or *Myriobiblion* gives us revealing information about a relationship between Maštoc̣ and Theodore of Mopsuestia. He tells us that he has read three discourses or treatizes against the Persian religion written by "Theodore the Priest" and addressed to "Mastoubios of Armenian origin": Θεοδώρου πρεσβυτέρου, περὶ τῆς ἐν Περσίδι μαγικῆς ἐν λόγοις γ́. Ἀνεγνώσθη βιβλιδάριον Θεοδώρου Περὶ τῆς ἐν Περσίδι μαγικῆς καὶ τίς ἡ τῆς εὐσεβείας διαφορὰ ἐν λόγοις τρισί. Προσφωνεῖ δὲ αὐτοὺς πρὸς Μαστούβιον ἐξ Ἀρμενίας ὁρμώμενον, χωρεπίσκοπον δὲ τυγχάνοντα.[1] Then he identifies this Θεόδωρος πρεσβύτερος with Theodore of Mopsuestia: Οὗτος ὁ Θεόδωρος ὁ Μοψουεστίας εἶναι δοκεῖ· τὴν δὲ γὰρ Νεστορίου αἵρεσιν καὶ μάλιστα ἐν τῷ τρίτῳ λόγῳ κρατύνων προαναφωνεῖ, ἀλλὰ καὶ τὴν τῶν ἁμαρτωλῶν ἀποκατάστασιν τερατεύεται.[2]

---

[1] *P.G.*, t. 103, col. 281.   [2] Ibid.

Unfortunately, the discourses referred to have not survived. However, there can be no doubt about the accuracy of Photius' information. He is well known as a scrupulous and trustworthy scholar of his time. Therefore, taking his testimony as true, we have to answer the question: Who was Μαστούβιος to whom these discourses were addressed?

N. Adontz was the first to take into serious consideration the testimony of Photius. After careful study of the ecclesiastical history of the period between 383 and 435, he suggested that Maštoç, the author of the Armenian alphabet, must have been the person to whom Theodore addressed his work. His arguments may be summed up under the following heads:

(a) The similarity of the two names is striking: Μαστούβιος = Maštoç, Mašt'oç, Maždoç, which is the original name of Mesrop as known to Koriwn and P'arpeçi.[1]

(b) The outstanding figure of that period in Armenian ecclesiastical and cultural history is Maštoç.

(c) The works of Theodore of Mopsuestia were translated into Armenian and spread in Armenia to such an extent that immediately after the Council of Ephesus Rabboula of Edessa and Acacius of Melitene, the followers of St Cyril and the holders of the Ephesian orthodoxy in the neighbouring regions of Armenia, became alarmed and gave urgent warnings to the Armenians. In fact, the subsequent troubles in the Church over the *Three Chapters* started from Armenia as Liberatus tells us.[2]

When and how did Theodore come to know Maštoç? The evidence provided by Photius points to a personal relationship. Theodore must have known Maštoç personally if he addressed, as he did, his work to him. It is reasonable to think that Maštoç

---

[1] See Abełean, *Koriwn*, Intr., pp. 18–19; Akinean, *Koriwn*, p. 69, n. 5, with full bibliography on this point.

[2] *P.L.*, t. 68, col. 963. We shall deal with this extremely important episode of Armenian ecclesiastical history in the next chapter. Here we only note the fact that there was some ground in Armenia for Theodore's reputation and influence. Adontz's thesis is argued "par des raisons tout à fait séduisantes" (Peeters, *Origines*, p. 210), in his study already quoted—*Maštoç and his Disciples*.

might have asked him to write the above-mentioned discourses, because in his own time Mazdaïsm was penetrating into Armenia. We saw that it was the official policy of the Persian Empire to assimilate the Armenian people through a Mazdaean mission in Armenia in addition to the political pressure brought upon them. Therefore, Maštoç might have needed the help of an outstanding Christian theologian and apologist to provide him with solid arguments to be given as Christian answers to the Mazdaean criticisms of the truth of Christianity, which was being challenged through an intensive wave of preaching. Furthermore, this had been especially successful among the Iranophile Armenians. We must also note that Eznik of Kołb, who took up the challenge and answered the criticisms in his *De Deo* (Book III), most probably used Theodore's treatises in his Refutation of the Persian religion.[1]

Adontz suggests that Maštoç might have met Theodore somewhere and at some time during his journey to East Syria in search of the Armenian alphabet. This is why he proposes the decade 383–92 as the period in which the date of the invention of the Armenian alphabet has to be fixed.[2] The argument for this suggestion, is that, according to Photius, Theodore wrote his treatises and addressed them to Mastoubios when he was a priest ($\pi\rho\epsilon\sigma\beta\acute{u}$-$\tau\epsilon\rho o s$). After 392 he was the bishop of Mopsuestia.[3]

Akinean thinks that Maštoç had been in Antioch and had studied under the famous teacher Libanius.[4] There he must have met Theodore with whom he continued to keep in touch after his return to Armenia.[5] Secondly, he suggests that it was on Maštoç's request that Theodore wrote his treatises.[6] His third

---

[1] P. L. Mariès, who has studied the text of Eznik's work very thoroughly, assures us that with all probability Eznik had used not only Theodore's treatises, but also the works of Theodore's teacher, Diodore of Tarsus. (See *De Deo*, pp. 85–91.)

[2] See Adontz, *Maštoç*, p. 43.

[3] See Amann, *Theodore*, col. 235–6; cf Devreesse, *Essai*, p. 3.

[4] See Mozley, *Libanius*, pp. 709–12; also, and particularly, Festugière, *Antioche*, pp. 91–139.

[5] See Akinean, *Maštoç*, col. 506.   [6] Ibid., col. 509.

suggestion is that when Maštoç went to East Syria he also went to Mopsuestia to consult his friend Theodore, now the bishop of the city. In order to substantiate his hypothesis he proposes to change the name of the city mentioned in Koriwn as Samosata into Mopsuestia, the Armenian form of which is Mamuestia.[1]

Furthermore, he suggests that Maštoç knew Ibas of Edessa personally. The name of the priest mentioned in Koriwn's text[2] as Abel must have been in the original form Hiba or Ibas. This priest was the person who revealed to the Armenian King, Vramshapouh, the existence of an Armenian alphabet in the possession of Daniel, the Syrian bishop. Maštoç must have met Ibas in Edessa, with whom he became very friendly and who must have helped him in his work.[3]

It is difficult of course to subscribe to Akinean's propositions because they are not based on any historical evidence. His dealing with the text of Koriwn is too arbitrary and the manuscript tradition does not lend support to it. One could reach any conclusion with so many alterations in the text. Many of his assertions reviewed above are in fact questionable at various points and they cannot give us any solid ground of certainty or even of strong probability.

But setting aside these proposed textual alterations and these unconfirmed hypotheses, it seems to us that it is highly probable that, if not Maštoç himself, at any rate his disciples, could have met Ibas in Edessa, because in the first quarter of the fifth century he was the most prominent figure of the School of Edessa; this was a time, we must remember, when Armenian students came to Edessa, a familiar place for Christian studies, as we said earlier. It must have been this personal acquaintance with Maštoç's disciples or Armenian students sent to Edessa[4] that made it both possible and easy for Ibas to translate the works of Theodore of

---

[1] Ibid., col. 515–17; cf Idem, *Armenian Alphabet*, col. 298.

[2] Koriwn, p. 44; cf Xorenaçi, bk. iii, ch. 52.

[3] See Akinean, *Armenian Alphabet*, col. 295–7; cf Peeters, *Origines*, p. 209; Idem, *Jérémie*, p. 21. (See Additional Note 2.)

[4] See Koriwn, p. 74; Xorenaçi, bk. iii, ch. 60.

Mopsuestia into Armenian, works which were to cause such a storm in the Armenian Church, as we shall see later.

What can we conclude from all these fragmentary indications?

P. Peeters, who was for the first time to treat the history of the origins of the Armenian alphabet in relation to the doctrinal orientation of the Armenian Church and against the background of Eastern Church history as a whole, has the firm conviction that "il n'est pas contestable que, au temps de Maštoç et de Sahak, l'Église d'Arménie, dans sa parfaite inexpérience spéculative, ait commencé par accepter, en toute innocence, les enseignements de l'école théologique d'où le nestorianisme est sorti."[1]

In Peeters' mind this doctrinal situation in the Armenian Church was a well-established one and was created by men who had already adopted a definite theological attitude. This is easily seen in his thesis when he tries to show that the later pro-Ephesian position of the Armenian Church was the opposite of this one,[2] and that no relationship with Alexandria or familiarity with Alexandrine theology ever existed. He says: "Pas un mot du récit (of Koriwn), pas une allusion, rien ne laisse entrevoir qu'ils (i.e. the leaders of the Armenian Church) aient un seul instant songé à l'Égypte: on peut étaler une plus sereine ignorance de

---

[1] *Origines*, p. 226. Again, after studying the historical indications we reviewed above and which hinted at the relationship of Armenian Christianity with the Antiochene tradition—via Syriac Christianity—he suggests that the theologian cannot stop there. He must draw conclusions. Therefore, himself being a theologian, he goes on to say: "Devant un tel ensemble de preuves convergentes (*sic*) force lui sera de reconnaître que la littérature arménienne est éclose sous le signe de Théodore de Mopsueste et qu'elle a commencé de s'épanouir dans un terroir saturé d'influences nestoriennes. (*Origines*, p. 217).

[2] Ibid., p. 218. Even the later Monophysite position of the Armenian Church is understood by him as a departure from the earlier doctrinal position. He says: "Avant d'évoluer vers le monophysisme le plus exagéré (*sic*) l'Arménie avait commencé par subir l'attraction de l'école d'Antioche. Elle a fait ses premières classes sous des maîtres dont Théodore de Mopsueste était l'oracle. Personne ne conteste qu'elle les ait répudié d'assez bonne heure et que les ayant quittés, elle ne leur a pas ménagé les anathèmes et les invectives. Mais cette conversion n'abolit pas le passé que les historiens arméniens ont un peu volontairement oublié, et que rien n'autorise à déclarer invraisemblable à priori" (*Jérémie*, p. 23).

l'hellénisme alexandrin et une absence de prédilection plus voisine de l'indifférence pour la christologie de S. Cyrille."[1]

We can go quite a long way with Peeters in his analysis of the relation of the Armenian Church to the Christian tradition of East Syria. But we cannot reach the same conclusion, for the reasons given below.

We do not need to repeat what we have perhaps overemphasized already in this chapter. But let us put this as one of the postulates of our interpretation of the doctrinal situation of the Armenian Church at this stage: There had been a close traditional link between the Armenian Church and the Syriac-type Christianity in East Syria and North Mesopotamia and, therefore, it is reasonable to conclude that Armenians had been in contact with the Antiochene Christian tradition through Syrian influence. But this influence was not an exclusive influence or even the dominant one. This assertion is the point where we begin to depart from Peeters' interpretation, in which the Antiochene influence is seen and evaluated rather unilaterally.

We have already shown that especially during and after the time of St Gregory the Illuminator there had also been a strong Greek influence, which was not Antiochene in its origin or character and had come mainly from Caesarea. Now it can easily be shown that in the time of Maštoç, even in view of his possible relationship with Theodore and the story of his journey to East Syria, the Antiochene tradition was not everything in Armenian Christianity and was not even predominant, as has sometimes been imagined.

It is certain that Sahak Catholicos stood at the very centre of Armenian Church history in the first four decades of the fifth century. He was not only the leader *ex professio* of the cultural movement but he also occupied a central place in the political affairs of his time. His work did not consist simply in helping or encouraging Maštoç in his achievements; rather it had the character and the scope of a guiding, planning, and co-ordinating

[1] *Origines*, p. 218. Again, he stresses this fact a little further on. (See pp. 231–2; cf *Jérémie*, p. 17.)

action. He did not back the work of Maštoç, but directed it with such skill and efficiency that the whole course of fifth-century history is seen to be overshadowed by his eminent figure. It is obvious that especially those cultural activities in Armenia which followed the invention of the Armenian alphabet, were carried on under his direct guidance, active participation, and close supervision.[1]

On the political scene, Sahak played the rôle of a mentor to the Armenian Kingdom. He knew the situation in all its complicated phases and at all its sensitive points, because he considered himself—as well as did the people—as the man responsible for tackling it with the utmost care and wisdom. The dilemma which we described in the previous chapter[2] had to be solved by him rather than anyone else. He tried, and, in spite of all the unavoidable hindrances and some temporary failures, succeeded to a great extent in securing a period of comparative peace for Armenia. He achieved this by being faithful to the Persian overlords and, at the same time, by consolidating the foundations of Armenian independence in terms of a strong cultural and national self-consciousness, which became the major factor in Armenian history throughout the fifth century and afterwards. For fifty-one years he dominated the scene of Armenian history and provided the Armenian Church with a period of peace. In fact, it was under his catholicate that the "Golden Age" was reached, he himself being primarily responsible for its achievement. Thus, he went twice to Ctesiphon to give assurance of Armenia's loyalty to the Persian Government which constantly suspected the Armenians for their relations with Byzantium.[3]

Again, Sahak also held that highest authority to which the Armenian feudal lords could appeal in cases of conflict with their

[1] See for historical evidence of this P'arpeçi, bk. i, chs. 10–11; cf Xorenaçi, bk. iii, ch. 54; Koriwn, p. 76; also Ormanean, *Azgapatum*, col. 276 ff; Akinean, *Sahak*, col. 475–6.

[2] See above, pp. 72–4.

[3] See, for the supreme importance of Sahak's rôle in the life of the Armenian people in the fifth century, Ormanean, *Azgapatum*, col. 225–326 (a summary, col. 322–3).

king or discord among themselves. And although they did not always follow his advice or directives, yet they could never disregard him.[1] We must never forget that Sahak was the last descendant of St Gregory's family, which was still held in the highest veneration by the Armenian people as a natural expression of their gratitude to St Gregory the Illuminator for his great work of converting Armenia to Christianity.

Yet with all his pro-Persian policy, inspired undoubtedly by the needs of the situation, Sahak, this great and authoritative figure, was a Hellenophile in his heart and mind as far as his relationship with foreign Churches was concerned. We have already noted that his father, St Nersēs the Great, was educated in Caesarea and had encouraged and strengthened the Hellenophile influence in Armenia. Most probably he was sent by his father to Caesarea and Constantinople for his advanced studies.[2] His knowledge of Greek and the superiority of his education over any other Armenian of his time is something that is equally testified to by both Koriwn[3] and P'arpeçi.[4] It was with this mastery of the Greek language and literature that he became so efficient and proved so successful in his leadership of Armenian intellectual life in the fifth century, centred, as it was, on the translation movement.

With all his precautions to avoid any clash with the Persians, Sahak did not sever his relations with the Greeks. These relations were maintained through the Byzantine section of Armenia. Right from the beginning of his catholicate he was suspected of Byzantinophile inclinations. Consequently, he was summoned to Ctesiphon with King Xosrov soon after the partition of Armenia. There he cleared himself from all stains of suspicion,[5] and whereas

[1] This is clearly shown in the episode of the dethronement of the last Arsacid King, Artašēs. See the story related in detail by P'arpeçi; bk. i, chs. 12–16; cf Xorenaçi, 63–7.

[2] See Ormanean, *Azgapatum*, col. 257–8. He was even born in Caesarea. See Idem, *Azgapatum*, col. 163–4; cf Akinean, *Sahak*, col. 472–3.

[3] See pp. 74, 76.

[4] Bk. i, ch. 10, where it is said that he could compete with Greek intellectuals with his masterly knowledge of the Greek culture.

[5] See Xorenaçi, bk. iii, chs. 50–1.

the Persians dethroned King Xosrov, they permitted Sahak to continue his catholicate. Surely this was a move made with the idea of winning the confidence of the Armenians and thus preventing them from shifting to the Byzantine side. Therefore, given all these circumstances, it is legitimate to think that the most powerful man in the Armenian Church had no direct relations with the Antiochene Christianity and, what is more important, that he had close links with Byzantium.

That this link with Constantinople was not broken off by the partition of Armenia is evident from the events which followed the invention of the Armenian alphabet. In fact, the Byzantine section of the country was always regarded as an integral part of Armenia by Sahak, Maštoç, and all those leaders of the Church whose deepest and constant concern was the preservation of the unity and solidarity of the Armenian people. King Xosrov had tried through negotiations with Byzantium to extend his rule over that part of Armenia also,[1] and if Sahak sympathized with this policy, that can be explained only by his firm conviction that Armenians in the Byzantine section should be cared for and not be left to their fate at the hands of the Byzantines.[2] Sahak kept in close touch with that part of Armenia and through it maintained his relations with Constantinople.

It was with this fundamental concern for the Byzantine Armenians that Sahak endeavoured to spread the use of the newly invented Armenian alphabet among the Armenians in the Byzantine section.[3] But it was not so easy to achieve this aim. The rulers of

[1] See P'arpeçi, bk. i, ch. 2; cf Xorenaçi, bk. iii, chs. 49–50.

[2] See Xorenaçi, bk. iii, ch. 54. The situation on which the Armenian Church lived in the Byzantine section could not have left Sahak indifferent.

[3] According to Xorenaçi's account it was Sahak himself who went there and directed the work personally (bk. iii, ch. 57). But on the request of the Armenian *naxarars* he returned to Persian Armenia to settle the discord which had arisen among them and to secure national unity. Thus, when he left the Byzantine section he entrusted the work to Maštoç (bk. iii, ch. 58). According to Koriwn's account, the initiative was taken by Maštoç himself and the work also done by him. There is no mention of Sahak (see pp. 64–8). It seems to us more likely that Sahak himself had designed the work for Maštoç and his journey to Constantinople. Such an important work, so close to Sahak's heart and mind, could only be

the Byzantine section could not allow the spread of the Armenian alphabet because it came from the Persian section and, more important than that, it was not consistent with their own policy, the ultimate end of which was the total integration of the Armenian Church into the Byzantine. So Maštoç and Vardan, the grandson of Catholicos Sahak, were sent to Constantinople to get permission from the emperor for the alphabet to be used.[1]

We need not go into the details of Maštoç's journey to Constantinople and his missionary work in Byzantine Armenia. What is immediately relevant to our purpose is to note that this visit to Constantinople was a decisive moment in the history of the Armenian doctrinal orientation. If, chiefly for political reasons and partly for cultural and traditional reasons, the Armenians had been kept for a while in close contact with the Antiochene tradition through their link with Syriac-type Christianity, their links with Constantinople, equally traditional and cultural, were not altogether broken. They were loosened, but not destroyed. Their re-establishment meant that the Antiochene influence was not an exclusive element in Armenian Christianity. Moreover, that strengthening would carry with it a weakening or a decrease of the Antiochene influence. The visit of Maštoç to Constantinople brings to our consideration the following two points which are of great importance in understanding the doctrinal situation of the Armenian Church at this juncture.

1. On his way to Constantinople Maštoç "took a great number [lit. "a multitude"] of disciples to the city of Melitene; he entrusted them to the holy bishop of the city who was called Acacius, and left [there] as head of the disciples the one called Leontius, a

---

directed by him. This is evident not only from his former connections with Constantinople, but it also can be deduced from Koriwn's narrative itself; here Koriwn speaks of the whole work of Maštoç as being directed by Sahak. In fact, Maštoç used to report to him at the end of every mission he took in the remote provinces of Armenia or in the countries outside Armenia, such as Caucasian Albania and Georgia (see Koriwn, pp. 64, 70, 74).

[1] There is a difference between the two accounts of the event which deserves attention. (See Additional Note 3.)

faithful and truth-loving [lit. "truth-worshipping"] man."[1] This Acacius was none other than the well-known supporter of St Cyril and a determined opponent of Nestorius. Later, he took part in the condemnation of the latter at the Council of Ephesus. Afterwards he became the defender of Cyrilline christology against the Nestorians or Nestorianizers.[2] As we shall see a little further on, he was the man who opened the early stages of the controversy on the *Three Chapters*, more precisely, over the writings of Theodore of Mopsuestia, a controversy which started in Armenia. His close connection with Armenian doctrinal history can be explained by his intimate relation with Maštoç, and particularly by his well-established authority and influence on the Armenian students entrusted to him. Later we shall see what influence these students were to have in Armenia when they returned to their country and when the Nestorian controversy raged over the eastern provinces of the Byzantine empire.

How can we explain the action of Maštoç, if we assume that he was a convinced Antiochene, whose theological mind was formed under the influence of Theodore of Mopsuestia and other pioneers in what later came to be Nestorianism? We think that his personal relationship with Theodore of Mopsuestia—which we assume to be a highly probable fact even if not historically established—or his journey to East Syria for the accomplishment of his work did not imply that he adhered to the Antiochene theology as such. Otherwise he would have been very reluctant to entrust his students to the care of one of the most anti-Antiochene theologians of that time.[3]

[1] Koriwn, p. 66; cf Xorenaçi, bk. iii, ch. 57. The date of Maštoç's journey falls between 419 and 425, the date of the death of Atticus, the Patriarch of Constantinople, whom Maštoç had met. Akinean puts it in 419/20 (see *Maštoç*, col. 533), Peeters in 422 (see *Origines*, p. 212), Manandean in 420/22 (see *Critical History*, p. 275.)

[2] See Rouziès, *Acace*, col. 242-3. Lightfoot speaks of Acacius' doctrinal position in the following words: "Altogether his antagonism to Nestorian teaching was not only persistent but intemperate" (*Acacius*, p. 14a).

[3] P. Peeters, while stressing the pro-Antiochene theological position of the Armenian Church, has not been able to avoid the difficulty found in the passage just translated from Koriwn. He has recognized the fact, but it seems that he has

2. The second important point is this: The visit of Maštoç to Constantinople reopened the way for the Armenian Church divines to have direct contact with the cultural life of the imperial city. That road of communication had practically been closed to them after the partition of Armenia, which had prevented them, on political grounds, from proceeding to Caesarea and Constantinople. We have in Koriwn two explicit testimonies to this effect. In the first case, after the return of Maštoç from Constantinople when the literary activities were being more and more intensified, two students, Yovsēp' (Joseph) and Eznik were sent first to Edessa on a mission "to translate from the Syriac language into Armenian the traditions (i.e. the literary heritage) of their (i.e. of the Syrians') holy Fathers".[1] Having done this and having sent their translations to their teachers, Sahak and Maštoç, "they went forth to Byzantium, where they studied and became erudite and were appointed translators of the Greek language".[2]

This happened, we must remember, just before the Council of Ephesus. They were soon followed by two others, Leontius and Koriwn, the author of the *Life of Maštoç*.[3] Most probably, as we shall see in the next section, this happened soon after the Council of Ephesus. These cases are those recorded in the historical documents. It is reasonable to think that many others also would have followed these disciples, and the later history of the fifth century indeed provides us with more names. This communication with Constantinople, and presumably with other non-Antiochene centres of Christian culture, towards the end of the first quarter of the fifth century and during the time of the Nestorian controversy in Constantinople, was to play a determining rôle in the doctrinal orientation of the Armenian Church. The Ephesian doctrine which later became the rock of the Armenian christological position came to them through that same channel: from Contantinople to Armenia via Melitene.

---

not worked out its implications carefully. (See *Origines*, pp. 217–8; cf *Jérémie*, pp. 17–19.)

[1] Koriwn, p. 74.   [2] Koriwn, p. 74; cf Xorenaçi, bk. iii, ch. 60.

[3] Koriwn, pp. 74–6.

Before closing the study of this period we must note carefully that the communication with Constantinople had some consequences in Armenia which are not unimportant for elucidating our point. When in 423 Artašēs, the son of Vramshapuh, was nominated King of Armenia,[1] the deepest desire of St Sahak was fulfilled.[2] But Iranophile elements in the country later opposed King Artašēs and asked Sahak to join them in bringing charges against their King before the Persian Court. Sahak declined their invitation and advised them, in a fatherly way, not to carry out their intention, which seemed to him to be striking a blow at Armenia's autonomy at its most sensitive point, the Arsacid Kingdom.[3] But in spite of his counsel they went to the Persian King and asked him to dethrone Artašēs. Their request was immediately granted and, with Artašēs, Sahak Catholicos also was deprived of his Catholicate, which was now transferred to Surmak, a representative of the Syrophile faction.[4]

Now, there are two things which seem to us to be of great significance for the understanding of the ecclesiastical situation of the time:

1. According to Xorenaçi's account of the event the accusation brought against St Sahak and King Artašēs was that they had been maintaining close relations with Byzantium. In fact, when the Armenian naxarark' came to Sahak to ask his support for their accusations against the King, Sahak told them that they must wait a little while and bear with patience the mistakes of the King until "we could find a way out of this situation [by the help of] the Byzantine emperor Theodosius".[5] And this, we have to note carefully, fits perfectly into the story of St Maštoç's mission to the

---

[1] See P'arpeçi, bk. i, ch. 13.

[2] Xorenaçi says that Sahak had sent two Armenian princes, Sembat and Vardan, on a special mission to the King of Persia, Vram V (420–38). This latter, having "forgiven" the transgressions of the Armenians, appointed Artašēs King of Armenia (bk. iii, ch. 58).

[3] As Grousset has said it in a penetrating remark, "c'était, on peut le dire, le suicide de l'Arménie antique" (Histoire, p. 183).

[4] P'arpeçi gives us the full story in a dramatic fashion. (See bk. i, chs. 13–14.)

[5] See Xorenaçi, bk. iii, ch. 63.

Byzantine section of Armenia and his visit to Constantinople. It is obvious that the pro-Byzantine orientation openly expressed in these two events had caused some uneasiness and anxiety to the Persian Court and to the Iranophile elements in Armenia.

2. It is equally important to note also that the Armenian *naxarark'* who went to Ctesiphon to complain before the King of Kings, had with them a "certain priest by the name of Surmak, from the provinces of Bznunik', from a village called Arckē, of the family of the province's priests. Having joined the Armenian *naxarars* who had broken away from the counsel of the Catholicos, St Sahak, he spoke words unfair and more abominable than [those] of the Armenian *naxarars* against King Artašēs before the Persian nobility, thus pleasing the Armenian *naxarars*, because some [of the Armenian nobles] had promised him the Catholicosal throne of Armenia."[1]

Surmak came from that province in south Armenia—Bznunik'—which had always been under Syrian influence. He was the first of the three "catholicoi" in Armenia who were appointed by the Persian Court on the request of the Iranophile Armenian *naxarars* and whose reign was meant to achieve the breaking-off of the Armenian Church's relationship with the Church in the Byzantine Empire, a relationship which was being gradually affirmed during the last ten years, as we have shown already. Surmak and his two successors, Brk'išoy and Šmuēl (Samuel), were all of them recognized successively as the responsible heads of the Armenian Church at the Persian Court during the last decade of the Catholicate of Sahak, who had always been regarded as the real head and leader of the Armenian Church by the Armenian people themselves.[2] The scope of our study cannot permit us to go into the details of this story which is so clearly and extensively related in both P'arpeçi and Xorenaçi. It is interesting, for instance, to

---

[1] P'arpeçi, bk. i, ch. 14. Xorenaçi is more explicit here (bk. iii, ch. 64).

[2] It is worth noting that these three catholicoi have not found places in the official list (the Armenian "Liber Pontificalis") of the Armenian Catholicoi. They have always been regarded as foreigners imposed on the Armenian Church by their political masters.

notice how these prelates display the same ways of life as the bishops of the Persian empire,[1] how they soon become disliked by the Armenian *naxarars* and how Sahak still remains the head of the Church.

At length, on the request of the Armenian *naxarars* Sahak was accepted by Vram V once more as the official head of the Church, with authority only in spiritual matters. At the same time Šmuēl was recognized as having authority in secular and political matters. The political interest of the Persian Government in Armenian Church affairs cannot be more clearly seen than in this action. It is interesting to note that when Sahak was given back his spiritual authority he was warned by Vram V with the following words: "I make you swear by your own faith to remain faithful in our service and not to contemplate insurrection and be misled by [your] erroneous common faith with the Byzantines. [If you do so] you will be the cause of Armenia's destruction at our hands and our name will be changed from benefactor into evil-doer."[2]

This was then the situation of Armenia at the time when the Nestorian controversy started in Constantinople which prepared the way for the Council of Ephesus. The two Christian traditions in Armenia were still competing with each other and trying to win and maintain the upper hand. The Syriac influence was being weakened under the mighty figure of St Sahak, who rallied around him St Maštoç and the brilliant group of the first generation of the Armenian "Translators", that notable team of intellectuals who shaped the pattern of Armenian literature and laid the foundations of the Armenian doctrinal position.

It was obvious that in spite of the last attempt of the Syrophile elements to take the lead in Armenian Christianity with the direct help of the Persian Government,[3] the tide of Hellenophile

---

[1] See P'arpeçi, bk. i, ch. 4; Xorenaçi, bk. iii, ch. 65.

[2] Xorenaçi, bk. iii, ch. 65. See a summary of these dramatic events in Tournebize, *Histoire*, pp. 499–512.

[3] René Grousset has termed the situation which is just outlined above as a "Tentative de rattachement de la chrétienté arménienne à l'église syriaque" (*Histoire*, p. 184). It is highly significant to find in the councils of the Church, under the Persian rule, the names of "bishops from Armenia". Thus, in the list of

influence was not halted. On the contrary, it grew steadily. The temporary and, indeed, very limited success of the Syrophiles had not sufficient strength to shake the foundations of the Greek-type Christianity which was now being consolidated through the intensive work of the "Translators" and particularly through the cultural relations with Constantinople. In fact, it was so firmly established under the reign of St Sahak—and mainly through his labours—that it overshadowed the Syriac type and started it on its way to weakness and decadence. However, this is not to say that the latter was uprooted or eliminated altogether. In the second half of the fifth century it still struggled to survive. But the battle was already a lost one.

What can we deduce from this story? What are the points in it which are relevant to our immediate purpose?

(*a*) The Armenian Church was not committed to one particular school of Christian theology in the first quarter of the fifth century. It had maintained its character of a two-fold Christianity which we described earlier. The interplay between the two Christian traditions of Greek and Syriac origin and influence had not yet disappeared. The whole course of the fifth century is marked by the conflict between the two.

(*b*) If the Antiochene theological tradition is associated with the Syriac-type Christianity in Armenian Church history, then the reflection of that theology through Syriac influence on Armenian Christianity was not dominant, but was counterbalanced

---

the bishops of the councils of 424 held by Dadjésus (see Labourt, *Christ. Perse*, pp. 119–25; Wigram, *Assyrian Church*, pp. 120–5) there is the name of "Artašahr év. d'Arménie" (see Chabot, *Synodicon Orientale*, p. 285). Again, later in 486, in the council held by Acacius (see Labourt, *Christ. Perse*, pp. 141–54; Wigram *Assyrian Church*, pp. 163–6) there is the name of "Moïse d'Arménie" (see Chabot, *Syndicon Orientale*, p. 299). With these indications can we conclude that in the southern provinces of Armenia there were dioceses dependent on the Catholicosate of Seleucia, i.e. under the jurisdiction of the Syro-Persian Church? The Persian influence was so strong in these bordering regions that such a supposition is not unthinkable at all. If this is true, then it is legitimate to think that Surmak, Brk'išoy, and Šmuēl came from this section of the Christian Church in Armenia when the Persians tried to bring the Armenian Church under tight control by associating it closely with the Syro-Persian Church.

by the Greek type, through Cappadocian and Constantinopolitan influence.

(c) If the Armenians turned to centres of Syriac Christian culture to find assistance in shaping their own alphabet, it was done partly for technical and partly for political reasons. Their traditional links with East Syria and North Mesopotamia made this move all too possible and natural. But it is significant to note, at the same time, that the general pattern of the Armenian alphabet was derived from the Greek.

(d) In the third decade of the fifth century and immediately before the Council of Ephesus, the strengthening of the Armenian Church's relationship with Constantinople was a decisive moment in the history of the doctrinal orientation of the Armenian Church during the Nestorian controversy; and this orientation played a vital part in their later attitude to the Council of Chalcedon, as we shall see.

Now, in view of these points, which we believe represent in a schematical form—and in the limits of the existing historical evidence—the true picture of the ecclesiastical situation of the time, what is to be our estimation of P. Peeters' thesis, which seems to have found a place in recent studies of the problem by Western scholars?

We think that he makes too much of the relationship of the Armenian Church with the Antiochene tradition. In other words, he reads too much doctrinal significance into events which do not by themselves have theological implications or doctrinal consequences. It is equally an exaggeration to distinguish so sharply the doctrinal divergences of the Antiochene and Alexandrian Schools by representing these two theological traditions as opposed to each other and mutually exclusive. In fact, these two traditions existed side by side in one and the same Church, and the differences between them were revealed only later, namely in the course of the Nestorian controversy.

Finally, these two traditions became so sharply opposed to each other that it was impossible to hold them together. Until the first quarter of the fifth century both had their lawful place in the life of the Church. Therefore to be connected with one of them did not necessarily mean to be committed to its later interpretations or developments. Briefly, we think that Peeters reads back the conflict between the Antiochene and Alexandrian christologies too far.

It is, again, misleading to try to find relations between the Armenian Church and Alexandria. Given the circumstances in which Christianity was introduced and spread in Armenia one cannot expect to see any regular or constant contact with Alexandria itself. Later, after the Council of Ephesus and, more particularly, after the Council of Chalcedon relations were established for understandable reasons. At this early stage, Armenians could know the Alexandrian tradition only through their contacts with Cappadocian Christianity and with Constantinople. Here, again, Peeters' way of putting the problem—in an "either-or" fashion—is not justifiable from the historical point of view.

Therefore, returning to the problem of the relationship of the Armenian Church to the Antiochene tradition, we can say with confidence that this relationship did not mean that the seeds of Nestorian christology were planted in Armenia. If this were the case, as Peeters wants us to believe,[1] then it would be impossible to understand such a sudden change as the adherence of the Armenian Church to the Council of Ephesus. It would simply be a betrayal of a former position, which would have left its traces in history and literature.

We now turn our attention to later episodes of importance in the development of the doctrinal situation of the Armenian Church.

[1] "La littérature arménienne a commencé à s'épanouir dans un terroir saturé d'influences nestoriennes" (!) (*Origines*, p. 217).

4

THE HISTORICAL BACKGROUND (3)
The Ecclesiastical Situation
Between Ephesus and Chalcedon

In the course of the first decade of this period the doctrinal position of the Armenian Church became established with such a firm foundation that the succeeding years of bitter christological controversies could never shake it. Therefore, it is most important to see how this happened and in what way it affected the relations of the Armenian Church with the other Churches of the Byzantine Empire. The process which led to the establishment of that position is to some extent described in five documents containing the correspondence of Acacius of Melitene with Sahak Catholicos and the Armenian *naxarars*—three letters[1]— and of Proclus, the Patriarch of Constantinople, again with Sahak Catholicos—two letters.[2]

[1] The text of these three letters exists only in Armenian. It is published in the famous *Book of Letters* (see pp. 14–21). A Latin translation has been made by Dom B. Mercier and incorporated in the article of M. Richard. (See *Acace*, pp. 394–400.) A French translation is made by M. Tallon, *Livre des Lettres*, pp. 29–44. I use the Armenian text as printed originally in the *Book of Letters*.

[2] The letter of Proclus, generally known as the "Tome of Proclus", in its present Armenian text is a mutilated and, indeed, a very confused document. Vardanean tried to reconstruct it. The first parts of the letter which were not found in the *Book of Letters* were discovered by K. Tēr-Mkrtč'ean in the *Florilegium* known as "Seal of Faith" (see pp. 109–12). Vardanean inserted them in his edition. He used also the Greek text and Syriac translation. See the Greek text in Mansi, v, pp. 421–38; Migne, *P.G.*, t. 65, col. 856–73. A new edition by Schwartz, *A.C.O.*, t. iv, vol. 2, pp. 187–95. The Syriac translation is found in the Chronicle of Zachariah of Mitylene. See Land, *Zachariae episcopi Mitylenis aliorumque scripta historica*, iii, pp. 103–15; the English translation in Hamilton and

All of these letters come from that period of christological disputes and ecclesiastical disturbances which upset the life of the Church in the East from the Council of Ephesus to the Council of Chalcedon; but more precisely, they belong to the years between 432 and 438. We have already outlined the situation of the Church in this period.[1] We must remember that the issues, in their actual state, were crucial ones. On the one hand, the Antiochenes were struggling by every means to save their tradition, which was so deeply stricken at Ephesus. On the other hand, the Cyrillines were trying to complete their victory on practical grounds by removing all the obstacles in the way of the expansion of the christology sanctioned in Ephesus and still opposed by bishops and theologians, especially in the eastern provinces of the Byzantine Empire.

Now, the Armenians were not present at the Council of Ephesus, which was convened in such a haste and urgency by Theodosius II. But it seems that the immediately subsequent consequences of the Council echoed in Armenia, whence there started a whole controversy over the writings of Theodore of Mopsuestia, a controversy that stirred once more the ecclesiastical situation in East Syria, Cilicia, Antioch, and Constantinople. That was the beginning of the controversy later to be known as the controversy of the *Three Chapters*. Although it was closed for some years with the death of Cyril in 444 and with the Council of Chalcedon (451), which now became the centre of the christological disputes, it was to be reopened in the sixth century and to create a real storm in the Eastern Church for more than half a century.[2]

To what extent and in what way did the beginnings of the controversy affect the doctrinal orientation of the Armenian Church? This is the fundamental question with which we are

---

Brooks, *Syriac Chronicle*, pp. 24–8. I have used the Armenian text as reconstructed by Vardanean (see *H.A.*, vol. 35 (1921) col. 12–25), giving at the same time the references of the corresponding passages in the Greek text of Migne and Schwartz.

[1] See above, pp. 35–8.

[2] See above, pp. 53–4.

concerned here while dealing with the history of the origins of the *Three Chapters*.

The Armenians were not informed directly or officially of the decisions of the Council of Ephesus. The canons set up in the Council were not sent to the leaders of the Armenian Church. Later, they were brought to Armenia by Armenian Church divines who had been sent to Constantinople to pursue their advanced theological studies. But soon after the closure of the Council the news must have reached the leaders of the Armenian Church, as can be inferred from the documents related to this controversy.[1]

At this new, Ephesian, phase of the fifth-century christological controversy, Armenia became involved in it through active participation and in a direct way, and sometimes in a responsible rôle. Therefore, turning now to the documents mentioned above, let us see what we can learn from them concerning the doctrinal orientation of the Armenian Church.

1. The Letter of Acacius to Sahak

Chronologically the letter of Acacius to Sahak[2] must be taken first into account. It was written soon after the Council of Ephesus, most probably in 432.[3] It opens with an assertion that in Christ all peoples are made one.[4] That unity,

> was shaken by the malicious heresy of Nestorius, who was the bishop of the city of Constantine; when he was found a heretic he was deprived of his dignity (i.e. episcopacy); so we became aware that this fierce wolf had attacked the holy Churches, and in some places had won the simple-minded to his ill-will (i.e. malignity). Caught by the fear that a stain [of the heresy] might have gained space also in your Churches, and having in mind the common good we deemed it good to advise you that these people are moulded in no other [disease] than in the Jewish disease;[5] for they are mistaken

---

[1] See Additional Note 4.   [2] See *B.L.*, pp. 14–15.
[3] See Richard, *Acace*, pp. 405–6; Tallon, *Livre des Lettres*, pp. 22–3.
[4] He quotes Col. 3. 11; cf Gal. 3.28.
[5] The christological teaching of Nestorius or of the Antiochene School as a whole was characterized by their opponents as "Jewish", because the Jews did not

about the descent (i.e. Incarnation) of the Lord [that is to say] about his passing like a man through all suffering except sin.[1]

After this general warning he tries to show briefly, on the basis of the Scriptural evidence,[2] that it is one and the same Lord, one and the same person who lived and acted as the God-man. He criticizes those who think of Christ as a person no greater than the Apostles and the Saints.[3] He complains about people who accuse him of Theopaschite inclinations[4] which he rejects categorically by saying:

But we not only do not accept their (i.e. his accusers') interpretation, but also we anathematize those who dare say that God even in his nature underwent the sufferings, and consider the immortal as mortal and the incorruptible and the unstained as corruptible; they do not look into the Scriptures and not into the teaching of the 318 Bishops of Nicaea.[5]

It is important to translate the concluding passage:

When you receive this letter offer to God continuous prayers for my weakness. But we fear that people might be found [in your country] who follow the teaching of Theodore of Mopsuestia and [might

---

recognize in Christ the Godhead and regarded him simply as a man. Therefore those who separated Christ in two were likened to the Jews. This appears several times in the fifth-century doctrinal documents of the Armenian Church, as we shall see.

[1] B.L., p. 14.

[2] It would be interesting to refer to some of these passages which may help us in understanding his conception of the unity of Christ's person. See John 9.35-9; 2 Cor. 13.13; Matt. 9.28; cf John 6.53.

[3] The target of his attacks was perhaps that extreme type of christology which could not be dissociated or distinguished from Adoptionism. He exaggerates in his interpretation of the Antiochene christology which, in all probability, he had in mind.

[4] He refers, as Richard has shown convincingly, to the incident which happened in Chalcedon immediately after the Council of Ephesus when delegations from the two sides, Alexandrians and Antiochenes, were advocating before Theodosius the truth of their respective christological systems and Acacius was suddenly caught out by the Antiochenes for teaching Theopaschism in his utterances at the meeting. (See Richard, Acace, pp. 402-3.)

[5] B.L., p. 15.

have fallen victim to] the pernicious venom of Nestorius and who might exert influence on the simple-minded. For, as regards the writings left by the former[1] and especially as regards the one written on the Incarnation, when this problem [of their heresy] was revealed, the holy bishops assembled in the city of Ephesus decreed that they all should be burnt. Therefore, take care to keep the faith without confusion (lit. "muddiness") so that you may receive the final justification in purity.[2]

There are problems which emerge from this letter and which have to be met and answered where possible. But before doing so —and in order to see them in the general context of the whole situation—let us present the evidence of the other documents that are closely linked with this.

2. The answer of Sahak to the letter of Acacius

In the first place, Sahak thanks his colleague, bishop Acacius, for his care for the preservation of the orthodox faith in Armenia. He tells Acacius that he is very much pleased with his advice and message.[3] He openly says that it was with a real satisfaction that he was informed about these things, because, he adds, "We were well content with ourselves in being and remaining in our familiar ignorance by having taken refuge in our ignorance like in a solid fortress."[4] Then he blames and deplores those who go astray from the truth and fall into various heresies. He adds:

But I myself wonder how some people try and strive, beyond the limits of the law, to comprehend the incomprehensible; besides, I think that the men like these do not know at all the Scriptures and their power, but have regard only to the Jewish dregs.[5]

---

[1] The Armenian article znora surely refers to Theodore and not to Nestorius. For the reasons see Additional Note 5.

[2] B.L., p. 15.

[3] Richard, well acquainted with the Patristic literature of the fourth and fifth centuries, shows a very high appreciation of Sahak's letter to Acacius. After saying that he will not comment on it in detail, he adds, "Notons pourtant le caractère fleuri du style, que n'alourdit aucune citation biblique, la modestie du ton et la grande prudence en matière de dogme" (Acace, p. 406).

[4] B.L., p. 16.   [5] B.L., p. 17.

With this kind of general statement he proceeds to condemn such people. The only clear indication of any specific heresy is found in the following statement:

> There is no science as gloomy and depressing as the one which distinguishes by name two sons or two Lords in Christ; [by this] they openly declare their impudence without fear and without shame.[1]

Then he promises to persecute these men if they appear in Armenia: "If we suddenly find here men of those [heretics] not only we do not accept or persecute them, but also we do not hesitate to bring them under heavy punishment."[2] In his turn, he exhorts his colleague to watch diligently and to cast out the evil from the Church of Christ, especially as he has the privilege of the emperor's protection and support.[3] Finally, he concludes by answering the last paragraph of Acacius' letter in the following important passage:

> Therefore, our Lord and Father, do not hesitate to remember us in your holy and acceptable prayers, and if there is anything erroneous in the contents of our letter, because of our ignorance, do rectify and be not slow in strengthening our weakness. But as regards the heresy which you wrote us to abhor, at this time, by the grace of God, nothing of that sort has reached [us]; however, if there is something of that venom hidden, surely we will endeavour to extirpate that obstacle so that we can glorify Christ in concord.[4]

3. The Letter of Acacius to the Armenians

This is the title of a curious document which follows, in the series of the documents of the *Book of Letters*, the answer of St Sahak to Acacius. As can be seen in the first paragraph, it is addressed to "the honourable and virtuous Armenian *naxarars* beloved and servants of Christ, both to the seniors and the juniors".

---

[1] Ibid.   [2] Ibid.

[3] A remark which is quite eloquent in showing us how Sahak envied his colleagues in the Byzantine empire. This reflects his feeling of the heavy burden put upon his shoulders by the dilemma of the Armenian Church's situation under the Persian rule or overlordship, as we tried to expound it in the previous two chapters.

[4] *B.L.*, p. 18.

Acacius first gives the reason for his writing to them. He says that the followers of the teaching of Nestorius and Theodore did spread the poisonous and pernicious doctrine of their masters even in Armenia. Therefore in such times of trouble,

> We thought it worthy and right to write to you as to God-loving people, that God by his grace make your saintly and truthful teachers stand firm and unshaken on the foundation of the true faith and not yield to the fierce wolf to find time for stealing anyone from Christ's flock.[1]

Then he explains how the times predicted by Paul[2] have come to pass. The situation now is so much troubled that Acacius reminds the Armenians of Christ's challenging question: "Nevertheless, when the son of man comes, will he find faith on earth?"[3]

> But those who fear God must keep firm to the religion of the Fathers and to the teaching of the 318 holy bishops; [that is] the foundation which they taught as the rule of faith with great veracity and deliberation and by the command of the Holy Spirit and [in accordance] with the teaching of the Apostles and of the Gospels, and which we recite always in our churches.[4]

Again he mentions Nestorius and Theodore as men who tried to shake that foundation on which the Church was built. Therefore they became responsible also for other people's deviation from the faith in which people were received into the Church through baptism. But they were soon defeated. The evil was overcome by the Council of Ephesus. The Nicaean faith was re-established. And now,

---

[1] B.L., p. 19.

[2] The quoted passages are Acts 20.29, 30; 2 Thess. 2.3.

[3] Luke 18.8.

[4] B.L., p. 20. It is generally believed that the insertion of the Creed into the Eucharistic worship dates not earlier than A.D. 476. Its inclusion is thought to be the work of Peter the Fuller, the Patriarch of Antioch. (See Kelly, *Creeds*, pp. 348 ff.) Have we, then, in Acacius' letter information revealing earlier use of the Creed in the Eucharistic worship? Was it possible that Peter got the idea from an existing practice in some Churches? An investigation may prove perhaps useful and profitable.

if anyone teaches anything outside it (i.e. that faith) and preaches two sons, one from Mary and another, the Word, who is from God, or if anyone confesses God as being convertible and changeable in becoming flesh, let him, whoever he may be, be anathema; for it is not we who anathematize that kind of people but St Paul [himself when] he says[1]: "But even if we, or an angel from heaven, should preach to you a gospel more than you received, let him be anathema."[2]

Once more he affectionately urges the Armenian *naxarars* not to depart from the orthodox faith in which they had been brought up. Here, he specifies more clearly the reasons of his writing to them. He says:

I thought it necessary to write this [letter] to your belovedness, because when Hon, Koth and Anĵn, our beloved priests, came to us, they told us about the good work you did, that you tied up and sealed the writings of Theodore.[3] Now, let no one persuade you to give them again to those who readily and pleasingly welcome them for the destruction of those who accept them and hear [to them]; for, if Nestorius was removed from all the Churches how would Theodore and his books and teaching, which have the same ideas and the same harmfulness, be acceptable? Do recognize this kind of people as being false prophets, fraudulent cultivators disguised in the appearance of the servants of Christ; guard yourselves from those people and consider them as [having been] anathematized, and do not accept the false news which they bring to you from the East.[4]

Finally, he reminds them of his own humility or unworthiness, adding that it was only the care for their salvation that impelled him to write these things. And again exhorting them to remain faithful to the true faith, he blesses them in the name of the Lord.

These three documents, which we have summarized and translated in extracts, put before us problems of considerable significance for the understanding of the doctrinal situation of the Armenian Church. But before tackling them we must give an

[1] Gal. 1.8. [2] *B.L.*, p. 20.
[3] In the text it stands as *Diodor*, "Diodore" (see *Erratum*). We translate it Theodore (*T'ēodor*) thus departing from other scholars' doctrinal interpretation of the letter. See Additional Note 6.
[4] *B.L.*, p. 21.

account of the other two documents and must complete the evidence provided by this corpus of the correspondence we have already referred to, in order to understand the situation in a wider context and in a clearer picture.

4. The Tome of Proclus

We need not give a very detailed summary of this famous christological document which has already been studied because of its extremely important christological doctrine formulated in the aftermath of the Council of Ephesus. In fact, we may remember, it was written at a very crucial moment in the post-Ephesian period—the beginning of the controversy over the writings of Theodore of Mopsuestia, which was the opening phase of the question of the *Three Chapters*, as we have already noted. It was agreed upon by the two leaders of the two groups opposing each other in the christological battle: John the Patriarch of Antioch and Cyril the Patriarch of Alexandria. Constantinople, Antioch, and Alexandria joined hands together in 435 through the signatures of their patriarchs on a christological exposition—indeed an event of singular importance.

It is only natural, therefore, that such a document has drawn the attention of so many scholars. Here, however, we study the Tome not in its general lines as far as its christology is concerned, but especially in its connection with the doctrinal situation of the Armenian Church. Therefore we must use the Armenian text, which displays differences from the Greek text of great significance.

In the preface of the letter which has been lost in the present Armenian text—the first two sections of Migne's edition—and which we follow in the original Greek text, Proclus first shows his sympathy with the leaders of the Armenian Church for the troubles which they suffered at the hands of heretics. Then he tells them that those who are not capable of seeing spiritual things preach foolishly, because their vision cannot transcend the visible, earthly aspects of the things they speak of. He speaks of the virtues which the Greeks had taught and he adds that they are not sufficient; only the Christian virtues may enable us to see the truth.

Then follows a brief statement, made in confessional terms, on the doctrine of Christ's person. The basic assertion here is that the Word of God became truly man without suffering (i.e. without passing through human experience)—ἀπαθῶς—and took upon himself the form of a servant; this, however, does not mean that his nature was changed or that he added something more to the Trinity.[1]

In the next section he presents an *apologia* of the faith; he shows how important it is to hold steadfastly to the right faith. Those who teach things contrary to that faith, let them be anathematized as St Paul said (Gal. 1.8).[2]

The succeeding passage is a purely christological one, in which Proclus shows that Christ became man in the truest sense of this word, that is to say, Christ underwent human experiences "by necessity".[3] Thus "nowhere does the Evangelist say that he (i.e. the Word) came and entered [a] perfect man; but he says that he became flesh by having descended into the nature itself."[4] However, he adds that by saying, "He became flesh" he did not mean that his nature turned or was converted into flesh. His divine nature was above convertibility or corruption.

The key words for Proclus' christology are the two Scriptural expressions: "He became flesh" and "He took the form of a servant". When these two "are understood in the orthodox

---

[1] See Vardanean, col. 12–13; cf Migne, col. 860; *A.C.O.*, iv, 2, p. 188.

[2] Vardanean, col. 13; cf Migne, col. 860; *A.C.O.*, iv, 2, p. 189. Here, there is a gap in the Armenian text. Most probably the missing passage (25 lines in Migne and 14 in *A.O.C.*) was left out by the compiler of the "Seal of Faith" (see above, p. 111, n. 2). The reason for this omission must have been the non-christological content of the passage, as the Greek text shows. In fact, the compiler was concerned with such testimonies of Church Fathers which could be used directly as christological arguments, in support of the anti-Chalcedonian position.

[3] The Armenian word is *i harkē*; the Greek ἀναγκαίως.

[4] Vardanean, col. 14; cf Migne, col. 860–1; *A.C.O.*, p. 189. Here, again, there is a gap in the Armenian text (7 lines in the Migne and 5 lines in *A.C.O.*) presumably for the same reason as the previous omission.

sense they become seeds of salvation for us". He explains the unity in Christ in metaphysical terms by saying:

> As there can be no unity in [the state of] two different things—for, if that is the case, then there is no unity (but duality)—likewise the one as (in the sense of) perfect accord (union) is not divided into two.[1]

Again, in the next section, he emphasizes the unity of Christ being God and having become truly man without being

> mutilated in anything from his incorruptible and stainless nature. . . . He became man and he saves [us] through [his] sharing in the sufferings, he who is of the same race and of the same lineage [as man]; he paid the debt of the sins for all by [his] dying as [a] man; he, as evil-hating God, obstructed him who had the power of death, that is to say, Satan.[2]

The opening words of the passage which follows this, are important and revealing: "Thus it is not so that Christ is one and God the Word is another[3]—God forbid!—because the divine nature does not know two Sons." After this basic assertion Proclus goes on to show how absurd is a christology in which duality (ἄλλος καὶ ἄλλος type of teaching) has found a place. He explains, furthermore, how contrary is such a doctrine to the way of life which Christ lived on earth and which is described so clearly in the Gospels.[4]

But just here comes the objection to his conception of the unity

[1] Vardanean, col. 14; cf Migne, col. 861; *A.C.O.*, p. 190.

[2] Vardanean, col. 15; cf Migne, col. 861; *A.C.O.*, p. 190. It is very significant to note that one can describe Christ acting *as* God and *as* man; more precisely *according* to his divine or human nature. But this can be done only after having conceived him as *One* in his *being*. This is a very important point which appears over and over again in all the later Armenian theologians. This is, indeed, a conception of unity which sounds quite different from the doctrine of Leo as formulated in his Tome where he describes the two natures as being, so to speak, *centres of activity* in themselves. The logical conclusion was naturally the *division*.

[3] It would be perhaps helpful to quote the Greek text: οὐκ ἄλλος οὖν ὁ χριστὸς καὶ ἄλλος ὁ θεὸς λόγος (μὴ γένοιτο).

[4] Vardanean, col. 16–18; cf Migne, col. 864–5; *A.C.O.*, p. 191. Obviously in this passage he has in mind as his target those of the Antiochene theologians who distinguished very sharply between man and the Word of God in Christ.

of Christ's person. He faces it boldly. Here are both the objection and his answer given straightforwardly:

> If they (i.e. the opponents) say the Trinity is of one substance[1] and the Trinity is without passions and sufferings; and if the Trinity is without passions and sufferings, then the Word of God also is without sufferings; it follows that he who was crucified was someone other than God the Word who is without sufferings.[2]

Proclus first makes his opponents look ridiculous for this very weak objection, which he likens to a spider's web—even looser than that—and to script written upon water! Then he answers the objection by saying that it is not the Word God who suffered but the Word Incarnate. Everyone knows that the divine nature in itself is above all suffering. But God wanted to overcome death which is the chief of all sufferings, and, therefore, he became flesh through the Virgin. His becoming flesh or his taking the form of a servant did not diminish his Godhead, and it was through his body that he overcame the sufferings.[3]

The succeeding passage elaborates this point. Proclus says that it was necessary for our salvation that the Word should become man. However, in becoming man he remained the same. "It is the same that is both God and man, not that [he is] divided into two, but [that] he is and remains one and the same." Therefore Christ *is* the Word God.[4]

---

[1] The Armenian word is *miazor* "of the one (same) power". It stands for the Greek ὁμοούσιος.

[2] Vardanean, col. 18; cf Migne, col. 865; *A.C.O.*, p. 191. This is probably the ground for accusations charging Proclus of Theopaschism. Although Richard has tried to clear him from any responsibility in this respect, in so far as his authorship of the famous formula εἶς τῆς Τριάδος ἐσταυρώθη is concerned (see Richard, *Proclus*), yet there seem to have been rumours about Proclus' "Theopaschism"; for this reference and, more particularly, the way in which he makes the accusations look ridiculous, show this quite clearly (cf Amann, *Theopaschites*, col. 506).

[3] See Vardanean, col. 18–19; cf Migne, col. 865; *A.C.O.*, pp. 191–2. Here can be seen in an embryonic form, the doctrine of "economy" which, again, later became a corner-stone in the system of Monophysite christology.

[4] See Vardanean, col. 19; cf Migne, col. 865–8; *A.C.O.*, pp. 191–2. Scriptural passages such as 1 Cor. 8.6; John 1.1–3 are quoted in support of this statement.

Again, some may bring forth passages from the Scriptures[1] where Christ is spoken of as a man, and they may use them as arguments in asserting the separation they have in mind. But they are either ignorant or malicious, because they do not see the meaning of the Scriptures in the right way. For it is all too evident that in the beginning Christ was not a man but only God. When he became man he took our nature in its complete form. And it is because of this that "as he is of the one substance of the Father according to the divinity, he is also of the same generation of the Virgin according to the flesh". Then they must accept that Christ is not a man as different from God the Word, but "the same God the Word who created the world, gave the Law, inspired the Prophets and, in the end, took flesh and chose the Apostles for the salvation of the Gentiles and the peoples".[2]

Having thus refuted the heretics, he exclaims: "Let us flee from those trouble-makers and from the overflowing waters of the filthy fallacy." He mentions by name Arius, Eunomius, and Macedon. He invites the recipients of his letter to join him in following St Paul's exhortation (Eph. 2.14) and let the heretics dread the condemnation of those who introduce newly invented impieties and divide into two him who united the divided.[3]

There follows rather a long passage in which he illustrates the point that, according to the Scriptural evidence taken from both the Old and New Testaments,[4] Christ is one. He who was born of the Virgin, he who in the course of time grew in stature according to the flesh, he who bore all the sufferings of the flesh, is he who was before Abraham and through whom the world was created.[5]

In the closing section[6] he first repeats his exhortation that the

[1] Namely Acts 2.22; 17.31; John 8.40.
[2] Vardenean, col. 20; cf Migne, col. 868; A.C.O., p. 193.
[3] See Vardanean, col. 20–1; cf Migne, col. 869; A.C.O., p. 193.
[4] See John 8.58; Rom. 9.4, 5; Exod. 4.22; Eph. 4.10; Gal. 1.15.
[5] See Vardanean, col. 21–3; cf Migne, col. 869–72; A.C.O., pp. 193–4.
[6] See Vardanean, col. 23–5; cf Migne, col. 872–3; A.C.O., pp. 194–5.

faithful followers of Christ should worship him in the right way, because they have "the mind of Christ".[1]

Then he gives the reason why he wrote this letter. He says:

> We wrote all these things to your belovedness, because we became aware[2] (lit: "we heard") that some people, evil-speakers and foolish, have fallen upon your country and want to contort the purity, the unadorned, unartificial beauty of the orthodox faith with malicious books and by adversity and fallacious, false-pretentious knowledge.

He reminds his readers of St Paul's warning against the insidious people[3] and of the only foundation of Christ's Church[4] which must not be confounded with any human teaching.

Here are a few lines which are not found in the Greek text. They are of the greatest importance for our immediate purpose. So I translate them:

> Now, hold [together] steadfastly in one spirit and as one person; be, by faith, athletes of the Gospel and not stricken by anathema and condemnation with Nestorius and Theodore who had been his teacher and who showed forth the evil plant and the malicious novelties which exceeded the denial of the Jews and, like the heresy of the Arians and others who deviated from the glory of the holiness and from the right faith; they were anathematized by all the peoples, and their books [containing] perverse ideas were burnt before all the people. You, too, keep yourselves safe from them and do the same as the assembly of the bishops did, and let no one regard this temporary shame[5] as his own and inherit the eternal shame and be condemned and destroyed with them in the hell.[6]

---

[1] See 1 Cor. 2.16.

[2] Here we have an important difference between the Armenian and Greek texts. In the Greek we read: Ταῦτα δὲ πρὸς τὴν ὑμετέραν ἐπεστείλαμεν ἀγάπην ἐκ τῶν ὑμετέρων προτραπέντες λιβέλλων ὧν πρὸς ἡμᾶς διεπέμψασθε. We shall speak of the significance of this difference later when we try to reconstruct the doctrinal situation as represented in these documents.

[3] Col. 2.8.   [4] See 1 Cor. 3.11.

[5] As Tallon suggests (see *Livre des Lettres*, p. 71) this "shame" must be the shame of having followed for a while these false doctrines. The author of this passage wants to place the responsibility on the originators of the heresy and urges his readers not to consider it as their own personal belief.

[6] Vardanean, col. 24.

After this digression, the Armenian text agrees with the Greek. The concluding words are worth translating:

> But you keep firm to the teaching which you received from the Holy Fathers who were assembled in the Synod of Nicaea and who affirmed the holy and glorious faith; which doctrine [was taught] by the holy and blessed Basil and Gregory[1] and by all who are like them, and who maintained the holy faith in holiness and concord in their own lives, and whose names are written in the "Book of Life" (Phil. 4.3).[2]

5. The answer of Sahak and Maštoc to the letter of Proclus

The elaborate form of this letter is surprising. Moreover, in many places exactly the same phrases are used as those found in Sahak's answer to Acacius, which we have already reviewed. The differences consist mainly in the addition of some passages which are concerned with the faith in general, and with the doctrine of Christ's person in particular. Therefore, we shall not give a full account of this document but shall present briefly these differences.

The first part of the letter is very similar—only with slight elaborations in the expression—to the first sections of the answer to Acacius. The first difference is noticed in the passage in which Sahak and Maštoc tell their colleague that they have sent messengers to the neighbourhood of the catholicosate and have given them strict orders to warn the people not to listen to such "barbarians" (i.e. heretics) and not to accept their pernicious and destructive heretical teaching. Whereas, in the letter addressed to Acacius, Sahak had promised to persecute such people *if* they ever appeared.

Another difference is seen in the passage which immediately follows this one. Here we have a confession of faith which opens with the words of the Nicene Creed and is continued with formulas taken directly from the *Didascalia* 318 *Patrum Nicaenorum*.[3]

---

[1] In all probability he refers to St Gregory of Nazianzus.

[2] Vardanean, col. 24–5; cf Migne, col. 873; *A.C.O.*, p. 195.

[3] Lebon has attempted to reconstruct the Greek text by a retroversion. (See his *Symboles*, p. 850.)

On the specific problem of the Incarnation, here is their view briefly stated:

> Concerning the Incarnation[1] of the Son we believe as follows: He took upon himself to become perfect man from Mary the God-bearer ($\theta\epsilon\acute{o}\tau o\kappa o\varsigma$) by the Holy Spirit by assuming soul and body truly and not feignedly; it is in this way that he achieved the salvation of our humanity; he truly underwent the sufferings, not because he himself was indebted to the sufferings—for Godhead is exempt from sufferings—but [it was] for us [that] he took upon himself the sufferings, was crucified and buried and the third day rose and ascended into heaven and sat at the right [side] of the Father, and he shall come [again] to judge the quick and the dead.[2]

Then they attack the heretics who

> contrive to find two sons and two temples in their minds (i.e. imagination); they [dare] to think without fear and without shame, and their shameful [thoughts] they declare openly [and] with impudence. For, our Lord Jesus Christ by the will of his Father had compassion upon the wandering of men. The Word which proceeded from the heart of the Father wanted to please him by becoming flesh through the covering of the Holy Spirit and in the womb of the holy Virgin. He received the flesh worn out by the treachery of Satan and turned into corruption [in order] to restore [it] in body, soul, and spirit so that the first creature created incorruptible might appear at the second birth [i.e.] at the resurrection of the dead; he took real (i.e. true) flesh for us and sowed in us, by faith, the divinity, and wrought miracles and signs so that we might become faithful believers in his divinity. He took upon himself thirst and hunger, fatigue and sleep, not that [his] divinity was being defeated (i.e. overcome) in the sufferings of the flesh, but that [he could] shut the shameless mouths and the tongues sharpened with iniquity which already are prepared to speak blasphemies; they (i.e. these latter) say [that] his coming did not take place in truth but by feigning, [that is to say] in false appearances to the eyes. He endured to take upon himself the slaps and the insults, the cross and the death not as if he

[1] The Armenian word is *marmnazdeçut'iwn* which literally means "putting on himself the flesh".

[2] *B.L.*, p. 10.

himself was indebted or worthy for them, neither was he worthy for the death [in which] he died, because the Godhead is immortal. But [he died] so that he might abrogate through the Gospel and [his] precious blood the dishonour which came [to us] because of our sins and make us worthy for washing.[1]

Then, after the exposition of this simple and orthodox faith, they attack those who depart from it. In the same way as Sahak had asked Acacius, they ask now also Proclus to watch diligently and to use all the imperial power of the King (i.e. the Byzantine emperor) to sweep away these heresies; on their part they promise to do the same thing to those who appear here and there in their country. In exactly the same words as those addressed to Acacius they ask for Proclus' prayers.

Finally, in the last passage there is a short paragraph where Theodore of Mopsuestia is mentioned:

> And that there are here disciples ("followers") of Theodore of Mopsuestia, at this time, by the grace of God, nothing like that has been revealed. But if it is hidden in the rust of impurity, surely we will endeavour to extirpate that obstacle and put away the scandal, so that we may become worthy to render glory to God for the concord [among us] like the unity which is glorified among you.[2]

These five documents, happily preserved, illuminate to a great extent our understanding of the background of the Armenian doctrinal position *vis-à-vis* the Council of Chalcedon. But, at the same time, they are not completely self-explanatory: they pose a number of questions which we have to answer by examining other sources of information. Moreover, there are contradictory statements in them which have to be explained, if possible, by the help of other sources. To give some examples: What do we understand precisely by Acacius' allegation that Theodore's works had been translated into Armenian? Why in the Armenian text of Proclus' letter is the name of Theodore *added*? Why, in the answers to both Acacius and Proclus, does Sahak Catholicos almost deny the existence of followers of Theodore in Armenia? Why

[1] *B.L.*, pp. 11–12.　　　　　　[2] *B.L.*, p. 13.

did Acacius write two letters instead of one? Why did he address the second to the Armenian feudal princes and not to the head of the Church? Who are the three priests mentioned in this second letter and what is their part in the controversy? And there are many similar questions. It becomes obvious that we have to look for further information about the doctrinal situation in Armenia elsewhere in order to reconstruct the true picture of that situation, which is only hinted at in these documents.

6. *The Testimony of the Armenian historiographers*

Looking into the Armenian sources themselves we find no great help. The Armenian writers of the fifth century give us no direct and open evidence on this controversy as such. They speak of the clash between Syrophile and Hellenophile orientations, but hardly mention names or give precise information.

However, we find two testimonies which are exceptions and cast some light on the situation. The first comes from Koriwn, who at the end of his "Life of Maštoç" having completed the account of the life and work of St Sahak and St Maštoç and before relating their death, introduces the following passage, which stands somewhat out of the context of his narrative.[1] Here is the translation:

> In that time there were brought into Armenia fallacious and frivolous books left by a certain Greek whose name was Theodore.[2] On this [matter] the bishops of the Churches assembled in Synod notified

[1] Akinean suspects the authenticity of this passage. He thinks that there are expressions in it which are not familiar to Koriwn's style. Again, the place of this passage in Koriwn's text—in the closing section—as it stands to-day does not seem to be the proper context. Therefore he removes it from where it stands now and inserts it in an earlier section in his own edition of Koriwn's work. In this section Koriwn speaks of the journey of Maštoç's disciples to Constantinople. That seems to him the proper context of the passage in question, because the controversy over Theodore's writings was connected with the disciples of Sahak and Maštoç, as we shall see later. (See Akinean, *Koriwn*, p. 44, and particularly pp. 104–5, n. 75.)

[2] All the manuscripts have it as *T'ēodios* (Theodios) which obviously is a mistake of transcription. In all the printed texts of Koriwn's work it is put as *T'ēodoros* (Theodoros). (See Abełean, *Koriwn*, p. 44; Fenteglean, *Koriwn*, pp. 59–60.)

and instructed the worshippers of the true faith, Sahak and Maštoc. These with their truth-loving diligence removed them (i.e. the books) away and rejected them by casting them out of the frontiers of their country so that no diabolic smoke be added to [their] luminous doctrine.[1]

The second piece of evidence comes from Movsēs Xorenaçi who, years after the controversy, writing the general history of Armenia refers to the same episode in more precise and clear terms. In fact, he devotes a whole chapter[2] to the Council of Ephesus where, after a brief description of the Council as such, he adds this singularly important passage:

> And because Sahak the Great and Mesrop did not happen to be at that Council, Cyril the Alexandrian and Proclus and Acacius, the bishops of the cities of Constantinople and Melitene, wrote to them and warned them, because they heard that some of the heterodox disciples taking [with them] the books of Theodore of Mopsuestia, the teacher of Nestorius and the disciple of Diodore, had gone to Armenia. Afterwards, our Translators whose names we mentioned before[3] came [back] and found Sahak and Mesrop in Aštišat of Taron, and handed them the letters (i.e. of the Church Fathers referred to) and the canons of Ephesus, six in number, drawn up under regulated headings and the accurate copy of the Scriptures.

It is surprising that in the succeeding passage nothing is said about the consequences of the reception of the letters and the six canons of Ephesus. The other fragmentary information provided by these two writers concerning the doctrinal situation of the Armenian Church, namely the sending of the students to Byzantium, we shall take into account later when we attempt a reconstruction of the situation as a whole. We may now turn to foreign sources.

7. The evidence of the foreign sources

In the first place, we have a very important account of some events closely connected with this situation in Innocentius Maroniae:

---

[1] Koriwn, p. 86.

[2] Bk. iii, ch. 61: "On the Council of Ephesus which was [convened] for [the case of] the impious Nestorius."

[3] See bk. iii, ch. 60, where he speaks of these Translators going to Byzantium.

Incipit sancti Innocenti Episcopi Maroniae de his qui unum ex Trinitate vel unam Subsistentiam seu personam Dominum nostrum Iesum Christum dubitant confiteri. Here I quote the Latin translation of the passage which is concerned with the problem under discussion, from Schwartz's edition.[1]

Post Nestorii damnationem, cum sectatores eius mortiferos libros illius in publicum proferre non possent, quia et anathematibus a sancta synodo quae primum apud Ephesum conuenerat, editis et imperiali constitutione prohibiti fuerant lectitari coeperunt iam Theodori Mampsuestanae ciuitatis episcopi, qui quondam Nestorii magister extiterat, circumferre uolumina et simplices quosque mortiferis laqueis inretire. Tantum uero studii gesserunt per eum eiusdem in Nestorii dilatare contagia, ut ipsa uolumina eius ad laesionem et interitum simplicissimarum, ut dictum est, animarum in linguam Syrorum Armenorum Persarumque transferrent. Sed ubi haec agnouerunt beatae memoriae uiri Rabbula Edessenae et Acacius Melitinae ciuitatis antistites, scripserunt in Armeniam sanctis episcopis ne ea susciperent, apostolice denuntiantes atque dicentes: uidete canes, uidete malos operarios, uidete concisionem. (See Phil. 3.2). Ciliciae uero episcopis insimulantibus eosdem uiros Rabbulam et Acacium quod non ex caritate hoc, sed ex aemulatione atque contentione fecissent, in unum omnes Armeniae regionis sanctissimi conuenientes episcopi duos venerabiles presbyteros Leontium et Abelium ad urbem regiam Constantinopolim destinarunt; qui libellos pro more facientes nec non et unum uolumen blasphemiarum Theodori deferentes secum beatissimo Proclo Constantinopolitanae urbis archiepiscopo supplices obtulerunt, scire desiderantes quaenam doctrina, utrum Theodori an Rabbulae et Acacii episcoporum uera esse probaretur. Beatissimus itaque Proclus et libellos Armeniorum et uolumen Theodori diligenter examinans, admirabilem illam ad Armenios scripsit epistolam; quam sumens Basilius quidam diaconus Alexandriam uenit et libellos Armeniorum suis annectens obtulit beatissimo Cyrillo eiusdem ciuitatis antistiti. Quibus, ut fertur ualde permotus aduersus Theodorum et Diodorum mirabile uolumen explicuit. Post haec antefatus Basilius Constantinopolim ueniens alios libellos composuit et sancto archiepiscopo Proclo porrexit, cuncta quae beatissimo Cyrillo antehac obtulerat suis libel-

---

[1] See *A.C.O.*, t. iv, vol. 2, pp. 68 ff.

lis adsocians. Sed beatissimus Proclus et priusquam Basilii preces acciperet, Armeniorum, ut dictum est, libellis et Theodori uolumine, qui iuxta Nestorii similitudinem pro Trinitate quaternitatem docere deprehendebatur, instructus, illam superius nuncupatem scripsit epistolam. Puto namque quia secundam post haec edidit paginam, propter quod Basilius in suis libellis unam tantum Alexandriam se detulisse memorauit; uerumtamen, siue prius hanc seu postea scripserit, sic in ea docuit, libros Theodori esse uitandos sicut Arii Eunomiique blasphemias.

This is reproduced with only slight differences by the Cartagenian deacon, Liberatus (sixth century) in his *Breviarium Causae nestorianorum et eutychianorum*.[1]

The letter of the Armenians addressed to Proclus, which is mentioned in the passage quoted above has fortunately been preserved in a Syriac translation and published by P. Bedjan in his Syriac edition of Nestorius' *Heraclides*.[2] Here I reproduce it in a French translation made by Mgr Dib and incorporated in an article by Mgr R. Devreesse.[3]

Copie de la lettre des évêques et des prêtres de la Grande Arménie à Proclus, évêque fidèle de Constantinople, au sujet des écrits de Théodore de Mopsueste.

Léonce et Abel, prêtres de la Grande Arménie, et les frères qui sont avec nous, au saint et aimé de Dieu, évêque de l'Église catholique et apostolique, Proclus.

Nous croyons, ô Révérend, selon la tradition de nos Pères, les évêques de la ville de Nicée, et nous confessons la vraie foi orthodoxe. Des hommes habitant en Orient sont venus chez nous. Ils voulaient nous troubler comme on trouble des gens simples, ayant apporté avec eux un écrit de Théodore, évêque de Mopsueste. Ce Théodore, en effet,

---

[1] See *P.L.*, t. 68, col. 989–90: *De Nestorianorum Scandalo et monachis Armeniae.*

[2] See Appendix I, pp. 594–6. It is taken from a manuscript of the British Museum (No. Add. 14,557) of the seventh century. (See preface, pp. xxxix–xl.) A Greek reconstruction is attempted by Schwartz, see *A.C.O.*, t. iv, vol. 2, Praefatio, pp. xxvii–xxviii.

[3] See *Trois Chapitres*, pp. 543–65. Reprinted in *Essai*, pp. 136–7 whence I have quoted it here.

ainsi que nous le savons par les écrits du saint Mar Rabboula, évêque d'Édesse, et de Mar Acace de Melitène, qui l'ont bien montré, est un homme pervers et un perturbateur de la foi qui est imperturbable. Des hommes sont venus de Cilicie à nous et ont attaqué Acace, le saint évêque de Melitène, et le religieux Rabboula, évêque d'Édesse, disant que ces derniers ont rejeté par inimitié et par haine les écrits de Théodore. Aussi, à cause de Ta Pitié, les saints évêques ont-ils jugé à propos de nous envoyer ici pour apprendre exactement de toi si ces livres et leurs auteurs sont vraiment pervers.

Nous te demandons donc de nous préparer des écrits pour que nous sachions, nos mandants et nous, si nous devons faire confiance à ceux qui sont venus de Cilicie avec les livres de Théodore, ou nous en tenir à l'écrit des saints évêques Rabboula et Acace. En outre, nous avons un ouvrage de Théodore. Nous te prions de voir si ce qui est écrit est juste, afin que, en considération de l'examen de Ta Sainteté, les hommes, les femmes et les enfants de la Grande Arménie et tout le peuple de la sainte Église s'attachent à la foi qui avait été prêchée d'une manière complète et ferme aux Romains, et que, avec eux, la grâce de Dieu aidant, les personnes venues de Cilicie pour nous induire en erreur trouvent leur voie dans le libelle de ta foi, se convertissent et adhèrent à la doctrine des Apôtres, affirmée par les 318 Pères. Quant à nous, nous confessons cette foi telle qu'elle est, d'un même cœur et d'une même âme. Nous sommes liés par toutes les artères les uns aux autres comme de vrais frères et à l'instar des membres qui composent le corps. Nous n'avons pas été troublés mais nos adversaires trament des complots. Soyons unis, puisque nous confessons un seul Seigneur, une seule foi, vraie et bien affermie dans nos âmes. Nous conserverons le souvenir de Ta Pitié.

We have now almost completed the presentation of the evidence at hand on the doctrinal situation of the Armenian Church in the period between the Council of Ephesus and the Council of Constantinople. Let us now attempt to reconstruct that situation as clearly as possible.

Given the fact that the Armenian Church was in relationship with Syriac-speaking Christianity we could easily accept, *a priori*, that some works of Theodore of Mopsuestia and other Antiochene writers could have been translated into Armenian.

But we cannot be very sure about it, not because there is nothing preserved of these translations,[1] but because when the great movement of translation took its full course after the invention of the Armenian alphabet in the thirties of the fifth century, Theodore's works were already becoming a matter of controversy by being considered as the real source of Nestorianism. Furthermore, the historical data which we reviewed above gives us quite clear indications of a special translation of a special work with a special purpose. That special work in question was Theodore's *De Incarnatione*.[2]

Therefore, the first fact which the historical evidence puts before us is the translation into Armenian of certain writings of Theodore, among them being, with all probability, his *De Incarnatione*. This happened immediately after the Council of Ephesus. We must not think, therefore, that Theodore's works were translated into Armenian just in the same way as were the works of a Chrysostom, or a Basil, or a Gregory of Nazianzus; that is to say, for general theological and educational reasons. At least, our sources cannot allow us such a conclusion.

We said that Theodore's "books" were translated for a definite, special purpose. What was it? Innocentius Maroniae's account gives us quite a satisfactory answer. After the condemnation of Nestorius, when his works were prohibited and it became

[1] The later official condemnation of the *Three Chapters* would have put these translations, if they ever existed, under some kind of "index" and surely they would not have any chance of survival.

[2] See Acacius' letter (above, p. 115); cf Innocentius' treatise (above, p. 130–1); the letter of the two Armenian priests (above, p. 131). See also the testimonies of the Armenian historians, who tell us that Theodore's writings were brought into Armenia by certain people and with a specific intention or a particular purpose. (See above, pp. 128, 129.) The explicit reference to a particular book raises no doubt or objection to our understanding of the passages referred to. But the word "books", used in the plural, may seem to refer to several writings. But it may also refer to the *fifteen* books of *De Incarnatione*. As Devreesse shows, Cyril, with Fecundus of Hermiane, mentions the *De Incarnatione* as βιβλία and Justinian, with Leontius of Byzantium, as λόγοι. (See *Essai*, p. 44.) Devreesse has made also an attempt to reconstruct the original plan of the work through the surviving fragments. (See ibid., pp. 44–8.) For its importance in the christological disputes of the time see Sullivan, *Christology*, pp. 44 ff.

dangerous to read them, the supporters of his teaching began to circulate Theodore's writings in order to rescue their doctrine from destruction, because that doctrine was basically the teaching of Theodore. Moreover, in order to propagate their doctrine, now stricken in the Byzantine Empire, they began to translate Theodore's works—again with all probability giving the first place to the *De Incarnatione*—into Syriac, Armenian, and Persian.[1] This must have been the cause of the campaign against Theodore's writings.[2] Armenia became the battlefield which decided the line that the Armenians followed later. Moreover, the battle itself provided an opportunity for clarifying the attitudes to Theodore's "orthodoxy" on the larger scene of the ecclesiastical life of the Byzantine Empire.

Again, confining our interpretation only to the evidence of these documents, we are fully justified in saying that there were in Armenia followers of Theodore who tried to propagate his teaching in the Armenian Church through the translations of his works, namely of the *De Incarnatione*. In this they were guided and helped by the representatives of the Antiochene School who struggled hard for the survival of their theology after the condemnation of Nestorius.

There are some points to be noted here. First of all, the initiative for this work came from outside. Koriwn and Xorenaçi do not give us any hint of the precise place or of the persons who started this work in Armenia. The terms they use are very vague on this point and very general indeed.[3] But in the letter of the two Armenian priests addressed to Proclus these people are identified as "people who live in the East". There is also a second indication to their identity. We are told that they had some connection with Cilicia, the stronghold of Nestorianism in the period immediately following the Council of Ephesus. This connection raises no

[1] For further historical evidence on this point see d'Alès, *Lettre d'Ibas*, p. 13; cf Peeters, *Jérémie*, p. 21.

[2] See Additional Note 7.

[3] See above, pp. 128, 129. Only Xorenaçi identifies the persons as "some disciples of Theodore".

doubt, because when Rabboula and Acacius warned the Armenians about Theodore, the two Armenian priests who went to Proclus said in their letter that "men from Cilicia" came to them in Armenia and accused Rabboula and Acacius by saying that they attacked Theodore out of personal enmity and hatred against him (and not out of their concern for the orthodox faith). Therefore these "Orientals" were people who came either from Anatolia in the west of Armenia—usually known in this time of christological controversies as the *Orient*[1]—or from the eastern borders of Armenia, i.e. from the Persian Church—the word being taken this time in a purely geographical sense. The first supposition seems more likely, because the Nestorian victory was not yet achieved in the Persian Church at this early stage.

Therefore we can say in conclusion that the first phase in the doctrinal situation in Armenia shows us an attempt to win Armenia to the Nestorian side.

The second phase is the counter-attack. We have already noted that in the third decade of the fifth century the Armenian Church had taken a decisive step towards the reopening of its relationship with Constantinople and other Greek Christian centres, Melitene being the nearest and the most frequently visited one among them. Acacius of Melitene had been the host of the "Father of Armenian Literature", St Mesrop Maštoç. He had taken care of the education of Maštoç's disciples who had been entrusted to him by the latter. Therefore, it was easy for him to know what was happening in Armenia, especially in the field of ecclesiastical life. Being himself a determined and devoted Cyrilline, he would try to have the Armenian Church on his side in the hard struggle against the Nestorianism surviving on the eastern borders of the Byzantine Empire. Thus, it is not surprising at all to see him opening the counter-attack with his letter addressed to the head of

---

[1] From the time of Diocletian, Cilicia, Syria, and some other neighbouring countries were constituted in a single administrative unit called the "Diocese of Orient", one of the twelve dioceses which were set up by Diocletian in his administrative reforms. (See Stein, *Bas-Empire*, t. i, pp. 70, 439 n. 25, 440 n. 36; see also maps 2 and 3 at the end of t. i.)

the Armenian Church, Catholicos Sahak.[1] His concern and active intervention is proved with his second letter written later and addressed this time to the Armenian *naxarars*.

In his first letter Acacius expresses himself very cautiously. He denounces categorically the teaching of Nestorius and Theodore. However, he is not so categorical when he comes to speak about the followers of Nestorius and Theodore in Armenia. He is "caught by the fear" that there might be found followers of them. Surely, he must have heard of some attempts made with the aim of propagating Theodore's "books" in Armenia. Otherwise, his intervention cannot be explained. At the same time, we know that he had always been an ardent and zealous advocate of the Council of Ephesus and a bitter opponent of Theodore and the Antiochenes as a whole. Why, then, does he approach the problem so cautiously?

The answer, we think, may be found in the fact that he was not informed officially or asked for anything by Sahak. In other words his information had reached him through unofficial channels. In all probability it was the Armenian students and visitors in Melitene who gave him the information. Therefore we presume that the reason for his cautious attitude was that he wanted to avoid the impression that he was intervening in the affairs of the Armenian Church by unofficial means. This was necessary if he expected, as he did, to find a friendly response from the official authorities of the Armenian Church.

Secondly, we must remember that this was the beginning of an attack which put under fire a man who had been, and still was, held in the highest esteem in that part of the world for many years before the Council of Ephesus. It is not improbable, as we already said, that Theodore might have enjoyed the same high respect also in certain quarters or circles in Armenia. Therefore, Acacius had to be very tactful in condemning the Armenian followers of such a person.

Why did he write the second letter and why did he address it so

[1] It is not improbable that he wrote this letter on Rabboula's instigation, as Richard suggests. See Additional Note 8.

generally "to the Armenians" and not again to Sahak as might be reasonably expected? Was it because Sahak had not shown the expected readiness to follow his advice strictly, as we shall see in a moment? Why did he urge the Armenian princes to carry on the anti-Theodorean campaign? Who were these *naxarars*? What authority did they possess? The documents themselves do not provide us with all the necessary and adequate answers. Nevertheless, we can make the following points.

First of all, there is one obvious reason for his writing. As he says, three priests[1] had come to him and informed him of the good works these *naxarars* had done by withdrawing Theodore's writings from the public. Here, in this letter, he seems more confident and sure about his knowledge of the introduction of Theodore's writings into Armenia, and therefore he is more emphatic in his denunciation.[2] It is quite evident that the anti-Theodorean movement had now[3] started in Armenia and Acacius was trying here to encourage it and to avoid any lapse in it.

Why did he write to these *naxarars*? This question brings us to the third phase in the doctrinal situation of Armenia: the response.

Sahak, in his answer to Acacius' letter, with all due respect and affection sincerely expressed, did not seem to be very much affected by Acacius' suspicion of the existence of Theodore's followers in Armenia. He openly denied the existence of those heretics, promising that if they suddenly should appear he would not hesitate to bring them under heavy punishment.[4]

How is this answer to be explained? Is there a contradiction between what Acacius knows and what Sahak comes now to deny? And if this is the case, what are the implications of this contradiction? Can it be explained by supposing that Sahak simply ignored the existence of such heretics or that Acacius'

---

[1] For the problem of the identity of these three priests, see Additional Note 9.

[2] See above, p. 118.

[3] The date of this letter falls between 433 and 435. See Tallon, *Livre des Lettres*, pp. 27–8. Richard's dating (A.D. 438, see *Acace*, pp. 410–11) is not acceptable.

[4] See above, p. 116.

suspicion was an exaggeration due to his over-zealous care for Ephesian orthodoxy now being challenged in the name of Theodore?

It is difficult to subscribe to either of these two suppositions, because, on the one hand, Acacius in his second letter confirms what he had said rather reservedly or hesitantly in the first, as we saw, and, on the other hand, Sahak gives the same answer this time to Proclus three years later, in 435, when the controversy had been intensified to such an extent that even Proclus was asked to intervene, as Innocentius relates and as the letter of the two Armenian priests confirms.

Therefore, there must have been a good reason for Sahak to deny the fact or, perhaps, more precisely, to minimize its importance. His attitude, however, was not the only response. Our documents have other things to say about the reaction of the Armenians to this twofold intervention of opposite sides in the christological controversy of the time. In that wider context of the Armenian reaction Sahak's attitude can be better understood.

According to Innocentius' record of the events, the Armenian bishops, being somewhat perplexed by the contradictory interventions of Acacius and Rabboula on the one hand, and of the Cilician bishops on the other, took counsel and sent two priests to Constantinople giving them a letter and a "book" containing "the blasphemies" of Theodore. These two priests presented the letter and the "book" to Proclus, and asked him to judge which teaching was right, Theodore's or Acacius'? On this request Proclus wrote his famous Tome.

The same story can be read in a more elaborate form in the letter of the Armenian priests themselves. These, Leontius and Abel, in a letter presented as being sent by the "bishops and priests of Armenia Major" and addressed to Proclus, say almost exactly the same things as Innocentius has related.

Everything is clear so far. But there are certain points in this letter which make us doubt its origin as represented by its title. Thus, whereas here, in the title, it is said to be the letter sent by the "bishops and priests of Armenia Major", in the text it is the two priests themselves who ask Proclus to give them a letter so that they and those who sent them might be assured whether the Cilician bishops or Rabboula and Acacius had the right teaching. This shows that the letter was not written by "the bishops and priests of Armenia Major", but by the two priests.

Furthermore, there is another ground for suspecting the validity of the origin of this letter. We have already noted that in the Greek text of Proclus' Tome there was no mention at all of Theodore of Mopsuestia, whereas at the end of the Armenian text, Theodore is denounced by name.[1] Again, in his answer to Procclus, Sahak uses almost the same words as those used in the answer to Acacius about the supposed heresy of Theodore having found place among the Armenians. He denies it once more.

Curious textual similarities and striking contradictions, indeed! How are we to explain them?

First of all, we have no ground to suspect the authenticity of the documents as such.[2] Therefore, we have to look into them in order to find, if possible, the necessary explanation. If, as the letter of the two Armenian priests suggests, "the bishops and priests of Armenia Major" sent a delegation, with a letter and a volume containing extracts from Theodore's writings, to Proclus, and, secondly, if Proclus as he himself says, wrote the Tome "being impelled by the letter[3] you sent to us" (ἐκ τῶν ὑμετέρων προτραπέντες λιβέλλων ὧν πρὸς ἡμᾶς διεπέμψασθε) how, then, could Sahak and Maštoç, the heads of "the bishops and priests of Armenia Major" say in their reply that there were no disciples of Theodore in Armenia?

The answer to this question can be found through an inquiry into the origin and nature of the two priests' "mission". That Sahak and Maštoç were not involved, in any way, in the so-called mission of these two priests, is clearly seen in their way of answering Proclus' letter. If they had requested his advice and

---

[1] See above, p. 124. [2] See Additional Note 10.

[3] He refers to the famous letter of the two Armenian priests in which Theodore is explicitly mentioned, the case of his writings and of his followers being the core of the whole story.

solicited his intervention in a conflict in their own Church, how could they be ignorant about it? Therefore, it is reasonable to think that the priests acted independently, without having obtained the consent—let alone the commission—of St Sahak and St Maštoç.

They must have acted as representatives of an anti-Theodorean group in Armenia and presumably on instructions given by Acacius himself. We know already from Koriwn and Xorenaçi that one of the priests, Leontius, "a faithful and truth-loving man", was the chief of the disciples who were entrusted to the care of Acacius by Maštoç on his journey to Constantinople.[1] Therefore he had been in an immediate and most intimate relationship with Acacius by having him as his guide in his studies. Naturally, he would have been deeply influenced by Acacius' christological position and would have become a supporter of it in such a time of controversy as this.

Furthermore, Koriwn tells us that Leontius and he himself went to Constantinople where they joined the other Armenian students, Eznik among them, and after completing their studies returned to Armenia with him, bringing with them the canons of Ephesus and an accurate copy of the Greek Bible—the Septuagint.[2] Can we see in this journey the so-called and self-appointed mission of the two Armenian priests?

Adontz has no doubt about it. Leontium is *Łewond* and Aberium[3] is *Koriwn*. If Koriwn had such a direct connection with the mission aimed at the condemnation of Theodore, he would have spoken differently about the introduction and translation of Theodore's writings. But we saw how vague is his information. But, more important than that, if Proclus' Tome was written in 435 then this mission could not have coincided with the journey of Leontius and Koriwn, because Eznik returned to Armenia

---

[1] See above, p. 102 ff.   [2] See Koriwn, pp. 74-6.

[3] Adontz had not seen Innocentius' text, where this name is put as "Abelium". He used Liberatus' text in which Abelium had become Aberium. This change of *l* into *r* is the basis of his argument in identifying Aberium with Koriwn. Of course, with Innocentius' text, which is the source of Liberatus, that argument is automatically ruled out.

earlier than 435 (probably in 432–3). And Koriwn himself tells us that they—himself and Leontius—returned with Eznik.

We think, therefore, with Fr Inglizean,[1] that this mission was a self-appointed one, carried on without the knowledge of St Sahak and St Maštoç. Leontius must have gone a second time to Constantinople. We suppose that on his return from his first journey he realized that the pro-Theodorean group in Armenia was expanding its propaganda. So, with Acacius' advice he must have gone a second time to Constantinople to ask for the intervention of the bishop of the imperial city. Surely, such an intervention would have a great impact on the leaders of the Armenian Church. In this time of frequent cultural contacts, Leontius' second journey to Constantinople could be very natural and easy. This time he was accompanied by Abelium (= *Abēl* or *Habēl*), most probably another disciple of St Maštoç.[2]

However, there is one objection to this hypothesis, which is otherwise well supported by the historical evidence. Why did Leontius not apply to his immediate superiors and teachers, Catholicos Sahak and Vardapet Maštoç? Is it possible at all to think that with his deep affection towards them he would disregard them? Was not his action rather some kind of underground activity?

Indeed, it is difficult to imagine that Sahak and Maštoç were not contacted by him or by the group of anti-Theodoreans. But when we read once more Sahak's answer to Acacius about Theodore's heresy having found a place in Armenia, we can understand what would have been his reaction to Leontius' or the anti-Theodoreans' request for immediate action against Theodore's followers. We think that even in their advanced age Sahak and Maštoç could not but be aware of the sympathy that some people in Armenia had for Theodore. Maštoç's relationship with the great theologian is indeed most important in this context. But being the leaders of the Church—more responsible and far-seeing churchmen than a

[1] *Three Chapters*, pp. 9–10.
[2] For the identification of these two persons, see Inglizean, *Three Chapters*, pp. 38–44. His proposition remains in the sphere of sheer probability.

Leontius or an Abelium—they surely would be reluctant to take drastic measures against Theodore for two obvious reasons: (*a*) Theodore was not yet condemned in the Church as a whole. On the contrary until then he had enjoyed a very high reputation. It was not so easy to declare him now a heretic. (*b*) More important still, most probably Theodore was being favoured in Armenia by those people who sympathized with Persia politically and with Syriac-type Christianity theologically and culturally. To condemn such a person officially and openly would serve the opponents of Sahak—who were, indeed, very active and successful at that time—as undeniable evidence of his attachment to the Byzantine Church, and, at the same time, of his antagonism to the Nestorianizing Church favoured by the Persian Government. Here we have to remember how sensitive Sahak's position was on this point. He had already suffered for his relationship with Byzantium and had been warned officially to remain faithful to the Persian religious policy, whereas Leontius and his colleagues, mostly influenced by Acacius and Rabboula and educated in Constantinople, were keener on theological issues and more enthusiastic in their likes and dislikes than Sahak and Maštoç. Moreover, the constant contacts with Melitene could have kept them alive and firm in their doctrinal allegiance. Those contacts would have impelled them to establish their doctrinal position in Armenia and make it the official position of the Armenian Church. The Council of Ephesus was already accepted by the Church. They had to confirm and protect it against Nestorianism.

This zeal of theirs explains sufficiently why they went as far as to embark upon the "mission" already referred to, and to try to bring in the intervention of Proclus in order to consolidate the Ephesian tradition by rallying Sahak and Maštoç to their side in an active participation in the anti-Theodorean movement. We do not think that this was a purely private or personal enterprise. Leontius and Abelium, in fact, were representing an important and influential section of the Armenian clergy. This must have given them the courage and the necessary support for such a daring enterprise in which Acacius' part is so transparent.

Thus, having shown the origin and the nature of this "mission", the textual alterations in Proclus' Tome can easily be explained. First, the title of this letter in its present text, "Letter of Bishop Proclus to St Sahak, Catholicos of the Armenians and to St Maštoç", indicates that the letter is directly addressed to Sahak and Maštoç, whereas both in the Greek text and in the Latin translation this address is lacking and we have instead the following opening words: Τοῖς θεοφιλεστάτοις καὶ θεοσεβεστάτοις ἐπισκόποις καὶ πρεσβυτέροις καὶ ἀρχιμανδρίταις τοῖς οὖσι κατὰ πᾶσαν τὴν 'Αρμενίαν τῆς ὀρθοδόξου ἁγίας ἐκκλησίας Πρόκλος ἐν Κυρίωι χαίρειν. This is literally reproduced in a fifth-century Latin translation: "Dei amantissimis et venerabilibus episcopis et presbyteris, et archimandritis orthodoxae sanctae per totam Armeniam Ecclesiae Proclus in Domine salutem."

There can be no doubt that this was the original title of the letter. In fact, it corresponds exactly to the beginning of the letter Proclus was presented with by the two Armenian priests. The words Πρόκλου ἀρχιεπισκόπου πρὸς 'Αρμενίους, περὶ πίστεως, or "Procli Constantinopolitani ad Armenios de Fide Epistola", which appear in the heading of the letter, are later additions by the compilers of the Patristic texts.[1]

Unfortunately, the first two sections of Proclus' letter have been lost in the Armenian text. So we cannot say whether the original long title was included there or was omitted. But most probably they would have been replaced by the address that now appears in the Armenian text and which has been translated above. The basic reason for this supposition is that the answer to Proclus' letter was written by Sahak and Maštoç. This means that they had been the recipients of the letter.

As Inglizean rightly contends, there must have been some good reason for this change. He argues against Vardanean's view that some feeling of national pride—i.e. by representing Proclus as writing to the leaders of the Armenian Church in person—must have caused this change.[2] He maintains instead that Leontius

---

[1] See Vardanean, *Proclus*, col. 7.   [2] See ibid., col. 6–8.

himself, who translated the letter into Armenian, made this alteration thinking thereby to influence Sahak and Maštoç by presenting the letter as addressed to them personally.[1]

A second change reveals more explicitly the nature of this "mission" and casts further light on the theological conflict in Armenia. Thus, where Proclus says very clearly that he was impelled by the letter of the Armenians to write this letter, in the Armenian text we are told that Proclus wrote it because he "heard" or "became aware of" the writings of Theodore and their harm to the people in Armenia. Why is there such a change in the Armenian text? As Inglizean suggests, Leontius must have introduced this change to conceal the fact that he and his colleague had presented to Proclus a letter which was supposed to be written by "the bishops and priests of Armenia Major". Sahak would be surprised, of course, if he realized that people in Armenia acted in the name of the Armenian hierarchy without his knowledge and consent. Therefore Leontius thought to avoid giving Sahak an impression which might affect negatively his reaction to the purpose of the whole mission.

Thirdly, the most important change is the introduction of Theodore's name into the Armenian text. Whereas in the Greek text Theodore is not mentioned at all—and this is perfectly consistent with Proclus' general policy—in the Armenian text we have him condemned by Proclus. The language used against Theodore is even sharper than Acacius' expressions in his first letter. What is the explanation of this third change? Simply because without it the whole mission—to fight Nestorianism through the condemnation of Theodore's writings—would have failed, and Proclus' letter would not have served the purpose that Leontius and his colleagues had in mind when acquiring it.

There remains, however, one more problem to be dealt with: how were these alterations made?

Inglizean has a straightforward answer: they were made by the two priests themselves, namely by Leontius, who had translated this letter and the other documents, i.e. Acacius' letters as well.

[1] See Inglizean, *Three Chapters*, pp. 31–3.

His argument is based on a remark made by Gatʻrčean that the language and the style of these documents are of the same calibre.[1]

But this answer cannot be accepted for very obvious reasons. For, if the purpose of Leontius' mission was to win Sahak's support for the anti-Theodorean campaign, then it would be unreasonable to think that he would not have presented the *Greek* text of Proclus' letter to Sahak and Maštoç. We cannot imagine Leontius handing to Sahak and Maštoç a letter from Proclus in Armenian! In fact, Sahak and Maštoç were competent hellenists and there is no reason to suppose any necessity for an Armenian translation. On the contrary, that would open a door to suspicion in Sahak's mind as to the sincerity of Leontius' presentation of the letter. Therefore it is more reasonable to think that the changes had already been made in the Greek text that was presented to Sahak and Maštoç, a letter which was later translated into Armenian to be kept in the archives of the Catholicosate.

Who would have dared to make these alterations in Proclus' letter? We can make two alternative suggestions.

(a) The alterations were made in Constantinople itself, most probably by the deacon Basil who played an important part in the story of Proclus' Tome. Innocentius' narrative leaves no doubt that Basil played a prominent rôle in the condemnation of Theodore.[2] His journey to Alexandria, his relation with Cyril and then his return to Constantinople and his zeal for the condemnation of Theodore—all these episodes make us think that he might have been responsible for the alterations, or at least the addition of the passage in which Theodore is explicitly condemned. The last paragraph of Innocentius' account quoted above is very significant. It suggests that something was added to Proclus' letter, either by himself personally or with his consent. The second letter, to which refer the words: "Puto namque quia secundam post haec edidit paginam", could have been the one sent to the Armenians. Indeed, in the second letter Theodore's writings were denounced. That was the direct answer to the request of the Armenians.

(b) On the other hand, it is not unthinkable that Acacius might have intervened here again. Leontius on his way back to Armenia passed very naturally through Melitene where he had studied and where his former teacher Acacius knew all about the troubles in the Armenian Church, and with all probability about Leontius' mission itself. Thus we are tempted to think that he might have made the alterations in order to make Proclus' letter effective for the anti-Theodorean campaign, which had been carried on under his personal leadership. This can be deduced from some expressions in the section added to Proclus' letter concerning Theodore's heresy. A simple comparison will reveal the similarities between Acacius' first letter and this added passage. Here again, the intensified tone in denouncing Theodore is easily understood by supposing that in the interval between Acacius' first letter and Proclus' answer Theodorean propaganda had been strengthened in Armenia. In other words, it reflects a further stage in the growing tension between the two factions in the Armenian Church.

Before closing our observations on this complicated and confused situation, which we tried to elucidate by the available data of the historical evidence, there is one thing which may be put forward as an objection to our attempt at reconstructing that situation in this manner. It can be stated in the following way: given the supreme authority and the highest prestige that both Sahak and Maštoç enjoyed amongst their own people, and, secondly, taking into account the deepest love and respect that their disciples constantly showed towards them, it does seem to us, at first sight, that the way in which these two Armenian priests tackled the problem of the doctrinal controversy in their own country showed a disloyal and unfaithful attitude towards their teachers. It is somehow incompatible with the general atmosphere of deep affection, constant obedience, and enthusiastic collaboration.

But looking deeper, we can say that these disciples did not regard their task or mission as something contrary to the basic convictions and wishes of their masters. These basic convictions were clearly expressed in their attitude to the Council of Ephesus which they accepted without the least hesitation. But, as we have already explained, their hesitancy about entering into action against Theodore at such an early stage in the controversy was an act of well-balanced wisdom. And this in two respects: first, they could not denounce Theodore while the Church as a whole had not yet denounced him. Secondly, they were very sensitive about a possible interpretation of their action against Theodore—if they took that step—as being directed against the Church which was being favoured by the Persians, their political masters. On the other hand, their disciples having seen the christological controversy in its place of origin—Constantinople—and having been taught by people like Acacius, were more zealous concerning the doctrinal problems than their white-haired teachers.

Now, with Proclus' intervention the fourth phase of the doctrinal situation in the Armenian Church was closed. We do not know precisely what consequences it had.[1] But it seems that with the acceptance of the Council of Ephesus and with all the anti-Nestorian or anti-Theodorean campaign the Ephesian tradition became firmly established. It became the foundation-stone of Armenian orthodoxy, irremovable at any price and by any means, throughout the later years of bitter controversy over the Council of Chalcedon.

This, however, did not mean that everything was settled and the doctrinal situation in Armenia became one of a monolithic shape or of a peaceful state. The Council of Chalcedon was another instance to arouse the storm. The two main traditions in Armenian Christianity still had to fight each other. What happened, then, after the Council of Chalcedon and before its rejection by the Armenian Church? To this question we now turn.

---

[1] Only Koriwn gives us a hint by saying that on the receipt of Proclus' letter, Sahak and Maštoç discarded the writings of Theodore. (See above, pp. 128-9.)

5

THE HISTORICAL BACKGROUND (4)
The Ecclesiastical Situation
After the Council of Chalcedon

Soon after the controversy over the writings of Theodore, and on the apparent settlement of the doctrinal disputes with the victory of the anti-Theodorean group, the two great figures of the fifth century, St Sahak and St Maštoç, passed away with an interval of only six months. (Sahak died on 7 September 439 and Maštoç on 17 February 440.)[1]

Their successor now was one of their disciples, Yovsēp' (Joseph) who maintained unchanged the wisely devised and tactfully applied policy of his teachers, in the meantime firmly establishing the Ephesian orthodoxy and furthering the evangelistic and cultural activities of the Church.

The only important event in the ecclesiastical scene which is worthy of special reference in this context is the Council of Šahapivan[2] which was held for the purpose of removing all the pagan survivals still persisting in the life of the people. It was a council which dealt, predominantly on moral grounds, with the reformation of the Church, which had not yet been cleared of the ancient pagan customs and traditions. In the canons there are some references to the Messalian sect.[3] The nineteenth canon is

[1] See Dulaurier, *Chronologie*, pp. 135–6, n. 40; cf Manandean, *Critical History*, p. 260.

[2] See Melik't'angean, *Canon Law*, pp. 319–41; Akinean, *Šahapivan*; Ormanean, *Azgapatum*, col. 329–33.

[3] The Armenian word for this sect is *M'c'lneut'iwn* (= Messalianism), *M'c'lneayk'* (= Messalians). For its identification with Messalianism and for a study of its gen-

expressly directed against this heresy, which is described as a sect of very bad moral reputation. Otherwise, there are no doctrinal problems involved in this Council.

The Council of Šahapivan itself can be taken as a sign of a relaxed doctrinal situation in the Church. That comparatively peaceful time provided the leaders with the opportunity of dealing with internal affairs and of deepening the Christianization of their people.

Łazar Pʻarpeçi seems to reflect that state of peace when he closes the first book of his *History*. Thus, after relating the deaths of St Sahak and St Maštoç, he says: "And by the intercession of the departed, Armenia was granted [freedom] of the true religion until the twelfth year of Yazdgard, the King of the Persians and the son of Vram."[1]

That peace could not be maintained for very long. It had to follow the "Law" of Armenian history! The Persian King, Yazdgard II, realized that the free intercourse between Armenia and Byzantium was becoming perilous from the point of view of Persian politics. Armenia was drawing nearer to Byzantium in spite of the fact that it had been under Persian rule for half a century after the partition. Armenia's position in the political conflict between Persia and Byzantium was of the highest significance. Therefore drastic measures had to be taken.

The persecution started in 451, being well planned and carefully prepared between 449 and 450. The whole nation was engaged in the movement of resistance in the largest sense of the word, resistance which had a supreme significance as it was directly connected with the very existence of the Armenian people as such. After the battle of Avarayr (451) came years of intermittent attempts at dechristianization in various provinces of Armenia carried on in diverse ways by the Persians. With these attempts grew and spread also the reaction on the part of the

---

eral characteristics see Tēr-Mkrtčʻean, *Paulikianer*, pp. 42–5 (Armenian ed., pp. 61–76); Conybeare, *Key of Truth*, pp. 107–9; Akinean, *Šahapivan*, pp. 57–60; Melikʻ-Bašxean, *Paulician Movement*, pp. 64–79; Tournebize, *Arménie*, col. 301–2.

[1] Pʻarpeçi, bk. i, ch. 19.

Armenians. Not until 485 did there come a real settlement of the situation, when Vahan Mamikonean was recognized as Marzban of Armenia and complete freedom of worship was gained.[1] Vahan's rule (485–505) was a period of national recovery and reorganization. It was during this period that the Armenian Church authorities came to consider the Chalcedonian problem and to define their attitude towards it, which, in the end, resulted in the official rejection of the Council of Chalcedon.

Therefore, as we come nearer to the decisive moment, let us look into the situation more closely.

There has always been a general tendency, in circles of ecclesiastical scholarship, to think that the Armenians had been unaware and remained ignorant of the Chalcedon controversy for many years after the Council of Chalcedon. As Ormanean once wrote: "[The Chalcedonian] problem did not exist for the Armenians until the time of Catholicos Babgēn"[2] (490–516). Or, as Inglizean assumes as recently as in 1953: "Der schwere Kampf um Chalkedon und um das damit zusammenhängende *Henotikon* des Kaisers Zenon (482) scheint bis zum Beginn des 6. Jahrhunderts in Armenien keinen Widerhall gefunden zu haben."[3]

It is again generally assumed that during the catholicate of Babgēn, and somehow accidentally and indirectly—at the request and on the instigation of Syrian Monophysites—the Armenians took their decision against the Council of Chalcedon in—or even after—the synod held at Vałaršapat in 506.[4] The accuracy of this presentation of the Armenian Church's position has already been strongly challenged.[5]

At first, it would be difficult for anyone who is well acquainted with the post-Chalcedonian history, and, at the same time, with the history of the Nestorian expansion in the Persian Church, to imagine that Armenia could remain untouched by these stormy

[1] See a brief account of these events above, pp. 69–71.

[2] *Azgapatum*, col. 491.   [3] *Arm. Kirche.*, p. 366.   [4] See ibid., pp. 363–6.

[5] See Tēr-Minaseanç, Nestorianism, pp. 191–210; Malxaseanç, *Xorenaçi-Introduction*, pp. 14–28; Idem, *Xorenaçi-Riddle*, pp. 133–44; Abełean, *Literature*, pp. 374–80, also Appendix vii, pp. 658–73; but particularly Tēr-Mkrtč'ean, *Mandakuni*, pp. 89–94; Idem, "*Seal of Faith*"-*Introduction*, pp. lvii–lxvii.

quarrels which so deeply troubled the Church in the Byzantine and Persian Empires. Armenia was situated right in the middle of the two rival powers and there was no "iron curtain" on either side and no Great Wall of China around it! The pre-Chalcedonian history has shown clearly that Armenia was not virgin soil as far as the christological controversy was concerned. Therefore there are good reasons to think that the later phases of these controversies—i.e. the Chalcedonian disputes—would echo there very naturally and, indeed, very easily. The roads were opened by the controversy over Theodore's writings. If the troubled times of Armenia prevented the responsible leaders of the Church from taking part in the disputes, surely they could provide opportunities for the disputing sides to propagate their teaching. The argument that the Armenians could not deal with doctrinal problems *because of* political disturbances in their country is not a very strong one.

That these controversies actually did echo in Armenia is what must be shown now. In other words, the general statement that we have just made in hypothetical terms, however strong in itself, has to be substantiated by the factual data of the historical evidence.

Soon after the crisis of 451 when Catholicos Yovsēpʿ, St Sahak's successor, died (454), the Patriarchial See was occupied successively by two Catholicoi who apparently came from the Syriac-type section of Armenian Christianity. They were Melitē Manazkertaçi and Movsēs Manazkertaçi.[1] We do not know anything about their work. Only their names have survived, and yet they covered a period of ten years (Melitē: 452–6; Movsēs: 456–61). Why this silence over their Catholicates? Of course, the first answer can be found in the supposition that the Armenian historians were much more concerned with the history of the nation-wide movement of resistance and the martyrdom of the exiled ecclesiastical and political heads of the Armenian people, than with the works of these two Catholicoi. Secondly, it can be said that in such times of desolation and unrest, hardly any significant work could have been done.

[1] See Pʿarpeçi, bk. ii, ch. 62.

But, besides these two answers, perfectly reasonable and legitimate in themselves, there are some other factors which must be taken into account. Thus, as Tēr-Minaseanç has already guessed,[1] the feudal family—*Manazkertaçik'*—to which belong these two Catholicoi, was to some extent a rival family to St Gregory's in the fourth century. St Gregory's family was associated or identified with the Greek type of Christianity; these two Catholicoi could have been representatives of the Syriac type. In fact, their promotion to the Catholicosal See was an act in perfect accord with the religious policy of the Persian Government just in the aftermath of their attempt at abolishing Armenian autonomy on political, religious, and cultural grounds. We must note also that the province of *Manazkert* or *Manawazakert* is situated in the southern regions of Armenia where the Syriac tradition was most influential.

Furthermore, this supposition is confirmed by the way in which P'arpeçi mentions the names of these two Catholicoi. He says:

> After the death of the holy Catholicos Yovsēp', the lord Melitē, who was of the family of Manazkertaçik', succeeded him in the Catholicosate of Armenia; after him [came] the lord Movsēs, and he also was of the same family. And then, *according to the providence of God*, the lord Giwt succeeded in the Catholicosate of Armenia; a man abounding in the knowledge of Armenian and excelling [in the knowledge] of Greek.[2]

Then he goes on to praise Giwt's talents and relates his deeds at length.[3] Giwt (461–78), as we shall see, was a representative of the Hellenophile section, as P'arpeçi himself was. This characteristic way in which P'arpeçi records the succession of the Catholicoi makes it clear that he had no sympathy with the two predecessors of Giwt, most probably on account of their ecclesiastical orientation. Thus, whereas in P'arpeçi's record they simply succeed

---

[1] See *Arm. Kirche*, pp. 28–9 (Armenian edition, pp. 60–2).
[2] P'arpeçi, bk. ii, ch. 62.
[3] See P'arpeçi, bk. ii, chs. 63, 64.

each other, Giwt, on the contrary, is appointed "by the providence of God".[1] Is this an indication that Melitē and Movsēs were nominated by the Persian Government? We do not know exactly; but there is good ground to believe so.

The struggle between the two traditions in Armenian Christianity and especially the attitude of the Persian Government is more clearly seen in the following episode. Giwt had been accused before King Peroz for his disloyalty to the Persian Government and for his relations with the Byzantine emperor. The accuser, Gadišoy, was a leader in the Iranophile faction which had got the upper hand in Armenian affairs after the battle of Avarayr. Giwt was summoned to the Persian Court. Peroz did not deem it worthy and honourable to judge him personally, so he sent messengers and put before him the accusations. Giwt answered by saying that the charges which were made against him were not all lies. There were things justly said and things which were put wrongly. Thus, that he loved Christianity and the Christians was true; heaven hated those who had gone astray from the truth. But that he was disloyal to the Persian King was wrong.

> As regards my relations (lit. "goings and comings") with Byzantium, the things were not as he (i.e. the accuser) thinks and tells, for he is a liar; [I do that] because I was educated and made my studies in Byzantium, and [because] I have many acquaintances and fellow-students there. Moreover, the kind of vestments [we use] we buy from there, because they are not found anywhere else; so we are bound to buy it from there when we need it. But [as regards] the obedience of citizenship, even our law (i.e. the Christian teaching) prescribes that we should render it to the proper and worthy masters.[2]

When Giwt's answers were taken to the King, he recognized in him an intelligent man. So he sent his messengers back and put before him the following alternative proposal: He would

[1] He later says that Giwt was *not* appointed by the Persian King. He was soon deposed by the latter, as we shall see a little further on.

[2] P'arpeçi, bk. ii, ch. 64.

recognize him as Catholicos[1] and give him all honours if he accepted the Mazdaean faith and worshipped the sun; if not, then he would take away from him his Catholicosal office and also his episcopal dignity. Giwt chose the second, but added that his episcopacy could not be taken away from him by any man, not even by death, and that martyrdom was closer to his heart than the denial of Christ's true faith. Peroz, on hearing Giwt's answer, deprived him of his Catholicosal function, but at the same time afflicted him by not giving him the happy chance of martyrdom, because, he said, these Christians honour their dead more than their living.[2] The episode in itself is quite eloquent and needs no further comment. It reflects the general atmosphere and bears direct witness to the attitude of the Persian Government.

That in Armenia this tension between the two traditions had become more strained in the second half of the fifth century in general and in the third quarter, in particular, is still more clearly seen in two documents of the fifth century: (a) the letter of P'arpeçi to Vahan Mamikonean[3] and (b) the last chapter of Xorenaçi's *History*: "Lamentations on the removal of the Armenian Kingdom from the House of the Arsacids and the end of the Catholicosate (lit. "arch-episcopate") of the House of St Gregory".[4] In these two documents we have allusions to conflicts, persecution, heterodoxy, etc. What do they mean? Let us first examine them.

P'arpeçi, who had studied in the "country of the Greeks"

---

[1] He said: "Until now your authority was held without my order, and it was the vassals (= the Armenian *naxarars*) who gave you that great office, and you have no confidence whatsoever from me."

[2] The whole story is related by P'arpeçi in a most attractive way. The dramatic setting of the episode makes the reading most enjoyable indeed. See bk. ii, ch. 64.

[3] This letter which was sent to Vahan Marmikonean, was written in Amid, where Łazar P'arpeçi had taken refuge while he was being persecuted in Armenia by his opponents. In it he exposes to the Armenian *marzban*, a former classmate of his, the fallacy of the accusations brought against him. In fact, it is a plea of self-defence. Usually it is published at the end of P'arpeçi's *History*. M. Emin made a separate edition in Moscow, 1853. But the text as published in the critical edition of P'arpeçi's *History* is more accurate. I have used this latter. (See Bibliography.)

[4] See bk. iii, ch. 68.

(Byzantium),[1] had met strong opposition in Armenia, where people whom he calls "Armenian *Abeghas*"[2] had been bringing many charges against him. Most of the accusations were of a moral nature in the wider sense of this term. At least one of them, however, had a doctrinal significance. His enemies charged him with "heresy". But P'arpeçi declines to name the heresy, because it was, as he says, such an abominable one that he did not deem it decent to write it down.[3] It is difficult, therefore, to identify it. The identification becomes more difficult when we are told by P'arpeçi that ". . . concerning the heresy of Armenia, of which they speak, it is anonymous as regards its teacher, and unwritten as regards its teaching".[4] He gives us the impression that they accuse him of a heresy without specifying their charge. Therefore, under these conditions, it would be sheer conjecture on our part if we attempted to identify it in precise terms and with specific names. We do not wish to embark on that line of conjecture.

However, we note a very significant passage in this letter in which P'arpeçi's doctrinal position is seen quite clearly. Thus, after saying that he had been charged with heresy, he immediately goes on to justify himself in a long passage in which his self-defence is made on the following two grounds:

(*a*) "I have studied Greek literature extensively; I have read the writings of the Holy Fathers, who, inspired by the Holy Spirit, turned back the swords of the heretics into their own hearts and broke in pieces their bows, and taught us the saving doctrine. Therefore, those who have read their writings with deep affection can be safe from the arrows of the evil archers." He names the following Fathers: Athanasius of Alexandria, the two Fathers of the same name, Cyril of Alexandria and Cyril of Jerusalem, Basil of Caesarea, Gregory of Nazianzus who was called "the Theologian", and the "Apostle-like" martyr St Gregory the teacher

---

[1] "In accordance with the order of my teachers I was taken to Byzantium, where I dwelt [some] years" (P'arpeçi, p. 187; cf p. 193).

[2] A Syriac term—*awîla*—for monk. (See Tēr-Minaseanç̣, *Arm. Kirche*, p. 32; cf Malxaseanç̣, *Dictionary*, vol. i, p. 2.)

[3] See P'arpeçi, p. 192.　　　　　　　[4] P'arpeçi, p. 193.

of Armenia, and all those who, like them, followed the same path of sound doctrine;

(b) In the succeeding section of the same passage[1] P'arpeçi mentions the names of heretics whom the Church had anathematized and whom, therefore, he rejects. They are: Arius of Alexandria, Apollinarius of Laodicea, Nestorius of Antioch, Eutyches of Constantinople and "Kowmbrikos" (= Cubricus) the slave, who later changed his name into Mani and those who followed his teaching and were called after him Manichaeans.[2]

It is very important to note here that P'arpeçi has not mentioned any Antiochene theologian in the list of the orthodox "holy Fathers". On the contrary, he seems to be a representative of that School of Armenian theologians who, after the Council of Ephesus, took the line of Alexandrian christology, and, at the same time, continued to hold firm to the traditional link of the Armenian Church with the Cappadocian Fathers.

As we cannot tell precisely what the heresy ascribed to him was, and if, secondly, we put aside the moral charges brought against this heresy[3]—a common feature in the refutation of heresies—then we are not perhaps very far from the truth if we say that the heresy which might have been opposed by Nestorianizing Syrophiles—as the opponents of P'arpeçi were—was the anti-Chalcedonian and staunchly Cyrilline christology. This, in the mind of those people, was the greatest error, namely that, again in their view, it confused the two natures of Christ.

[1] Unfortunately there is a gap here in the text. The missing part seems to have been an important one for doctrinal reasons. It would certainly have explained the connection between these two points more straightforwardly and more clearly than it does now in the present mutilated state of the text.

[2] See P'arpeçi, p. 192.

[3] It could be that P'arpeçi's enemies charged him with Messalian heresy. They found in Messalianism a pretext to oppose him. Indeed, this heresy had a very bad reputation in Armenia. This seems to be the case especially when we take into account some other passages in the letter (namely p. 193). However, P'arpeçi knew well that what they actually aimed at in their opposition was not his "Messalianism" or the heresy which he declined to name, but his doctrinal attitude. Otherwise he would not take the trouble of putting forward the names of the Fathers and heretics we just mentioned. In fact, he brought them to justify himself.

This interpretation seems to receive some further support from the fact that the opposition was not directed against P'arpeçi alone, but also against other people who belonged to the same school of theology. The accusations against P'arpeçi were not purely personal but reflected ideological—doctrinal—features of a controversy in which two distinct groups or factions, opposed to each other, were involved. In this letter of self-justification or self-defence there are three persons mentioned by P'arpeçi who were persecuted even more fiercely than he, and all three were representatives of the Greek-type tradition and had gone to Byzantium for advanced studies. Their names were Movsēs, Xosrovik and Abraham.[1] Again, the names of St Gregory, St Nersēs, and St Sahak—three champions of Greek-type Christianity—are mentioned in this letter,[2] in which P'arpeçi links this fifth-century conflict with that of the fourth. This means that it had the same common background. The persons and the issues were changed; but the conflict at the basis was the same.

Movsēs Xorenaçi, in his famous "Lamentations" gives us a similar picture of the ecclesiatical situation in Armenia. According to his own story, he and others had been sent by Sahak and Maštoç to Alexandria.[3] When they returned to Armenia, their teachers had passed away. So, in his History, after relating their deaths he composed his "Lamentations", in which the post-Chalcedonian doctrinal situation of the Armenian Church is rather vaguely reflected. But we find some glimpses which serve to confirm what we saw in P'arpeçi's letter to Vahan Mamikonean.

First, he says that on the deaths of the two blessed men "the peace was disturbed, chaos reigned (lit. 'became rooted'), orthodoxy was shaken, and heterodoxy was established through ignorance". All these happened because the true shepherds (St Sahak)

---

[1] See P'arpeçi, pp. 202–3. Unfortunately there is a missing sheet in the manuscript just at this point. There could have been other names also mentioned there, and we could probably have some further evidence on the doctrinal nature of the conflict.

[2] See P'arpeçi, p. 203.　　　[3] See Xorenaçi, bk. iii, ch. 61.

and his assistant (St Maštoç) had passed away and there was no Joshua to succeed Moses. Therefore, "now battles from within and terrors from without; terrors from the heathen and battles from the schismatics (i.e. heretics)". He deplores the fact that on their return from Byzantium there was no one who would rejoice in their achievements and could appreciate their academic progress. Then he adds: "Who, then, will restrain the daring of those who oppose the sound doctrine [and] who, being divided [among themselves] and dismembered, change many teachers and alter books, as one of the Fathers had said?" These people mocked and despised Xorenaçi and his fellow-students. "Who then will shut their mouths?" he exclaims. Then, invoking Jeremiah's Lamentations he invites the prophet to come and lament over the miseries of the Armenians. Finally, he denounces all those who caused these miseries—vardapets (i.e. Church divines), monks, bishops, disciples, lay people, princes, judges, etc.

Now, what do all these allusions to "orthodoxy" and "heterodoxy", to "battles of schismatics or heretics", to "opponents of sound doctrine" mean? First of all, we must say that it is more than probable that the opponents here were the same people as those who fought P'arpeçi and his colleagues or friends. The chronological proximity of the two cases—both of them in the second half of the fifth century—on the one hand, and the similarity of Xorenaçi's and P'arpeçi's theological background—both of them came from centres of theological traditions such as Alexandria and Byzantium—on the other, leave no doubt about it.[1]

It is obvious that Xorenaçi and his friends were victims of those Syrophile elements who took advantage of the Persian persecution in Armenia to bring the Church of Armenia under the influence of the Persian Church, which was undergoing at that time

---

[1] We must remember that P'arpeçi mentions a "Movsēs" as one of those people who were being persecuted with him. If we accept the identification of this Movsēs with Xorenaçi (See Tēr-Mkrtč'ean, "Seal of Faith"-Introduction, pp. lix–lx) then our supposition becomes very convincing.

the process of Nestorianization, as we shall see in a moment. Having studied in Alexandria and having passed through Byzantium, Xorenaçi could not have any other doctrinal position than that of a staunch anti-Nestorian, and therefore, anti-Chalcedonian.[1] For him "orthodoxy" was the Cyrilline christology and "heterodoxy" nothing other than Nestorianism, which in his own view and, indeed, in the view of many others of his time, had been reaffirmed or reinforced at Chalcedon. Hence the immediate association of Nestorianism with Chalcedon.

The situation as described in these two documents and as seen through the episode of Giwt's deposition by the Persian Government is understood in a further light when we see it in connection with the situation of the Church in the Persian empire.

Mgr Tisserant, speaking of the period between 424 and 484 of the history of the Persian Church, rightly remarks: "C'est pendant ces soixante années que se fixe l'avenir de l'Église de Perse."[2] We know what that future came to be: an adherence to Nestorian christology. How was this reached? The Nestorian sources are not very helpful in answering this question straightforwardly, but scholars have found some valuable information from Monophysite sources though they have used them very cautiously for understandable reasons.

During this period and with a background of dyophysite Antiochene christology, the Persian Church became the host of the Nestorian refugees who either fled from or were driven out of the Byzantine Empire. Chalcedon had not troubled them at all. On the contrary, they had good reasons to welcome it had there not been the political barrier. In fact, their doctrinal teachers were recognized by that Council as genuinely orthodox. There was nothing new for them in Chalcedon, it reaffirmed what they had always believed and followed. But soon the anti-Chalcedonian

---

[1] It is a very naïve belief to assume that Xorenaçi was a Chalcedonian, as Malxaseanç has contended. (See *Xorenaçi-Introduction*, pp. 14–28; *Xorenaçi-Riddle*, pp. 133–44.) His view cannot stand any critical approach. It has already been refuted successfully by Abełean, *Literature*, Appendix vi and vii, pp. 653–8, 658–73.

[2] Tisserant, *Nestorienne*, col. 173.

movement became a matter of concern for them and was deeply resented. Incidentally, this is a very characteristic symptom of the close association of Nestorianism and Chalcedonism. The man who understood the danger and led the opposition was the famous Barsuama already condemned in the second council of Ephesus (449).[1]

Labourt, who has studied very carefully all the available evidence on this period, especially the information about Barsuama's activities, shows that he and his supporters were alarmed by the resurgence and expansion of Monophysitism under the reign of Zeno (474-91). This meant to them the weakening of their Dyophysite position. The definition of faith officially drawn up and approved in the council of 486 was a reassessment of their doctrinal attitude and, at the same time, a repudiation of the Monophysite position which was understood by them, as the Definition itself shows, as teaching the mixture or confusion of the two natures of Christ.[2] In 489, by the order of Emperor Zeno, the "School of the Persians" in Edessa was purged of its Nestorian teachers and students. They "prirent alors le chemin de la Perse sans espoir de retour. À la première étape, Barsauma les arrêta. Il fonda à Nisibe une école qui devint rapidement célèbre."[3] Thus, Barsauma and his followers started a real war against the Monophysites and drove them to the Byzantine provinces. They were supported by Peroz. According to Monophysite writers they even had recourse to bloodshed.[4]

Now, it must be observed that the new stronghold of Nestorianism—Nisibis—was very close to Armenia and the earlier

---

[1] See Bardy, *Barsauma*, col. 948–50.

[2] See Chabot, *Synodicon Orientale*, p. 302; cf Tisserant, *Nestorienne*, col. 177.

[3] Labourt, *Christianisme Perse*, p. 141. See about all these events and his critical analysis of them, pp. 131–41; cf Wigram, *Assyrian Church*, pp. 142–71, particularly pp. 153–5; Tisserant, *Nestorienne*, col. 173–8; Tisserant, *Narsai*, col. 27; Duval, *Histoire d'Édesse*, p. 216.

[4] Labourt, whose approach to these sources is even over-critical, says: "Il est possible qu'il y ait eu quelque sang versé; mais il ne foudrait pas admettre les chiffres fantaisistes de Barhébraeus" (*Christianisme Perse*, p. 140). For Peroz's religious policy, see Duval, *Histoire d'Édesse*, p. 199.

relations between the two had been more than friendly.[1] The publication of Zeno's *Henoticon* (482), the councils of 484 and 486, and the closure of the School of Edessa (489), followed by the emigration of Nestorian theologians to the Persian empire, were successive events with serious consequences for the Persian Church. The situation in Armenia could not remain unaffected. In fact, we have quite important historical evidence for an attempt intended to win Armenia to the Nestorian side. The person mentioned in connection with this attempt is none other than the same Barsauma.

Thus, a tenth-century Armenian historiographer, Thomas Arcruni relates the story of Barsauma's coming to Armenia and his failure in rallying the Armenian Church to the Nestorianized Church of Persia. He says:

> In the time of Peroz, King of Kings, there was a certain man of the heresy of Nestorius by the name Barsauma, who was [only] nominally a bishop, and who holding firm to the Nestorian heresy and bringing forth before Peroz calumnies against the Armenian *naxarars* committed many bloody crimes.
> . . . [This Barsauma] came to *Arznarziwn*[2] and to the province of *Mokk'*[3] in order to sow there the seeds of the Nestorian heresy.
> . . . When Meršapuh, the prince of the Arcrunik', heard this . . . he sent him (Barsauma) [a message] to leave the frontiers of the

[1] An example of this closeness is the story of St James of Nisibis who has always been regarded and venerated as a most popular saint in the Armenian Church, with many rich traditions about his life and work in Armenia. "C'est chez ces derniers [i.e. the Armenians] qu'il a obtenu le plus de popularité ayant été mis en relations d'amitié avec saint Grégoire l'Illuminateur" (Tisserant, *Jacques*, col. 293). See an exhaustive study on the Armenian traditions concerning St James of Nisibis in Peeters, *Jacques*, pp. 312–39, 342–73.

[2] *Arznarziwn* is undoubtedly another, rather lengthy, form of *Arzn* or *Arzan* which is situated in South Armenia. Definitely it is Arzn or Arzan that is meant here. This can be seen very easily when we compare it with Michael Syrus' passage which is quoted below and in which it is written as *Arzôn*. This province was not far from Nisibis (see Map 1). See Chabot, *Synodicon Orientale*, pp. 272–6, etc. See Index, p. 666. Honigmann writes it as "Arzanène". See *Evêques*, pp. 129, 130; Vööbus, *Syrian Asceticism*, pp. 295, 324.

[3] *Mokk'*, another southern province of Armenia situated eastwards to Arzan (see Map 1).

province; he did not touch him, but because of the Persian king[1] he only threatened him severely by sending him messages.[2]

Thomas Arcruni surely takes this story from some oral tradition, as the title of the chapter suggests.[3] That tradition must have been quite widespread and well known, because it is recorded also in a Syrian source, the Chronicle of Michael Syrus. In relating Barsauma's works in Nisibis and Ctesiphon this famous Syrian historian tells us that he (Barsauma) compelled Acacius, the Catholicos of the Persian Church, to accept Nestorianism as the official doctrine of the Church.[4] Having done this,

Bar-Çauma s'en alla sur la frontière d'Arménie et arriva à Arzôn. Les Arméniens lui addressèrent des menaces en disant: "Si tu ne retournes pas, tu rendra compte, par nos mains, du sang des fidèles."
—Ce scélérat écrivit au roi des Perses en disant: "Les Arméniens sont revoltés contre toi."—Le roi fit connaître la chose à ses conseillers qui l'engagèrent à ne pas susciter une guerre civile et à ne pas diviser son empire à cause des querelles des chrétiens. Alors, il écrivit au prince d'Arménie de venir. Les Arméniens répondirent: "Si tu ne dois pas changer nos lois, ni nous envoyer à la guerre contre un autre peuple que les Turcs, avec notre croix marchant à notre tête, puisque nous sommes chrétiens, nous viendrons faire un pacte et des serments; sinon, nous ne viendrons pas."—Le roi, conseillé par ses grands, agit selon le désir des Arméniens, et fit revenir Bar-Çauma. Et (ainsi) les Arméniens échappèrent au nestorianisme.[5]

---

[1] The relation of Barsauma's mission to the policy of the Persian Government is clearly seen in this remark. Barsauma was being supported by Peroz. Therefore to touch him would mean to be hostile to Peroz. When we remember that it was the same Peroz who deposed Catholicos Giwt, the religious situation in Armenia becomes still clearer.

[2] Thomas Arcruni, *History*, pp. 88–9.

[3] The anachronisms and the confusions of some historical facts which appear in his record of the story as a whole have been studied by Tēr-Minaseançֺ. See *Nestorianism*, pp. 196–7; cf Idem, *Arm. Kirche*, pp. 37–8, 56–7 (Armenian edition, pp. 80–1, 122–4).

[4] See Michel Le Syrien, *Chronique*, vol. ii, pp. 437–9.

[5] *Chronique*, vol. ii, p. 439. That in the days of Peroz there was a definite attempt for the Nestorianization of the Armenian Church is supported also by the testimony of a Georgian writer of the ninth century, Arsēn Saparaçi. In his treatise on the separation of the Armenian and Georgian Churches he says that "King Peroz

The differences seen in these two accounts of the same tradition must not allow us to discredit the tradition as a whole. Such divergences are common features in the formation and development of oral traditions. The major basic fact is the same in both Thomas Arcruni and Michael Syrus: Nestorianism became a serious menace for the Armenian Church in the second half of the fifth century. It was openly and officially introduced into Armenia with a definite policy of making it the official doctrine of the Church in the last two decades of the century. The Armenians rejected it deliberately and with an unyielding opposition.

Besides this attempt made by Barsauma, there seems to have been another made on a smaller scale and on individual rather than official initiative, some ten or twenty years before. We have a valuable reference to it which removes all doubt of its authenticity. In the days of Giwt (461–78) three "heretics" came to Armenia and began to spread their false teachings. They were saying that the Virgin Mary was not θεοτόκος and were refusing to say for the Cross "God's Cross". Giwt wrote a letter to David the Invincible—a famous Armenian Christian philosopher—asking him to compose a treatise on the Cross and to refute the teachings of these heretics.[1]

In these two cases, which fortunately have found a place in the historical records, we can see not merely individual, isolated instances. Once having appreciated the ecclesiastical situation in both the Persian and the Byzantine Empires, it is reasonable to read in these two surviving cases a general tendency—expressed surely in other ways and instances which have not been recorded —which aimed at the total Nestorianization of Armenia. This was a perfectly justifiable policy when seen through the eyes of the

---

compelled the Armenians to follow the teaching of the ungodly Nestorius; but the Armenians categorically rejected this " (Melik'set'-Bek, *Georgian Sources*, vol. i, p. 35).

[1] Giwt's letter and David's treatise are contained in the work published under the name of David the Invincible in Venice, 1833. Unfortunately, the book is not at my disposal, so I give the instance as represented in Ormanean, *Azgapatum*, col. 423–4; cf Tēr-Minaseanç, *Nestorianism*, pp. 198–9.

Persian Government on the one hand, and from the doctrinal standpoint of the Persian Church on the other.

We know what was the reaction of the Armenian Church to these attempts. The rejection was the natural consequence of their acceptance of the Council of Ephesus and their fight against the writings of Theodore of Mopsuestia. As Grousset, speaking of the last quarter of the fifth century, puts it so straightforwardly, "l'Église arménienne était toute entière dressée contre le nestorianisme".[1]

Here we face a very important problem: Why in this whole story is the Council of Chalcedon not mentioned? In fact, in all the historical and theological literature of the fifth century, there is not a single mention of the Council of Chalcedon by name. But this question raises another one closely linked with it and preliminary to it: Does the absence of any specific mention correspond necessarily to a state of ignorance about it? In other words, does this silence mean that the Council of Chalcedon was unknown to the Armenians until the first decade of the sixth century? It is not reasonable to think so.

The reasons for giving this straightforward answer can be found in the following points:

1. We have two treatises, written sometime during the last two decades of the fifth century which in fact are directed against the Council of Chalcedon, although they do not mention it by name. The first is John Mandakuni's *Demonstration*,[2] and the second Movsēs Xorenaçi's *Treatise*.[3] On the authenticity of these two documents we shall speak in the next chapter when we come to present the christology contained in them. Here we take it for granted.

The doctrine refuted in these documents is undoubtedly the doctrine formulated in the Council of Chalcedon. This becomes

[1] *Histoire d'Arménie*, p. 235.

[2] *Of the blessed John, the Armenian Archbishop [Catholicos], Demonstration of why to confess the Saviour "Of Two Natures" or "One Nature".* (See *B.L.*, pp. 29–40).

[3] "[*A treatise*] *of the blessed bishop Movsēs Xorenaçi, the great Rhetor.*" (See *B.L.*, pp. 22–8).

obvious when we read them carefully, as we shall try to do later, again in the next chapter. The mere title of Mandakuni's *Demonstration of why to confess the Saviour "Of Two Natures" or "One Nature"*, shows a direct connection with the terminology which became the central issue in the Chalcedonian problem. But here we are not concerned with the internal or textual evidence. We give two reasons for the assertion that these documents were written with a view to refuting the doctrine of the Council of Chalcedon.

First, the *Demonstration* of John Mandakuni has always been regarded as directed against the Council of Chalcedon. Thus, in a seventh-century compilation of Patristic fragments, *The Seal of Faith*, the *Demonstration* is quoted extensively under the following title which needs no comment: "Of John Mandakuni, the Armenian Catholicos from the Refutation of the Council of Chalcedon which is called Demonstration.[1]

Secondly, in the treatise of Movsēs Xorenaçi we have obvious influences from the Armenian translation of Timothy Aelurus' *Refutation of the Definitions of the Council of Chalcedon*. These influences are seen not only in textual similarities[2] between the two, but also through the list of Church Fathers and those writings which are mentioned in Xorenaçi,[3] and which are found in Timothy's *Refutation*. The dependence of Xorenaçi on the Armenian translation of Timothy's work can be seen very easily through a comparison. To mention them in the order of Xorenaçi's text, these Fathers are: Basil the Great, John of Constantinople (Chrysostom), Julius of Rome,[4] Cyril of Alexandria,[5] Erectheus,

---

[1] See *Seal of Faith*, pp. 130–3. Here the extract from the *Demonstration* corresponds exactly to the text as printed in the *Book of Letters*.

[2] Such similarities can be seen also between the *Refutation* and Mandakuni's *Demonstration*, as Tēr-Mkrtč'ean has already shown. (See *Seal of Faith-Introduction*, pp. lix–lx.)

[3] See *B.L.*, p. 26.

[4] See *Refutation*, pp. 8–9, 132, 156–7, 177–8, 186–7, 259–62; cf Cavallera, *Timothée*, pp. 355–6.

[5] See *Refutation*, pp. 161–2, 178–9, 62–3, 68; cf Cavallera, *Timothée*, pp. 348–51.

bishop of Antioch in Pisidia,[1], Gregory of Neocaesarea,[2] Ephraim Syrus,[3] and Gregory of Nazianzus.[4]

2. Besides these two documents which by themselves provide us with positive arguments, there is the translation of Timothy Aelurus' *Refutation*, the influence of which we have just detected in Xorenaçi's treatise. The date of this translation has been a matter of controversy since the discovery of Timothy's work in Armenian translation in 1907. There have been, as there still are, two main positions in this controversy. To state them broadly, the first holds that the translation was made in the middle of the sixth century as the editors of the Armenian text first fixed it.[5] The argument for this dating is provided by external evidence: testimonies from later writings such as the letter of Photius to Zacharias, the Armenian Catholicos,[6] the anonymous treatise called Διήγησις and commonly known as *Narratio de rebus Armeniae*,[7] the treatise of Arsēn, Catholicos of the Georgians (ninth century) on the separation of the Armenian Church,[8] and an Armenian document recently found and published by P. Ananean.[9] It is obvious

---

[1] See *Refutation*, pp. 276–7; cf Cavallera, *Timothée*, p. 352.

[2] See *Refutation*, pp. 21, 92, 189; cf Cavallera, *Timothée*.

[3] It is surprising that there is no citation from Ephraim in the *Refutation*.

[4] See *Refutation*, pp. 22–5, 142, 160, 193–4; cf Cavallera, *Timothée*, pp. 353–4.

[5] See Tēr-Mkrtč'ean and Tēr-Minaseançj, *Refutation*, Preface, pp. xv–xvii. It must be said that later Tēr-Mkrtč'ean changed his view and adhered to the second position. (See *Seal of Faith-Introduction*, p. lix.)

[6] See the passage in question, in Tēr-Mkrtč'ean and Tēr-Minaseançj, *Refutation*, preface, p. xvi, taken from Papadopulos–Kerameus; *Fotija*, pp. 179–95. I have used the passage as quoted in the Preface; cf Garitte, *Narratio*, pp. 133–4, which contains the Armenian text with a French translation.

[7] This is a brief historical treatise which speaks about the relationship of the Armenian Church with the Byzantine. It relates the whole story from a strict Chalcedonian point of view. The author tries to show that the Armenians had always been united to the Byzantine Church but later, in the middle of the sixth century, were separated. Afterwards they returned to union several times, but always lapsed. (See Garitte, *Narratio*, pp. 26–47, the Greek text). Professor Garitte who made the critical edition with a masterly historical commentary, places the date of the writing about A.D. 700. (See ibid., pp. 382–400, particularly p. 398.)

[8] See the Armenian translation in Melik'set'-Bek, *Georgian Sources*, pp. 34–7; cf Garitte, *Narratio*, pp. 130–3, where there is the Georgian text with a French translation.

[9] See *Dowin Document*, pp. 112–13.

that all these documents have a common source. They are closely interrelated.

Now, in these documents it is said—indeed in varying forms and imprecise expressions—that the works of Timothy Aelurus and Philoxenos of Mabboug were translated into Armenian at the Council of Dowin (552-4). The works were brought to the Armenians by Syrian Monophysites who came from the neighbouring southern provinces of Armenia to secure the support of the Armenian Church for their position in a controversy against the Nestorians.

On the other hand, Galust Tēr-Mkrtč'ean considering the internal chronological evidence provided by the *Refutation* itself[1] showed that the date of the translation falls somewhere between the years 480 and 484.[2] His arguments were so convincing that those scholars who still could not accept an early translation of Timothy's work, proposed, too arbitrarily, various textual alterations in the chronological data in order to fit it to their own calculation.[3] It would be a very long digression for us to enter into the details of this dispute, and as there are no new or important indications for the clarification of this problem, the mere presentation of the various views of the scholars will not serve our immediate purpose in any way.[4] However, from what we have

---

[1] See *Refutation*, p. 277.

[2] Tēr-Mkrtč'ean, *Timothy*, p. 572.

[3] See Akinean, *Timothy*, pp. 21-2; Manandean, *Hellenizing School*, col. 442 (H.A., 1926). Ananean, *Dowin Document*, pp. 127-8.

[4] Fr P. Ananean has already gathered together all these views in his third article on the document already referred to. (See *Dowin Document*, pp. 117-31.) He has come to the conclusion that both sides are equally justified when seen only from the positive data of their argumentation. But he says that in order to decide which position is likely to be on the side of the truth one must see the translation in the context of the ecclesiastical situation of the time. And as for him, the Armenian Church could not have dealt with the Chalcedonian problem before the sixth century, therefore the middle of that century is the proper context in which such a translation could have been made. Moreover, he argues, the translation had to be authorized by the Church leaders. Therefore the translation in a Council can be accepted more easily and reasonably than a translation made on private initiative and responsibility. As the Armenian Catholicoi were not opposed to the Council of Chalcedon in the fifth century, so they could not have authorized such

already said in this chapter an early translation of Timothy's work *was* possible. We can make only the following observations in support of that possibility.

(*a*) One of the main arguments against the possibility of a translation towards the end of the fifth century has been based on the general view of the origin of the "Hellenizing School" in Armenian ancient literature. This School produced a period in Armenian literature when the Armenian language became literally dependent on the Greek. In other words, the Armenian translators began to follow the Greek texts in a servile manner, by reproducing the Greek words in Armenian forms. It was a School which opened also a new path in Armenian literature through translations from "profane" or secular literature, such as philosophy, especially from Neo-Platonist writers and from Aristotle.[1]

Until recently it was thought that the origins of the School could not be traced to the fifth century, which was the "Golden Age" of Armenian Literature and which had the purest language tradition. But lately, this general view has been strongly challenged and the philologists of Soviet Armenia especially have come to the definite conclusion that the Hellenizing School started in the second half of the fifth century,[2] presumably after the return of the second generation of Armenian students, the "Translators" as they are called, from the centres of Greek culture.[3]

---

a translation. With all these presuppositions, then, he accepts the date of the translation as 552/56 or 560/64. (See *Dowin Document*, pp. 121–7.) We cannot accept this dating for the simple reason that the presuppositions behind it are not well founded, as has become evident from what we have said in the previous two chapters.

[1] See for the history and general characteristics of this School, Manandean, *Hellenizing School* (on the characteristics, see col. 227–32); Abełean, *Literature*, pp. 101–9; K'iparean, *Literature*, pp. 104–9; Thorossian, *Littérature*, pp. 93–6; Gabrielean, *Armenian Philosophy*, pp. 305–437.

[2] See Abełean, *Literature*, pp. 101–04, 106–07.

[3] Those people whom P'arpeçi mentioned in his letter could have been representatives of this School. Indeed, it is more than probable that the doctrinal controversies constituted a major factor in the formation of this School. Theological terms such as $ο\dot{v}σία = \bar{e}ut'iwn$, $φ\acute{v}σις = bnut'iwn$, $\dot{v}π\acute{o}στασις = An\check{j}n$, $πρ\acuteoσωπον =$

Now, the translation of Timothy's work is undoubtedly a production of this School. Its language is markedly Hellenist. Therefore, as we come to see more and more clearly the beginning of the Hellenizing School as dating at least from the last quarter of the fifth century, there is no difficulty at all in envisaging the translation of Timothy's work being done as early as 480–4.

(b) We have already noticed in Mandakuni's and Xorenaçi's treatises the influence of the Armenian translation of Timothy's work. As these two documents come from the fifth century, there is a solid ground to accept the translation as being made in 480–4.

(c) The external evidence for a translation in the middle of the sixth century comes from later periods, not before the end of the seventh century. As we have noted, all the documents containing this evidence have a common source. Therefore they must not be taken as independent pieces of evidence testifying to the same thing from different sources. Moreover, all of them come from the Chalcedonian side. In fact, they try to show that the Armenians first accepted the Council of Chalcedon and then, in the middle of the sixth century, rejected it because they were misled by the Monophysite Syrians. The biased theological attitude and the inaccurate historical presentation of the facts in these documents are obvious, and it is therefore difficult to accept their evidence without any critical approach. Again, it is difficult to imagine that the translation of Timothy's and Philoxenos' books took place at a Council, as the authors of these documents would have us believe. They surely needed more time than the sessions of a Council would allow them. Furthermore, is it not reasonable to think that if the Syrians brought Timothy's work to the Armenians together with that of Philoxenos, they would have brought its Syriac version, whereas the Armenian translation is made from the Greek in a rather stereotyped form? This is

---

dēmk and many others had to be defined carefully and clearly. Hence, the immense importance of Aristotle's "Categories". And we know that these disputes had already become important issues towards the end of the fifth century.

indeed a most important question that has never been asked in the discussion on the date of these translations.

With all these question marks we think that in the Council of Dowin (552–4) the Syrians might have stated and expounded their doctrinal position *on the basis* of Timothy's and Philoxenos' works which they had brought with them in order to prove their orthodoxy. It could be that later this was interpreted by the Chalcedonians as the cause of the separation of the Armenians.

In conclusion, as it is impossible to fix the precise date of these translations on direct and unequivocal evidence, and for reasons stated above, we definitely accept the view that the works were translated in the fifth century and most probably in the years between 480 and 484, as was suggested by G. Tēr-Mkrtč'ean.

3. Another proof that shows that the Council of Chalcedon was known to the Armenians is that with which Łazar P'arpeçi provides us. In his letter to Vahan Mamikonean he anathematizes, among other heretics, Eutyches. This necessarily implies his knowledge of the Council of Chalcedon. And as P'arpeçi himself was a Cyrilline and disposed against the Council of Chalcedon, and as Eutyches was also condemned by the opponents of Chalcedon, there is good reason to think that he was aware also of the controversies which followed that Council. In the same way, the second generation of the Armenian Translators—Giwt and those whom P'arpeçi mentions in his letter—who went to study in Byzantium and Alexandria[1] after the Council of Ephesus, and, later, after the Council of Chalcedon, they could not be ignorant of the burning issue of the time—an issue which was causing bloodshed and murder and even involving the Byzantine military forces.

Before concluding this chapter and after having contended that the Council of Chalcedon was already opposed by the Armenian Church in the fifth century, the question which we first raised remains to be answered: Why then is the name of the Council of Chalcedon absent from the literature of the fifth century?

[1] Cf Ormanean, *Azgapatum*, col. 315–16.

We can think of two reasons.

1. This was a time (482–500) when the Council of Chalcedon was not only discredited on the whole in the Byzantine Empire, but was completely disregarded or discarded particularly on the eastern borders of the Empire. The *Henoticon* had made headway in these provinces of North Mesopotamia and East Syria. It had become so influential that the Nestorians found it difficult to oppose this advance. Now, in this situation where the Council of Chalcedon did not appear on the surface of things or, in other words, when it was deliberately concealed under some kind of official disregard, it must not be expected that the Armenians would have opposed it as such. The choice for them was not explicitly or directly "either Chalcedon or anti-Chalcedon". They had to decide whether to adhere to the general doctrinal position as expressed and maintained in the *Henoticon* or to oppose it. That is clearly seen in and through the two documents we have already mentioned, the *Demonstration* of Mandakuni and the *Treatise* of Xorenaçi.

We have no record of any official or formal acceptance of the *Henoticon*, but its general theological position became the position of the Armenian Church in the fifth century and, indeed, even at the beginning of the sixth when they rejected expressly but not directly the Council of Chalcedon, as we shall see later.

Therefore, it is reasonable to think that in such a state of affairs one cannot expect an explicit anathema or an open rejection of the Council of Chalcedon, which was not even proposed to them for acceptance. The silence over it, then, is only natural. However, their doctrinal position in this period was anti-Chalcedonian without being directed against the Council as such.

2. The second reason is perhaps more important, because it has a direct bearing on the position of the Armenian Church. As constant attempts were being made to rally the Armenian Church to Nestorianism, and as this latter was opposing the position formulated in the *Henoticon*, it was possible that the Chalcedonian

christology, as well as the Chalcedonian cause, was identified with the Nestorian. That this was the case can be seen in the later events of the first half of the sixth century, when the Armenian Church rejected Nestorianism once more and this time together with Chalcedon, the two being simply inseparable. We shall see this in the last chapter. Surely the Nestorians were preaching the duality of Christ's nature. Chalcedon had distinguished very sharply between the two natures. Therefore, to refute one of these two doctrines implied necessarily the rejection of the other. And it is this refutation of the duality which we find both in the *Demonstration* of John Mandakuni and the *Treatise* of Movsēs Xorenaçi.

If here we do not find any explicit mention of Nestorianism[1] that must be explained by the caution which was imposed especially upon John Mandakuni as he was the Catholicos, the head of the Armenian Church. It must be remembered that 485 was the date when Armenia recovered its political autonomy. Mandakuni was the successor of Giwt, whose difficulties with the Persian Government could not have been forgotten so easily and so quickly. The autonomy of Armenia was obtained with the final consent of the Persian Government through an official pact.[2] Therefore this was a time when the Armenians had to be very tactful in not giving any pretext for the revival of a hostile policy towards their own country. For the previous twenty-five years (451–85) they had been suffering from persecution and desolation. So it was an act of wisdom to keep silence over the name of Nestorianism at that critical moment.

It was on account of these considerations, we think, that the Armenian Church while it opposed the Chalcedonian christology, in association with Nestorianism, did not reject the Council of Chalcedon as such, simply because it was not put before them as such. But their doctrinal attitude was already formed. The re-

---

[1] Except one single reference to Nestorius in the list of heretics given by P'arpeçi. (See above, p. 156.)

[2] See above, pp. 71–2.

jection of the Council would follow as a natural consequence, as we shall see.

Before studying the act of rejection, let us examine that doctrinal attitude more closely by means of an analysis of the documents in which it is embodied.

6

THE DOCTRINAL BACKGROUND

We should be deflected far from the central theme of our study if we attempted a thorough investigation of the whole corpus of Armenian Christian literature of the period preceding the rejection of the Council of Chalcedon by the Armenian Church. But it is essential to look into it and try to see the specifically doctrinal background of that rejection.

The strictly theological part of that literature is not a vast field; but it has not yet been sufficiently explored. Once we exclude from it the historical part, such as the works of Agat'angełos (Agathangelus), P'awstos Biuzandaçi (Phaustus of Byzantium), Koriwn, Ełišē, P'arpeçi, Xorenaçi, there remain few books which need to be taken into account for such a purpose as ours. To name them: (a) The *Teaching of St Gregory*, as embodied in Agat'angełos,[1] (b) the *Stromateis*[2] traditionally known under the name of St Gregory and often ascribed by scholars to St Mesrop Maštoç,[3] (c) Eznik's *Adversus Haereses*,[4] or *De Deo*,[5] and (d) the *Homilies* of

---

[1] *Vardapetut'iwn Srboyn Grigori* presented by Agat'angełos as being the record of St Gregory's preaching immediately after his release from imprisonment in a pit, where he had been put for having refused to deny Christ (Agat'angełos, chs. 22–98). It has also been ascribed to Mesrop Maštoç. (See K'iparean, *Literature*, pp. 57–8.)

[2] *Yačaxapatum*—Twenty-three homilies of moral content rather than doctrinal. (See Bibliography.)

[3] See Abełean, *Literature*, pp. 125–7; Weber, *Hatschachapatum*, Preface.

[4] *Ełc Ałandoç*, Venice, 1926 (3rd ed.). See the critical edition together with a French translation made by the late P. Mariès in *Patrologia Orientalis*, t. xxviii, Fasc. 3, 4, 1959.

[5] See Mariès' *De Deo d'Eznik*.

John Mandakuni.[1] First, we have to eliminate from this list Eznik's treatise, because christological themes are totally excluded from it.

When we look into the other three works we do not find any form of christological doctrine in the technical sense of this word, that is to say, a systematic presentation. The whole context and purpose of these writings are really foreign to the polemical character of the christological literature of the fourth and fifth centuries. In fact they were written for the instruction of the "simple soul" and, therefore, they teach Christian doctrine in a rather elementary form. The authors are primarily concerned with its moral aspects; the purely dogmatic elements are not given any significant or important place. Indeed, the authors had before them an audience newly converted from paganism, who needed the "milk" before receiving the "solid food"! It is not surprising, then, that the christological doctrine in its dogmatic aspects and in its polemical form, is entirely absent from these treatises. Perhaps we can better understand the character of these writings if we compare them with the homilies of St John Chrysostom or with those of St Ephraim Syrus, and not, for instance, with the treatises of an Athanasius or the Orations of Nazianzus.

With this important observation in view, let us now look at them separately.

1. *The " Teaching of St Gregory"*

In the *Teaching of St Gregory* we have an exposition of the record of God's saving deeds. That is to say, an historico-theological *exposé* of the scriptural narrative of God's relationship with man.

The author begins with a confessional statement on the Holy Trinity, the foundation of all Christian doctrine and the source of all Christian life. Then he relates the story of the creation as being the work of the Holy Trinity. He dwells upon the doctrine of man longer than on any other theme and shows his supreme and unique place in God's creation. Then follow the story of the fall, the narrative of Adam's generation throughout the centuries as recorded

[1] *Čaŕk'*, Venice, 1860. On the authorship of these homilies see Additional Note, 11.

in the Old Testament, the prediction by the prophets of Christ's coming, the act of the Incarnation, the life and work of Christ—given in very general terms and centred on the specifically divine and saving acts. Here he inserts exhortations to the people to follow Christ, because all that Christ did was done for them. Then come the Apostles as those who continue Christ's work through his Church. Finally, he closes his *Teaching* with the doctrine of the eschatological hope.

Now, in all these instructions one can hardly find any specifically christological doctrine as this is understood in the context of the christological controversies of the fourth and fifth centuries. However, there are some passages in the middle of the *Teaching*—when the author speaks on the Incarnation as such—where there are expressions which have a not unimportant significance. Thus we read:

> God the holy Son was sent from God (the Father); he took flesh from the Virgin [and became] perfect man with perfect Godhead; he showed forth the power of the divinity and exposed the weakness of the flesh.

A little further on he stresses the unity:

> Those who believed in the flesh [he] manifested to them his Godhead; and those who erred [in their belief concerning] the flesh they denied his nature (i.e. his human nature). For, he united [himself] to the flesh in [his] nature and mixed the flesh with his Godhead.[1]

Again,

> He is himself in the essence, as, indeed, [it is said] "He who is"; but when he willed he took the form of man and put on flesh and came into our image (lit. "likeness" or "resemblance").

He was truly embodied in the flesh as though he was infinite. He became true man. He is at the same time, by his divinity in heaven and on earth.

> Although he came into humiliation for our sake, yet he remains in his nature, as he himself says "I am the same and did not change".[2]

---

[1] Agat'angełos, xxxviii, pp. 275–6.   [2] See Mal. 3.6.

For although he took the form and the flesh of man, yet he mixed, unified, and submerged (lit. "sank") it in his divinity.[1]

Then he urges his hearers:

Believe in the Trinity; believe in the truth of the unity in utter silence [or] in silent faith. How can we, earth-bound creatures, search and know the unexplorable and unsearchable Highest? How can we who have beginning examine him who is without beginning and is incomprehensible?

The true faith is this: He descended and mixed [his] Godhead with [our] manhood and the immortal with the mortal, so that he could make us participants in the immortality of his Godhead; thus, when the Son of God, equal to the Father, came with his flesh to the right hand of the Father, he united (lit. "mixed") us to Godhead.[2]

Now it is not difficult to see in these expressions a strong emphasis on the unity. If we cannot show the direct connection of these expressions with Alexandrian christology—the historical evidence is not sufficiently strong—we see no difficulty at all in recognizing in them the influence of the Cappadocian Fathers, namely that of Gregory of Nazianzus.[3] Therefore, purely on theological grounds, we have here an important aspect of christology which—it is worth noting—has no connection with the Antiochene doctrinal tradition and gives us a hint to the theological milieu of the background now under discussion.[4]

[1] Agat'angełos, xl, pp. 281–2; cf p. 286.
[2] Agat'angełos, xl, pp. 285–6.
[3] If this is true, then the author of the *Teaching* cannot be Gregory the Illuminator, who had died in 325, before St Gregory of Nazianzus was born. In fact, Gregory of Nazianus has often used the words $\mu\hat{\iota}\xi\iota\varsigma$ (see Orat. xxx, 3: *P.G.*, t. 36, col. 105; Orat. xxxviii, 12: *P.G.*, col. 325; see also the *Seal of Faith*, p. 350), $\kappa\rho\hat{\alpha}\sigma\iota\varsigma$ (see *Carm.*, Bk. ii, sect. i, 1 612: *P.G.*, t. 37, col. 107; cf Gregory of Nyssa, *Ad Theoph.*; see also Mueller, *Opera Minora*, p. 126), $\sigma\upsilon\gamma\kappa\rho\hat{\alpha}\sigma\iota\varsigma$ (Epist. CI: *P.G.*, t. 37, col. 180).
[4] It is interesting to note that the longest passages quoted from St Gregory in the *Seal of Faith* are taken from the chapters we have quoted from the *Teaching*. The compiler must have noted the christological significance of the passages in the seventh century. (See *Seal of Faith*, pp. 146–55.)

2. The "Stromateis" or Yačaxapatum

The twenty-three homilies which constitute the contents of this work touch upon a large variety of themes. To give some examples: the Holy Trinity, the significance of faith, the constitution of the created beings, the virtues, abstinence, repentance, providence, martyrs, and so on.

The christological problem is not touched at all. We hoped to find something in this respect at least in the homilies on the Holy Trinity.[1] Only in the second homily entitled "On the distinctions (lit: 'properties') of the Holy Trinity" is there a passage[2] on the Incarnation where he speaks of Christ's work rather than of his person. The writer refers only to Christ's taking our human nature and passing through all human experiences except sin. As the homily was intended for the spiritual instruction or edification of the faithful, it is understandable that there is no further inquiry into the nature of the act of the Incarnation as such. On the other hand, there are elaborate assertions on the relationship and importance of the Incarnation to the believer. Christ became man so that we could become sons of God. Then follow statements on how to understand and live this message. Thus the whole tone of the passage, and indeed of all the homilies, is not dogmatic but spiritual, devotional, and moral.[3] Therefore this book cannot help us in our investigation of the doctrinal background.[4]

3. The Homilies of John Mandakuni

Like the homilies of St Gregory the Illuminator, those known under the name of John Mandakuni are almost exclusively devoted to the exposition of the moral teaching of Christ and the general principles of Christian doctrine, without any specific ref-

[1] Hom. i: "On the Most Holy Trinity", pp. 1–3. Hom. ii: "On the distinctions in the Holy Trinity", pp. 4–18. Hom. xxii: "On the unchangeable essence of God", pp. 202–5.

[2] See Hom. ii, pp. 15–16.

[3] We may note that the first homily and the first part of the second are quoted in the Seal of Faith, pp. 18–22.

[4] See a summary of the contents and quite a fair presentation of the nature of the work in Abełean, Literature, pp. 127–33.

erence to the christological problem of the time.[1] Even a quick look at the titles of the homilies will suffice to convince us on this point.

In only one of the homilies, "On the Holy Trinity and on the Nativity of Christ our Lord"[2] is there a passage in which the unity in Christ is emphasized. I translate it:

> The only-begotten Word by the will of the Father came to the earth and took flesh from the holy Virgin; he suffered, was buried, the third day rose and sat on the right [side] of the Father; he shall come again to judge the quick and the dead. He who was without mother as regards [his] essence and without father as regards [his] economy (i.e. the Incarnation), came to save us, the creatures. It is not possible for God himself to suffer; he could not die either. Therefore, he who was God came and became man, died and saved us, the creatures. No creator, saviour, and life-giver other than he was or will be, or is ever to be, but only the one, the only-begotten, the God who was born of the Virgin and made man. For, many men knew God, saw God, and spoke of God; but they [all] are called men in so far as their nature is concerned. Some in body went up to the heavens, but even there they are men as regards their nature, or angels, but never God. In a similar way, the Word of God came to the earth and became man and died as man; but according to [his] essence he is called God and not man; according to the economy [he is called] God Incarnate (lit. "made man") and not man deified (lit. "made God"). [Henceforth being] man both in heaven and on the earth, he is one and the same, united, through the union of the flesh and Godhead.[3]

In this last statement we have a clear indication of his way of conceiving the unity of Christ. But he does not go further and tell us how that unity is to be explained. This shows that here he was not concerned with the technical exposition of the christological doctrine. He did that in a special treatise, the *Demonstration*, as we shall see in a moment.

[1] Fr B. Sargisean, who has studied the homilies from both philological and theological points of view, has not found any important christological teaching in them. (See *Mandakuni*, pp. 231–2.)

[2] See *Homilies*, pp. 212–13.   [3] Ibid.

So, after this rapid review of the Armenian theological literature prior to the rejection of the Council of Chalcedon we come to dwell at some length on the two christological documents which we have already mentioned, and which come from the last quarter of the fifth century, a time when the Chalcedonian problem had come to the attention of the Armenian Church, as we showed in the previous chapter.

4. The Treatise of Movsēs Xorenaçi

In the *Book of Letters* we have a document under the name of Movsēs Xorenaçi and placed between the correspondence of Acacius with Sahak Catholicos and the *Demonstration* of John Mandakuni.[1] It is written in a language strongly Hellenist, which makes the understanding of it rather difficult. It is an apologia for the "One Nature" and, at the same time, a refutation of the "Two Natures". The arguments for his thesis are of a philosophical (dialectical) nature. The author has also given due weight to the scriptural evidence. The treatise reveals that he was a highly competent theologian, well versed in Greek philosophy as well as in Biblical exegesis. The last paragraph suggests that the treatise had been written as a letter to a person. Abełean thinks[2] that Mandakuni could have been that person. This is only a conjecture in the sphere of sheer probability. However, it is not difficult to find some affinities between this letter and Mandakuni's *Demonstration*.

Before coming to the actual presentation of its christology it is necessary to say something of its authenticity, which has been challenged by some scholars. Among these, Malxaseanç was the one who dealt with the problem at some length and argued categorically that the treatise was a forgery. Xorenaçi could not have written it, because he was a convinced Chalcedonian. This contention of Malxaseanç is the result of his own analysis and interpretation of the fifth-century ecclesiastical situation as represented in P'arpeçi's letter and Xorenaçi's *Lamentations*. For him the Syrophiles in Armenia were the anti-Chalcedonians and the

---

[1] See *B.L.*, pp. 22–8.   [2] See *Literature*, p. 65.

Hellenophiles the Chalcedonians. Therefore, as Xorenaçi was a representative of this second group it follows that he was a Chalcedonian in his doctrinal position. He also thinks that the Syrophiles, being not highly educated people, could not understand the subtle nuances of the Chalcedonian definitions.[1] How, then, could such a Chalcedonian theologian who had even been persecuted for his doctrinal attitude have written a treatise or a letter against the Council of Chalcedon? These arguments, of course, cannot stand up to the slightest criticism. They are deduced from generalizations that have no weight, because they are not supported by any historical or theological evidence. From what was said in the previous chapter it is evident that this interpretation is far from being acceptable to us, as it has been unacceptable to many others before us. The only concrete evidence which he brings forth to substantiate his view is taken from a ninth-century Georgian writer, Arsēn Catholicos Saparaçi, who in his treatise on the separation of the Armenian and Georgian Churches says that Komitas, the Armenian Catholicos (of the seventh century)

> interpreted (= translated?) the heretical writings of Timothy the Alexandrian who was called "Aelurus", Peter the Fuller who was called "Wolf", Severus, and other heretics; he entitled these writings in such a way that they were taken as the homilies of St Sahak and Movsēs, and through this sort of forgery he made the whole of Armenia accept the faith [of these heretics].[2]

Abełean, who has successfully refuted Malxaseanç's thesis, shows how ambiguous is this testimony and how unfounded the conclusion that Malxaseanç draws from it. How can one identify the forgeries so ambiguously referred to by Saparaçi with the Treatise of the *Book of Letters*. In fact, Arsen says that the works of Timothy, Peter, and Severus were put under the names of Sahak and Movsēs; whereas, in this treatise we have a very brief letter written by Movsēs himself. Although it betrays some influences of Timothy's *Refutation*, it is not a translation of any part of it.

---

[1] See Malxaseanç, *Xorenaçi-Riddle*, pp. 135–40.
[2] Melik'set'-Bek, *Georgian Sources*, p. 38.

The validity and value of Arsēn's testimony is questionable in itself. It we take it seriously, then we must believe that Sahak was a Chalcedonian! In fact, his death preceded the Council of Chalcedon by some twelve years! Then we have to accept also that Komitas was so foolish as to ascribe works written after 470—some even in the sixth century—to a person, the famous Armenian Catholicos Sahak, who had already died in 439. How could Komitas have made the Armenian *vardapets* of later centuries believe in such flagrant anachronisms? Komitas' life and work as we know it through the authentic sources of the Armenian historiographers cannot provide any context for such forgeries.[1]

Thus, accepting the authenticity of the document, let us look at its christology.

Xorenac̣i opens his treatise with a strong assertion of the idea of "One Nature". This idea put in the opening phrase remains the corner stone of his whole treatise. He says that as the living creatures being composed of many elements have but one nature, so one single creature's nature has to be one. In the same way, according to the divine Scriptures the Word Incarnate is one nature. Those who divide this unity are mistaken and have to be refuted.

No one can understand the "how" of God's work. It is simply unknowable like the formation of the bones in the womb of a pregnant woman. Thus, the great prophet[2] tells us that God with one command created the world and man; but he does not tell us how or of what he created them. Therefore, we have to confine ourselves to what the Scriptures say and not raise problems. Although Moses himself knew all the science of the Egyptians concerning the creation and the movements of the created things, he did not say anything from his own or from his acquired knowledge, but only that which the Holy Spirit revealed to him. Greek science can also show this, because the Greeks in their search for

---

[1] See for a thorough treatment of this problem Abełean, *Literature*, pp. 653–8; cf Tēr-Mkrtč'ean, *Seal of Faith-Introduction.*, pp. lix–lx; Idem, *Mandakuni*, p. 92.

[2] He refers to Moses who obviously is taken here as the author of the Pentateuch.

knowledge received assistance from Moses. Thus they understood man[1] as being constituted of four elements[2] and the soul of three parts.[3] Now, how is it that man, being formed of these elements, is said to be "one nature"? The two are not confused; that is to say, the flesh is not soul and the soul is not flesh. Each maintains its own properties. The distinctness of the two is not destroyed by their unity.

The Incarnation of the Word must be understood in the same manner. It we cannot understand how this happens, we need not be surprised, because the descent of Christ is above all miracles. Therefore, it is proper for the confessors of the truth to say "One Nature".[4]

> But if some, considering this answer impossible, suppose the contrary, as if it were proper to say "Two Natures" let them know that the same impossibility is recognizable in [the case] of man, and this [is seen] not only through philosophical categories but also in the divinely inspired Holy Scriptures.[5]

In fact, the Bible presents the flesh as created out of worthless clay and breath and soul by the breathing of the Uncreated. The Apostle also recognized this distinction.[6] Christ's teaching (i.e. the Gospels) shows more clearly that the spirit is more than the flesh.[7] It is not possible to conclude that these two natures are two entities endowed with will, and those who say so are supporters of Apollinarius and his followers, who preached a foolish and corrupted doctrine. In the doctrine of the Incarnation we must confess Christ One in his nature, because it is said "the Word became flesh" and that "he took the form (lit. "image", "resemblance", or "likeness") of a servant". The meaning of the Scriptures is clear: that which was taken by the Word was that which he did not have. Therefore, the two, the Word and the flesh, which were distinct, separate, became one. Those who find

---

[1] He means the physical nature of man, or simply, the body.
[2] *hoł* = soil, *ǰur* = water, *awd* = air, *hur* = fire.
[3] *šnč'akan* = psychic, *zgayun* = emotional, *banakan* = rational or intellectual.
[4] See *B.L.*, pp. 22–3.   [5] *B.L.*, pp. 23–4.
[6] See 1 Thess. 5.23.   [7] Matt. 6.25; cf 10.28; Luke 12.23.

this union (of the natures) to be impossible, should not confess in word the union of the persons.[1]

> It is said (in the Scriptures), "He who was in the form of God took the form of a Servant". You see, it says form *and* form; which form is then absorbed in the mixture according to their confession? For if [they think] that the union of the two natures results in confusion, then they have to understand the same for the persons. Indeed, their sayings are ridiculous ... because, as in the legendary tales, they create one head and two tails![2]

Then he attacks these preachers of duality, and deplores their position which runs contrary to the faith as proclaimed in the whole world, namely that "the Word after taking the flesh,[3] then soul[4] and the spirit[5] is one Lord Jesus Christ". Christ had always been confessed one in everything he did. He was not man at one time and God at another time. We do not know, he says, how these people came to this teaching or from where they took it.

After this attack on the "dividers", as he calls them, he puts before them an alternative proposition: "It is necessary either to put away this awkward division because of the proper union, or to deny it (i.e. the union or the Incarnation as such) altogether." He asks them: "Why do you like to mutilate it [by supposing] a half concord ("communion" or "union") as if two entities could not make one entity?"[6] He mentions by name a number of Church Fathers with references to the works of some of them in order to substantiate his view.[7] Then follows a list of Biblical

---

[1] The Armenian word is *dimaç* (Nominative case, *dēmkʿ*) which has been used very freely in Armenian christological writings. Generally, it can be said that it corresponds to πρόσωπον. Here it stands for ὑπόστασις, because obviously in this passage Xorenaçi tries to show that for those who say "Two Natures in one Person", this expression amounts to an empty notion if they cannot conceive a unity in nature. Undoubtedly we have here a direct indication to the Chalcedonian formula. This provides us with a further argument for our contention that Xorenaçi was in fact attacking the doctrine of Chalcedon without mentioning the name.

[2] *B.L.*, pp. 24–5.   [3] *marmin* = σῶμα.   [4] *hogi* = ψυχή.
[5] *mitkʿ* = νοῦς.   [6] *B.L.*, p. 25.

[7] The list, together with the references collated with the corresponding passages in Timothy's *Refutation*, is given above, pp. 165-6.

citations which are brought in to confirm his view. I give the references: 1 John 5.20; Isa. 7.14; Gal. 4.4; Isa. 63.9; John 9.35–8; 10.30; 14.9–11.

He assures his readers that it is impossible to find any scriptural evidence for two natures as separated or divided. If the opponents boast of their knowledge of profane philosophy and use it for affirming their position, let them come forward that their deficiencies may be exposed. Here he tries to trap his opponents in their own words:

> We already said a little earlier that the flesh is not soul nor the soul flesh; let us leave aside other things (arguments). Now, the one nature of the word is the divinity and the other (i.e. the human) stands in juxtaposition or is parallel [with it]. Which [part] of the human nature do they single out—the soul without the spirit or the flesh? [But] there is no need to speak that language if we believe that the flesh and the soul are one nature.[1]

Therefore, he concludes, in an ironical tone, their teaching is like a sepulchre which looks beautiful from outside, but is full of corruption.[2] Then he draws the conclusion of his argument in more serious terms:

> Here they (the "dividers") must be speechless in all embarrassment, and accept [their] defeat, because if they persist in saying two, then they tear apart the human nature and deprive the soul or the body from the salvation [wrought] by him who took it;[3] in the same way they cut into two the divine by uniting the person [of the Word] with the human person. But if they consent to confess the union, which is true, they will not then dare to proclaim the two loudly and without inhibition [lit. "with mouths without door"].[4]

He closes his treatise with an exhortation to glorify God and never to confess the Incarnate Lord as man and God separately but united, and finally, not to attempt presumptuously to understand the mystery which is unsearchable. The last paragraph, as

---

[1] B.L., p. 27.   [2] See Matt. 23.27.

[3] The Alexandrian tradition is strikingly shown in this soteriological approach to the understanding of the nature of the Incarnation.

[4] B.L., p. 27.

we have already noted, is addressed to a person to whom he sent this treatise as a letter. He was probably asked by him to write it.

5. The Demonstration of John Mandakuni

This is an attempt to demonstrate, as the title itself shows, why it is right to confess the Saviour "of Two Natures" (ἐκ δύο φυσέων) or "One Nature" (μία φύσις).

It is a longer *exposé* than Xorenaçi's.[1] Whereas in Xorenaçi's treatise—the work of an intellectualist theologian—we have an attempt at mainly philosophical justification of the unity of Christ's nature, here, in Mandakuni's *Demonstration*, we find a more Biblical justification of the same doctrine accompanied by a remarkably pastoral and irenical character. Its style is easier and more straightforward.

Its authenticity, although sometimes suspected, is now generally accepted. The main argument against its authenticity had been based on the Hellenistic linguistic characteristics which are found in it. But now that argument is ruled out, on the grounds of our new understanding of the origins of the "Hellenizing School" which was presented earlier.[2] Therefore we need not dwell on this problem at any length as the authenticity is generally accepted on the whole.[3] Let us turn to its christology.[4]

Just like Xorenaçi, he asserts right from the beginning that the Scriptures—"the Testaments of the Prophets and Apostles"— "nowhere mention the duality[5] of the two natures, so we ought to confess, in an unswerving confession of faith, the Word God [who is] in the Trinity as Incarnate (i.e. "become flesh")".[6] It is by the Holy Spirit that we confess Jesus as Lord.[7] The Holy

---

[1] See it in *B.L.*, pp. 29–40.   [2] See above, pp. 168–9.

[3] See Tēr-Mkrtč'ean, *Mandakuni*, pp. 92–4; Idem, *Seal of Faith-Introduction*, pp. lix–lxii; cf Abełean, *Literature*, pp. 378–9; Tallon, *Livre des Lettres*, p. 81.

[4] A schematical summary of the contents, under headings and sub-headings, can be found in Tallon, *Livre des Lettres*, pp. 103–4. It must be said that Tallon is the first scholar who has studied this document with a thorough investigation.

[5] The Armenian word is *aylut'iwn*, which Tallon translates "altérité". Here, the word points to the fact that the natures are not to be understood in the sense of "One and the other". Therefore the underlying idea is the duality.

[6] *B.L.*, pp. 29.   [7] See 1 Cor. 2.10.

Spirit teaches the truth. Those who assume that honour for themselves will be condemned. He, then, urges his people to walk in the royal path without turning to the right or to the left and always following the experienced navigator so that they may reach the safe harbour (lit. "the port of Salvation"). What can be that safe harbour if not the solidity of the unshakeable and true faith handed down by the Apostles and the Prophets? In other words, it means simply to believe in one Father Almighty, in his Word without beginning, and in the Holy Spirit. "As we believe in the Father Almighty, we triumph.[1] Our mind cannot understand this, because the Almighty comprehends everything [and] he remains incomprehensible." The "how", again, is above our understanding.

Then he attacks all those heretics who teach separation in Christ. If, he says, there really was a division in the inseparable union of Christ, then he himself would not have said, "I and my Father are one",[2] or, "He who sees me sees my Father",[3] or again, "Know and see that I am in the Father and the Father is in me".[4]

You see, he reveals himself as an image, a ray shone out for us from the light; he never speaks of the two things[5] as going side by side or as walking on parallel roads, each being distinct from one another, such as Peter and John travelling side by side to the [same] end; it is inappropriate to interpret these two (Peter and John) as one. As regards the various names of the Lord, our Saviour, those are not taught as implying many persons or various natures but One Lord Jesus Christ [together] with the flesh.[6]

The passage which follows is quite a long one in which he tries to show that those who speak of many natures and strive to search the divine being (which is unsearchable) are miserably mistaken; they resemble people who have fallen seriously ill; the orthodox doctors (i.e. the orthodox Fathers) used various methods to heal them from their sickness. In order to show them the truth,

---

[1] Cf 1 John 5.4, 5.   [2] John 10.30.
[3] John 14.9.   [4] See John 14.10.
[5] The Armenian word *omanç* suggests the idea of a person.
[6] *B.L.*, pp. 30–1.

they put before them the example of man's nature.[1] He justifies this method by saying that they had to use the dialectic discourse of those who fought the orthodox doctrine. Here St Paul is called on to justify this procedure (see 1 Cor. 9.20). Thus, as physicians approaching the heretics they examined human nature in order to show them that, as is obvious, the nature of the flesh and of the soul and of the spirit are different things, and yet man is one nature. But how he is one out of these different natures is something that remains unsearchable, and he who searches is cast into doubt.[2] At this juncture he asks:

So, if one cannot search the [nature of] man made one of many [natures][3] or his closest companion or even himself, how then would one be able to comprehend the Creator by defining the unexplorable mystery of the Incarnation? If such is the mystery, then it is not mystery. For, [in that case], the searcher who defines has to consider himself as being greater and higher than he who receives [upon himself] the definition. Do you see the shipwreck of this incorrect way of searching? It was for people of this kind that Paul said: "They made shipwreck of their faith."[4] For, we must not contemplate more than to confess him as Almighty and Creator and Lord.[5] In the same way, the Creation—how God created us out of nothing—is above all understanding. Only the Creator knows.

With these premises put so firmly, he proceeds to the teaching of the 318 bishops of Nicaea. He says that they taught contrary to those who denied that Christ was of the essence of the Father, or that he was one nature, i.e., the divine nature of the Word of the Father by whom all things were made.

It was this same Son who, as the Nicene Creed says, "descended, took flesh and became man, and was born in a perfect manner from Mary, the holy Virgin". After quoting this passage,

[1] He specifically mentions Apollinarius and shows how he and his followers erred and consequently lost the salvation promised to us.

[2] See 1 Cor. 2.11.

[3] This shows an apparent affinity with the *Treatise* of Movsēs Xorenaçi. Did Mandakuni know Movsēs' *Treatise*? Perhaps it was he who asked the latter to write it, as Abełean has suggested.

[4] 1 Tim. 1.19.   [5] *B.L.*, pp. 32–3.

he immediately denounces those who say that the "descending" was only in appearance and not in truth. He then refutes the doctrine which teaches that Christ became man in the sense that he inhabited the flesh by "complaisance and will".[1] He refutes the objection raised by such people, namely that the divine cannot be contained in space. His arguments are taken from Jeremiah 23.24, Isaiah 66.1, and Psalm 135.6. After all, God is omnipotent. In this sense he can unite with the flesh, otherwise "who, if not the impious can draw limits to the incomprehensible essence by showing it (i.e. the essence) in various places?" Then he advises his readers in a fatherly tone not to dabble in such troubled waters, which bring death, but to believe in the Incarnation and glorify it in wonder because it is above all miracles.[2]

Now he embarks upon the Scriptural evidence for his teaching. Starting from John 1.10, he first invites his readers to put aside all futile and misleading speculations concerning the natures and to turn to the message of the Gospels and to the predictions of the Prophets. What does he find there? The word "nature" was not yet heard when the New Testament writer said: "The life was made manifest, and we saw him, and now bear witness to him; for he who was with the Father was made manifest to us."[3] Some people seeing only the form of the flesh—which he truly was in becoming man—called him "Son of Joseph",[4] "Samaritan",[5] "blasphemer".[6] But those who were gifted with spiritual eyes, capable of grasping the intelligible, confessed him "reflection of the glory and stamp of the essence of the Father without beginning".[7] For "they heard from the life-giving Saviour and believed [what he said]: "I am in the Father and the Father is in me".[8]

---

[1] Tallon has already noticed—and rightly, I believe—that the christology of Theodore of Mopsuestia is implicitly being refuted here. Most probably, the Nestorians, whose activities in Armenia we have already discussed, were teaching Nestorianism clothed with Theodorean terminology. As we have already noted, Theodore was much more widely known and highly revered in this part of the world than Nestorius.

[2] See *B.L.*, pp. 33–4.   [3] See 1 John, 1.2.   [4] John 6.42; cf Luke 4.22.
[5] John 8.48.   [6] Matt. 9.3.   [7] Heb. 1.3.
[8] John 14.10.

Now, what would the searcher of the natures who calls himself Christian say here? Which nature did the disciples see? That of the Godhead, or that of the flesh? It is evident that they saw the flesh."[1]

The most obvious and incontestable evidence is found in Luke 24.39: "Touch me and see; a spirit has no flesh, neither bones as you see me have", and Mandakuni adds, referring to the flesh, "Which he took by his descent from David. They (i.e. the disciples) gazed upon him as upon one of men, yet, the Word was united to the flesh; [thus] he removed the difference of the separation. For he did not say, 'He who saw the nature of the divinity *or* of the flesh', but he said, without dividing, '*Me*'." Again, he quotes St John (3.13): "No one has ascended into heaven but he who is descended from heaven, the son of man who is in heaven."

> Now, where was the Son of Man? In heaven whence he descended, as it is said? Well, let them show us. If the flesh was heavenly [then] he could not have been called "Son of Man"; and if [it was] from the earth and from the descendants of Abraham, as I boldly do confess, how then was he in heaven? [This all becomes intelligible] if we understand it correctly; that is to say, in virtue of the inseparable union.[2]

In the next passage he says that if we believe in Christ's own words, then, we must put away all talk on duality or division. Otherwise we should resemble the Pharisee who said: "Thou art a man and makest thyself God."[3] Again, "If there was separation in the distinction then why are Jews condemned; for they put hands upon the man [only] out of the zeal they had for the invisible and incomprehensible nature of God."[4] If this was the case the Jews in fact surpassed the piety of their ancestors when they cried: "Take him away from us and crucify him."[5]

---

[1] *B.L.*, pp. 34-5. [2] *B.L.*, p. 35.
[3] John 10.33. [4] *B.L.*, p. 35.
[5] John 19.15. Other texts also are brought in, among them John 10.30, a kind of watchword for the Monophysite polemists.

He emphasizes the importance of Isaiah 53.5, because here the prophet shows both the reality and the excellence of Christ's wounds. Paul also called the Crucified the "Lord of Glory".[1] The prophet[2] in his turn predicted that God himself would come and save us and not send messengers or angels. Armed with these arguments, he exclaims: "O, the power of the word (the Scriptures) which overthrows the bands of the separatist, dyophysite heresy."[3] However, he does not stop here. He goes on to bring more evidence from the Scriptures. "Again here [Paul] shuts the mouths of those who, by distinguishing, teach separation; for he writes to the Corinthians[4] what he himself received, [namely] that 'Christ died for our sins', and in another place that 'He alone has immortality'.[5] Does he, in fact, preach two Christs? Here is what he himself confesses, namely 'One Lord is Jesus Christ' (1 Cor. 8.6)."[6] The Apostles and the Prophets have no place for the doctrine of the two natures. On the contrary, "they know one Lord: he who died and he who remained immortal".

Here Mandakuni brings in the analogy of the human body. He says that although in one body there are many members which are distinguished according to their functions, yet the togetherness of those many functions and the union in which they exist in the body make all the members one body and one man. We must understand the Incarnation in a similar way.[7] As the canon of faith (i.e. the Nicene Creed) says:

[1] 1 Cor. 2.8.   [2] See Isa. 35.4; cf 63.9.   [3] B.L., p. 36.
[4] 1 Cor. 15.3.   [5] 1 Tim. 6.16.   [6] B.L., p. 36.
[7] This analogy indeed shows a conception of unity in Christ which does not seem to be in accord with the Orthodox Monophysite conception as a whole. Surprisingly enough, Mandakuni himself, elsewhere in this same treatise, asserts a closer, more intimate kind of union than the one which is suggested in this comparison. It seems that there is an inconsistency here. Is it to be explained by the supposition that here Mandakuni was attacking those who separated the natures by giving each of them an activity of its own? Tallon contends that Mandakuni knew the text of Leo's Tome in which the separatist tendency is markedly strong. In it the natures are hypostatized. If our supposition is correct, then, this comparison becomes understandable: Mandakuni wanted to combat this separatist tendency by bringing in the example of the human body in which various functions of constituent members are not separate from each other, but united in the human nature.

The Word God took flesh and became man; thus he united to himself, in God-fitting manner, the body of our lowliness,[1] the whole soul and flesh, and the flesh truly became the flesh of the Word God. In virtue of this it is said of the Invisible that he is seen, of the Intangible that he is felt, crucified, buried, and risen in the third day; for he himself was [both] the passible and the impassible, the immortal who received death. Otherwise, how would the Father have given [his] Only-Begotten, or [how would] the Lord of Glory have been crucified? This is like the one body which is formed of many members, although these latter have not the same function. For the soul in itself does not suffer [any] wounding, neither the flesh affliction, and the Word is incapable of both. But in everything he is [the one] who suffers and [the same] who is impassible and because of that he is said to be man and God by having the definition of "God Incarnate".[2]

Again, he urges his readers not to follow the Dyophysites, because if they did, they would be condemned as the Jews were for having separated Christ. The opponents argue that the Word accepted the adoration as being addressed only to him; in the same way he received the outrages, not by his nature, but by his will. He says that Moses was called "god to Pharaoh",[3] or again we read in the Scriptures, "You are gods",[4] or "He who receives you receives me".[5] But these have to be understood as sheer appellations. Nowhere were these people said to be God. But he who was born of the Virgin is truly God. He quotes Isaiah 9.6; 53.8. It is this same Lord who appeared on earth and walked with men.

Again he stresses the fact that those who carefully study the Scriptures—the Prophets and the Apostles—will soon realize without any doubt that Christ is not considered *as* God, but *is* God. Therefore only the impious man can say that Christ—he who came to us—was not God, that is to say, he who was with the Father. He directs his readers to John 1.1; 7.27; 20.27–9. In this latter text we have the episode of the Apostle Thomas meeting Christ after the resurrection.

[1] Phil. 3.21. [2] *B.L.*, pp. 36–7. [3] Ex. 7.1.
[4] Ps. 82.6; cf John 10.34. [5] Matt. 10.40; cf John 13.20; Gal. 4.14.

In the concluding passage he asks his readers: Whom are we to follow? To consent to the testimony of the Prophets and the Apostles or to quarrelsome people who arrogantly speak of God and divide him with terrible separations? We cannot follow these latter

> because the Word is the Word of the flesh and the flesh is the flesh of the Word.[1] [This is so] not by supposition or reckoning [or] by the excellence of the honour, but by true union. For in all the Catholic Churches it is always proclaimed: "He shall come with the same flesh", with that which the disciples saw going up to the heavens, and to which the evangelist bears witness: "from the beginning they were eyewitnesses and ministers of the Word" (Luke, 1.2).[2]

Therefore, this being the true faith, let us flee from those who do not agree with it and by raising problems teach blasphemies. In doing this and in glorifying the Holy Trinity we can inherit the promised eternal life.[3]

There is no need to comment in detail on the christological contents of these documents. They are quite clear in themselves. However, it is perhaps necessary to draw some conclusions from them in the light which they themselves provide.

Given the evidence of the documents, it is not possible to think that the theological mind of the Armenians was a *tabula rasa* before the rejection of the Council of Chalcedon. It is necessary to make this assertion, because there are still people, and sometimes serious scholars,[4] who continue to repeat the old and totally uncritical

---

[1] Here there is a striking affinity with Cyril's 11th Anathematism in which the unity between the Word and the flesh is conceived as a very intimate one. It runs as this: "If anyone does not confess the flesh of our Lord to be life-giving and *the own flesh of the Word* himself conjoined to him in dignity, or having a mere divine in-dwelling, and not rather life-giving, as we affirm, because it became *the own flesh of the Word* who hath strength to quicken all things, be he anathema" (Bindley, *Ecumenical Documents*, p. 219; Greek text, Ibid., pp. 114–15; Armenian text in *B.L.*, p. 405).

[2] *B.L.*, p. 39.   [3] See *B.L.*, pp. 39–40.

[4] Among these is, for example, Fr V. Inglizean (see *Arm. Kirche*, pp. 363–70). We shall consider his view in the next chapter.

view that the Armenian Church Fathers in the fifth century were completely ignorant and inexperienced in theological thinking and, therefore, could not make any decision of their own concerning the doctrine of the Council of Chalcedon. Besides the monumental work of Eznik, whose philosophical and theological penetration alone could challenge categorically this traditional view, these documents provide us with solid arguments in changing the antiquated interpretation of the doctrinal situation of the Armenian Church in the fifth century.

Of course one can pick out certain passages from them which reveal perhaps a rather naïve approach to the problems. But those things are common to both the Chalcedonian and anti-Chalcedonian controversialists of the fifth century. In fact, the sixth century was the time when on both sides there were considerable developments. The doctrines of both sides went through a process of systematization which immensely contributed towards the understanding of the doctrinal definitions of the Council of Chalcedon and the monophysite position. The names of Leontius of Byzantium and many other neo-Chalcedonists on the one hand, and Severus of Antioch, on the other, are significant in seeing and appreciating this change. The Armenian theology of the later centuries, particularly that of the seventh, went through the same process.

The basic fact is that in these documents we have a theological refutation of the doctrine of the Council of Chalcedon. The total absence from Mandakuni's *Demonstration* of any specific mention either of the Council of Chalcedon, or even of Nestorius, is significant. In fact, the only names of any heretics are those of Apollinarius and of the Arians. This shows clearly that he was concerned with the doctrine as such, because the Council itself was already discarded and did not come to his consideration for acceptance *or* rejection. It is worth noting that this confirms what we said at the end of the previous chapter.

The one question that we find difficult to answer is this: Was Mandakuni refuting the doctrine of the Council of Chalcedon having before him the text of Leo's Tome or the Chalcedonian

Definition? Tallon, as we already mentioned, tries to show that there are similarities between certain aspects of the doctrine refuted in the *Demonstration* and certain passages of Leo's Tome.[1] There can be one objection to his suggestion. The expressions which he singles out could equally be taken as characteristic expressions of Antiochene christology in general. Secondly, how are we to explain Mandakuni's direct use of the Tome? Was this latter sent to the Armenian Church? How did he know it? One cannot find any reference to it in the literature of the fifth century. With these points in mind it seems more likely that Mandakuni knew the doctrine of the Council of Chalcedon through the work of Timothy Aelurus, which was translated in the years between 480 and 484, just at the time when he was the Catholicos of the Armenian Church.

Finally, it is necessary to note that the anti-Chalcedonian attitude of these documents was not arrived at suddenly. In other words, it was not the result of a particular event such as the translation of Timothy's *Refutation*. Rather it was the natural consequence of a traditional theological relationship with the thought of the Cappadocian Fathers which served them as a very general background. The major factor in shaping that christological attitude in a definite form was the translation of the Church Fathers such as Athanasius, the Cappadocian Fathers themselves, and Cyril of Alexandria. The movement of translation, as we know, had started earlier than 430 and continued throughout the century. The names of the Church Fathers just mentioned correspond to those given by P'arpeçi.[2] Especially after the campaign against the writings of Theodore of Mopsuestia and the strong opposition to Nestorianism, the Armenian Church had resolutely adhered to the Cyrilline christology which became the basic principle of the Armenian position in the whole doctrinal controversy that preceded and followed the rejection of the Council of Chalcedon.

These documents are the first-fruits of that decisive process.

[1] See *Livre des Lettres*, pp. 107, n. 1; 109, n. 2; 110–11, n. 9; 112, n. 1; 119, n. 2; particularly pp. 122–3, n. 9; 127, n. 5; 135.

[2] See above, p. 157.

7

THE REJECTION OF
THE COUNCIL OF CHALCEDON

The basic idea which we have constantly had in mind in attempting this investigation into the historical and doctrinal situation of the Armenian Church has been that the rejection of the Council of Chalcedon was not an event in the sense of a single, clear-cut action, but rather a process which passed through preliminary stages and came to a definite conclusion towards the end of the first decade of the sixth century.

Therefore, having studied, in the preceding chapters, those preliminary stages, we now come to see the point which the process reached and the kind of attitude that was taken by the Armenian Church at this juncture. For obviously it was at the beginning of the sixth century that the most decisive step was taken. In other words, it was at this time that the corner-stone of the Armenian Church's position regarding the Council of Chalcedon was laid.

In the Introduction to this study a sketch was given of both the traditional and recent critical views concerning the rejection of the Council of Chalcedon. We have already shown how, with the publication of the *Book of Letters*, the transition from the traditional view to the modern critical interpretation took place.[1] We need not enter into the details of the general discussion which followed. The important views have already been outlined and reference will be made to them in the exposition of the Armenian attitude which is under study in this chapter.

Now, we examine afresh the two documents in question[2] and

---

[1] See above, pp. 6–18.   [2] See *B.L.*, pp. 41–51.

try to see their historical and theological significance for our understanding of the Armenian Church's position regarding the Council of Chalcedon.

1. Letter from the Armenians to the Orthodox in Persia

Under this title we have a letter which is addressed to "all the bishops, 'chorepiscopoi', priests, deacons, anchorites, lay people, nobles, chiefs of villages, seniors and juniors, and to all the faithful of Persia who are under the reign of Kawad, King of Kings".[1] In a second passage we have the list of those people in whose names this letter was written. Thus, we read that the letter was sent by Babgēn, "the Armenian Archbishop[2] of Armenia Major" and twenty bishops of various provinces of Armenia—all of them mentioned by name and by diocese[3]—and priests, monks, anchorites, princes—fourteen of them mentioned by name and province. As the letter resumes at the end: "From the [Armenian] bishops, priests, monks, nobles, and peasants to your orthodox saintliness; rejoice in Christ's love".[4]

What does this letter tell us?

After these long passages, Catholicos Babgēn immediately gives the reason for his writing. He says:

In the eighteenth year of Kawad, King of Kings, when I, Babgēn, the Archbishop of the Armenians and the bishops, monks and naxarars were assembled together in the province of Ayrarat, in the city of Dowin, the capital of Armenia, some people came to us who said they were from your country (lit. "from those parts or regions"),

---

[1] *B.L.*, p. 41. But before coming to this general address, there is a long list of persons and places mentioned by name. When one compares these names with the names of the persons and places mentioned in the *Synodicon Orientale* (see pp. 301–17) the resemblance becomes obvious. Some of these have already been identified by Tēr-Minaseanç (see *Arm. Kirche*, p. 32–3, Arm. ed., pp. 71–3). Others are not difficult to identify. We have no space here to attempt this, nor is it directly necessary for our immediate purpose.

[2] The Armenian word is *ebiskobosabet*, which literally means "Chief of the Bishops".

[3] It is worth noting that almost all parts of Armenia were represented in this Council. Most of the dioceses were situated in the south.

[4] *B.L.*, p. 42.

[that is to say] from Tisbon (Ctesiphon), from Garmikan,[1] and from the province of Vehrartašir,[2] they told us precisely their names and the places of their inhabitance: Samuēl (Samuel), priest of the monastery of Maharǰan in the province of Karmikan, Šmawon (Simon), a priest of Berdošma,[3] the priest Axa of Perozšapuh,[4] the city of the Turcs ("Tačkac̣") in the province of Vehartašir, and Mara the scribe and their other colleagues. Standing in front of the whole assembly they had a letter (i.e. a writing) in their hands by which they confessed the right faith; they had put themselves to great efforts to find the true and orthodox doctrine of the Holy Trinity.[5]

These people having received permission from Kawad had come to the Armenians with a definite purpose: to assure themselves and their opponents that their faith was the same as that held by the Greeks, Armenians, Georgians, and Albanians.[6]

What was the particular issue which impelled them to come to the Armenians? The letter gives a straightforward answer. It says:

They (i.e. the delegates) gave the reason for their coming to us by saying: "We are subjects of Kawad, the King of Kings; we do continuously and earnestly ask God to grant him and all who are under his authority health, peace, long life and every good thing like these. The faith that we have is the true [faith] of the ancient Fathers, the three hundred and eighteen, who assembled in Nicaea in the time of the reign of the blessed Constantine; which faith the whole world did accept and upon which the holy, catholic, and universal Church was built, and which in the beginning was even proclaimed (lit. "taught") by the words of the Lord: "Go therefore and make disciples of all nations, baptizing them in the name of the Father and of the Son and of the Holy Spirit" (Matt. 28.19). This [testimony] was

[1] Beit-Garmaï or Garamée, situated in the north-west of Persia. See Levenq, *Bêth Garmai*, col. 1230–3. See Map 2.

[2] Beit-Ardašir, commonly known as Seleucia, situated near Ctesiphon. See Map 2.

[3] *Berdošmay*. This is the corrupted form of Beit-Aršam (*Bed-Arsam*). Here we have a reference to a very important figure of the Syro-Persian Monophysite Church, Simon of Beit-Aršam. See Additional Note 12.

[4] A city on the Euphrates situated in the west of Beit-Ardašir. See Map 2.

[5] *B.L.*, pp. 42–3.   [6] See *B.L.*, p. 43.

put as a high and mighty seal on everything [in Christian doctrine]. This faith was held in concord by our country and there appeared in it no impurity at all until the twenty-seventh year of the reign of Peroz.[1] But at that time the evil leaven which was hidden within unholy people appeared. [These unholy people] began to trouble the pure faith of the true Trinity and deceive inconstant people by fleshly desires. [Therefore] discord reigned and many fell sick with unbearable diseases. Even the leaders of this blasphemous heresy held councils in various places, sometimes in Gowntšapuh[2] and sometimes in Mesopotamia[3] (lit. "Assyria"). [Thus] Acacius, Barsauma, Mani, Yohanan, Paul, Mika,[4] and others in communion with them joined their voices to the teachings and impieties of Nestorius, Diodore, and Theodore.[5] They endeavoured [to accuse] us before the princes and the judges and [cause] us much trouble and bring perils upon us and upon all the orthodox of our country. And we not being able to bear such an evil, insupportable and bitter blasphemy, went to the king to prove [our innocence]. We came also to you being impelled by the same danger and trouble in order to find help by the witness of the divine Scriptures so that the traditions and prescriptions of the Holy Fathers might stand firm and immovable and that bodily and spiritual afflictions might not torment us every day because of doubts about these things.[6]

Having become aware of these troubles and also having seen the written documents containing their faith, the Armenian Catholicos with his bishops praises the spirit of endurance which the

[1] 457+27=A.D. 484, the date of Barsauma's council.

[2] The other name more commonly used for this place is Beit-Lapat, situated in the north-east of Ctesiphon. See Lantschoot, *Bêth-Lapat*, col. 1233–5, and Map 2. It was here that Barsauma held his famous council of 484.

[3] It refers to the western regions of the Persian empire where Syriac-speaking Christianity was most influential. We know that two councils were held in this part: the first by Acacius in 486 and the second by Babaï in 497, both in Beit-Aramayē in Seleucia.

[4] All these names except that of Mani appear in the Acts of the Councils of Acacius and Babaï. (See Chabot, *Synodicon Orientale*, pp. 301, 306–7, 310–11, 315–17.)

[5] The word is *T'ēodoroti* (= "Theodoroti") which can be taken as referring to Theodoret. But it seems more likely to signify Theodore of Mopsuestia. Later in this same letter, as we shall see, Theodoret also is denounced, together with Theodore.

[6] *B.L.*, pp. 43–4.

Persian orthodox (i.e. Monophysite) Christians had shown so admirably. Then he says that the Nicene creed is the basis of the true faith. The Armenian Church accepts the doctrine of the Council of Nicaea, in which Aristakēs, St Gregory's son and successor, took part and brought the Creed and canons to his own Church. He quotes the creed to show that therein lies the foundation of the orthodox faith. No definition of faith other than this canon or rule can be accepted. This is the faith that the Greeks, Armenians, Georgians, and Albanians have in common.[1]

Then he condemns the Nestorians in the following passage which I translate *in toto*:

But as Samuēl the monk and Simon the priest and their companions, the brethren whom you sent, told us that Babē, the Catholicos of Assyria[2] and the other bishops who are Nestorians, teach that God (i.e. the Word) was two sons: the one, God, the Word, equal to the Father, who descended from the heaven, and the other, Jesus, mortal man like us, who was born of Mary and who because of his becoming more righteous than any other man, was honoured and by grace called "Son of God", [thus being] only by name and not [truly] Son of God and equal to the Father. He was man created mortal like us; and because the Holy Spirit helped him he was able to defeat the Satan and overcome the desires (i.e. the passions) and because of his righteousness and because of his good works he was worthy of the grace and became the temple of the Word of God

Again they assert that it is right to separate and to say openly perfect God and perfect man, that is to say, the perfect God took the perfect man, Jesus Christ; and because he (i.e. the Word) loved him (i.e. the man), he made him worthy to be honoured with him in adoration; and [thus] the man who received the grace was honoured and wrought miracles and wonders by the Word of God who descended from the heaven and dwelt in him, that is to say, in Jesus, and the wonders which he did were multiplied in him. All the sufferings and the humility he endured in himself and was found mortal like

[1] See *B.L.*, pp. 44–5.

[2] It refers to Babaï, the Catholicos of the Persian Church (497–502). Here we have a more explicit and direct indication to Babai's attempts at consolidating Nestorianism and fighting the Monophysite elements in the Persian Church. The council of 497 was a landmark in that direction.

us [because] being of man's generation he was equal to us; [he was] son of God [only] by the Word of God.

Still they say that the voice which came from the heaven, "This is my beloved Son, with whom I am well pleased" (Matt. 3.17), was not for Jesus but for the Word of God who is equal to the Father and who came from heaven and dwelt in him.

Again they say that when he entered the upper room, where the disciples were gathered together, the doors were not closed, but the disciples had left them open because of their fear of the Jews.

The heretics again say that Jesus Christ was mortal man created equal to us and neither descended from nor ascended to the heavens, but he was like Elijah and Enoch who were taken into the air and have not yet seen God and never will see him until the resurrection.

These the Nestorians say against us taking their strength from the writings of Diodore, Theodore, Nestorius, Theodoret, and Ibas. Acacius, Barsauma, Mani, and Paul[1] and their colleagues set this [teaching] as the rule [of faith]. And they say that the Greeks, the Armenians, the Georgians, and the Albanians have the same rule of faith as we have.

We heard these things from these people (i.e. the delegates) as being what the Nestorians say.[2]

Now comes the answer to the request of the Persian Christians. It is indeed, very short, formal, categorical:

As you wished to learn from us about these things, we signify to you that we the Greeks, the Armenians, the Georgians, and the Albanians did never accept and will never accept these blasphemies. We do not believe [in them] and do not communicate with [the people] who say and teach such, but we anathematize them as Paul the Apostle said: "If any one should preach to you more than we preached to you, let him be anathema" (Gal. 1.8). The same [faith] was affirmed by the three hundred and eighteen blessed Fathers of the Council of Nicaea, themselves being filled with the divine grace. To the same rule of faith adhered the hundred and fifty orthodox bishops who were assembled in Constantinople for the same issue and with whom we accord and anathematize the opponents of that true faith and perfect, God-given canon.[3]

---

[1] See above, p. 199, n. 4.   [2] *B.L.*, pp. 45–6.   [3] *B.L.*, p. 46.

In the last passage Catholicos Babgēn tells the Persian Christians that this letter was sealed by him together with the bishops and the princes of Armenia. As Sergis, otherwise known as Babgēn, a man from Šoštri[1] in Xužistan asked for a special letter on faith in order to use it for silencing the heretics in his own country, Catholicos Babgēn wrote a letter on the faith in Armenian and in Persian. He, together with his bishops and Vard Mamikonean—the Marzban—together with the princes, sealed it with their rings. Samuel and Simon took it and gave a copy to Sergis and took this letter to their country.[2]

2. "Letter from the Armenians to the Orthodox in Persia"

This letter with the same title as the previous letter, immediately follows this latter in the Book of Letters. It is more directly connected with the central theme of our study. Therefore we must look at it very closely. Here, again, Catholicos Babgēn and Meršapuh, bishop of Taron,[3] and the other bishops of the various provinces of Armenia together with Vard Mamikonean and other princes[4] and all the nobles address this letter to their "beloved brethren, orthodox and faithful servants of God, the diocesan bishops, monks, and people [of Persia]".[5]

They wrote this letter because, as they themselves say, the priest Simon[6] came a second time to Armenia and informed them that the issues were not settled and that the opponents of the orthodox faith did not accept the letters from the orthodox[7] and

---

[1] East of Ctesiphon, known as Shoshder or Schouster in the province of Houzistan (see Map 2). This passage seems to be a little confused. For the first time the name of Sergis comes in and I have been unable to identify him. However, this shows that there were people among the delegates from the parts east of Ctesiphon.

[2] See B.L., p. 47.

[3] Taron was a very influential province in South Armenia. The bishop of Taron apparently had the status of a senior bishop. In fact, the name of Meršapuh appears first in the list of the bishops in the previous letter as well. (See B.L., p. 41).

[4] Only two of them are mentioned by name.   [5] B.L., p. 48.

[6] The same person, Simon of Beit-Aršam, as mentioned in the first letter.

[7] In fact Simon of Beit-Aršam had obtained many letters from the Monophysite Church leaders as Barhébraeus tells us. (See Additional Note 12.)

even rejected their (i.e. "the Armenians'") letter; on the contrary, those opponents, the Nestorians, renewed their attacks and once more troubled the holy Church this time "*being strengthened by the Council of Chalcedon*".[1]

These heretics actually "derive [their teaching] on the Holy Trinity from Nestorius, the evil-thinker; they divide the Incarnation (lit. "the becoming flesh") of the Lord from the holy Virgin Mary". Christ was indeed

> truly man and at the same time God, as we (Babgēn and his bishops) confess and worship [him], [i.e.] the fleshness (i.e. manhood)[2] together with the Godhead and the Godhead together with the fleshness; we confess according to that same tradition which we received from the holy Council of Nicaea, from the 318 bishops and adhere to the meaning of the canons set up by them, because in fact, they are true since they are [formulated] through the divine co-operation. We flee from and deny the false teaching (lit. "the lies") of Nestorius and of others like him [which teaching was confirmed] in Chalcedon;[3] we know these people as having departed [only] feignedly from both the Gentile and Jewish errors, for they confess the same Gentile and Jewish doctrines and seduce into error the minds of the innocents, that is to say, of the ignorant; they make the blind deviate from the road; their reward was assigned by the Holy Spirit through the prophet.[4] The holy Fathers by their unanimity in Nicaea openly broke off the line of their (i.e. the heretics') evil teaching; they anathematized by [the power of] the Holy Scriptures Nestorius, Arius, Diodore, Theodoret (Theodore?), Eutyches, Paul of Samosata, and all those who are like these, [for] these taught Christ's becoming man as being a confusion or that [he was] solely man and not perfect God in perfect flesh.[5]

Here they mention two people, the "great Ampelis", bishop of the city of K'erson (= Cherson), "a lover and a minister of the true faith", and Anatolis of Constantinople,[6] "a devout priest".

---

[1] *B.L.*, p. 48.   [2] *marmnaworut'iwn* = "corporeality".

[3] For the supreme importance of this phrase, I quote here the Armenian text: *P'axč'imk' uraçeal z'i K'ałkedonin stut'iwn Nestori ew ayloçn nmaniç.*

[4] Perhaps he refers to Isa. 59.10.   [5] *B.L.*, pp. 48–9.

[6] For the identification of these two people see Additional Note 13.

We are told that Ampelis wrote on the Incarnation[1] and added to his writing the *Twelve Chapters* (*Kephala*) of Cyril and the letter of the blessed Zeno (the *Henoticon*). Anatolis also confirmed these writings and taught that there was no addition to the Holy Trinity and that he who was born of the Virgin was God the Word, who is always glorified with the Father and the Holy Spirit.

Then they repeat again that the true faith is the tradition of the 318 bishops, which tradition was confirmed by the 150 bishops (i.e. of the Council of Constantinople). They denounce those who do not hold steadfast to this tradition but instead follow alien opinions and talk nonsense. They liken them to the people whom the Apostle describes as "fruitless trees ... uprooted" (see Jude 12). In fact "those who do not confess the Son deny also the Father" (see 1 John 2.23). They urge their readers to follow the Apostle's prescription.[2] There follows a brief statement of the orthodox faith, made in confessional terms, similar to those of the creeds. It was that faith which was given to them by the 318 bishops of Nicaea and by the bishops of Ephesus.[3]

Here they become more explicit about their doctrinal position, because they mention by name the heretics whom they anathematize and the Holy Fathers whom they follow. The heretics are: Nestorius, Arius, Theodore, Diodore, Theodoret, Eutyches, Paul of Samosata, Ibas, Acacius, Barsauma and Babaï. The Holy Fathers are: Ignatius (of Antioch), Athanasius, Basil of Cappadocia, Gregory the Great (Nazianzen), and the two other homonymous Fathers, Gregory of Nyssa and Gregory of Neocaesarea, Julius (of Rome), "the guide of the way of life for the westerns", Ambrosius, John (Chrysostom), Atticus (of Constantinople),

[1] Although the letter does not say clearly what he did write on, it is obvious that he wrote on the Incarnation, namely on the doctrine of Christ's person and nature.

[2] See 2 John 10.

[3] To our knowledge, this is the first time that the Council of Ephesus is mentioned in Armenian theological literature in an *official* context. In fact, here, in this document, the first three Ecumenical Councils are mentioned together. They were recognized by the Armenian Church as the basis of orthodoxy and have remained so until to-day.

Theophilus (of Alexandria), Cyril, Proclus, and Aristakēs, the son of St Gregory the Illuminator.[1]

> We have the faith [of these Fathers] which we already have written to you together with the Georgians and Albanians in each nation's own language. Now we confirm the same and send it through our brother in the common faith, Simeon the zealous priest, so that no one dare contradict and oppose it for our sake.[2]

The concluding passage is an exhortation to the faithful not to be shaken or scandalized by the heretics who still repudiate the right doctrine. Let God judge and condemn them. They tell their readers that they have ordered copies to be made of the letter of Ampelis and that of Anatolis the priest, presumably for their instruction. The letter ends with the following advice: "If any one of the heretics comes and turns to our holy faith, it is right to accept him, because the door of God's mercy is always open for those who are both confessors and penitents."[3]

There are two points which must be taken as preliminary considerations before attempting to draw conclusions on the doctrinal position of the Armenian Church at this stage. The first is that in these two documents we have an *official* declaration and, therefore, a most important piece of evidence as far as the doctrinal orientation of the Armenian Church is concerned. Here we have a conciliar act, a decision taken by the supreme authority of the Armenian Church in its spiritual and national aspects. The Catholicos with his bishops and the Marzban with other feudal princes act together.[4] Secondly, the two letters are closely linked

---

[1] It is highly significant to note again the closeness of this list of Church Fathers to that of the Fathers quoted in Timothy Aelurus' *Refutation*.

[2] *B.L.*, p. 51.   [3] Ibid.

[4] It is worth while mentioning that the participation of the secular authority is the expression of the participation of the laity in the work of the Church. In fact, this participation of the laity has been a permanent feature and a very characteristic mark of the Armenian Church authority and activity throughout its history. It has taken various shapes according to the particular social systems of the life of the Armenian people in different periods of history. But the basic principle and its constant application have always had their place in the life of the Church.

with each other and they have to be considered together. The second letter, in particular, cannot be understood unless it is linked with the first. In fact, the two represent the two successive phases or moments of the one action.

Now, from the first letter we learn that the Armenian Catholicos and bishops, together with the feudal princes, were assembled in a council at Dowin, when Christians from the Persian Empire came and asked for their intervention in the doctrinal disputes of their own country. Then, the first question that arises is this: What was the purpose of that Council? Was it convened for doctrinal reasons?

The documents themselves tell us practically nothing about the council as such. We do not find much help in later documents either. Only in the second letter is there a reference to the participation of the Georgians and Albanians in this council. This reference is confirmed by a document of the seventh century. Abraham, Catholicos of the Armenians (607–15), writing to Kiwrion, Catholicos of the Georgians,[1] reminds him of Babgēn's council in which, he says, Gabriel the Catholicos of the Georgians with his bishops took part and condemned the Council of Chalcedon and the Tome of Leo. He even gives the list of those Georgian bishops who, with Gabriel, were present at the Council. Therefore, we must consider the council of Babgēn as an important one and in all probability directly connected with the doctrinal issues of the time.

Ormanean suggests that this council was one of the ordinary, regular councils of the Armenian Church which were held from time to time for the purpose of reviewing the work of the Church and meeting the various needs of the people, in the constantly changing circumstances of Armenian history.[2] Tēr-Minaseanç supposes that the council was convened for the acceptance of the

---

[1] It was this Catholicos who accepted the Council of Chalcedon and consequently the Georgian Church broke away from the Armenian in the seventh century. (See for details Akinean, Kiwrion; Ormanean, Azgapatum, col. 625–37; Tamarati, Église Géorgienne, pp. 239–44; Goubert, Géorgie, pp. 119–27.)

[2] See Azgapatum, col. 502.

Henoticon and for other internal ecclesiastical problems.[1] It is indeed probable that the *Henoticon* was considered and perhaps served as the basis for the doctrinal policy of the Armenian Church, but our documents do not give us a sufficient reason to assume that the council was held specifically for the acceptance of the *Henoticon*.[2] We think that this council had some direct connection with the doctrinal problems of the time in general. In other words, it was not simply one of the so-called regular or periodical councils convened for general purposes or intended to deal with the internal affairs of the Church. The participation of the Georgians and Albanians makes it more convincing that there were some issues which had to be faced in common. For the Georgian and Albanian Churches had been and still were in the closest relationship with the Armenian Church. This latter occupied a central position in that part of the world, as these letters themselves show.

Let us then look at the general political and ecclesiastical situation of the time.

The eighteenth year of Kawad's reign was A.D. 506. Therefore, the council of Babgēn was held in 506 at Dowin. The war which had started between Kawad and Anastasius ended in 505/6.[3] Hostilities thus ended for a while, the Christians in the Persian Empire had greater liberty and this time the Monophysites were apparently being favoured. Anastasius, on his part, had supported "la propagande monophysite dans les provinces orientales et même au delà des frontières de l'empire".[4]

---

[1] See *Arm. Kirche*, p. 30 (Arm. ed., p. 72).

[2] The only positive proof for supposing that the *Henoticon* was taken into consideration is provided by Simon of Beit-Aršam. He says: "Quam denique sequuntur modo, ratamque habent triginta ac tres Episcopi regionis Gurzan, cum Regibus et Magnatibus suis: nec non triginta ac duo Episcopi majoris Armeniae Persarum, cum Marzabanis suis: et cum reliquis Orthodoxis Episcopis et christianis Regibus, a Constantino fideli Imperatore usque ad Anastasium Caesarem." (See Assemani, *Bibl. Orient*, vol. i, p. 355.)

[3] See Bréhier, *Anastase*, col. 1451; cf Christensen, *Iran Sassanide*, pp. 345–54; Bury, *Later Roman Empire*, vol. ii, pp. 10–15; Stein, *Bas-Empire*, pp. 92–101; but particularly Charanis, *Anastasius*, pp. 29–31.

[4] Bréhier, *Anastase*, col. 1454.

This was a move which carried the expansion of Monophysitism a step further than the point which Zeno's *Henoticon* had reached. We have already noted that Barsauma and Acacius had opposed the *Henoticon* very strongly. After the councils of 484 and 486, a third was held in 497 under the Catholicos Babaï. Although the important issue was the marriage of the clergy, yet the councils of 484 and 486 were confirmed.[1] This council was held by the permission of Zamasp (496-8/9) who had occupied the throne through a *coup d'état* against his brother Kawad.[2] After the short reign of Zamasp, Kawad came back to power. The Monophysites seem to have been favoured by him for some time.

The situation of the Persian Church during the years between 484 and 506 was a troubled one. It was a time when Monophysites and Nestorians were continuously fighting each other. The echo of this struggle is clearly reflected in the council of Babaï (497). In the acts of this council we read that two bishops, Papa of Beit-Lapat[3] and Yazdad of Rew-Ardašir, stood in opposition to the orthodox doctrine (i.e. Nestorianism) and refused to appear before the council. Here, measures were taken to punish them for having declined the summons of the council.[4] The persecution of the Monophysites had been carried to such an extent that even the Emperor Anastasius intervened.[5] Now, it seems that after the war between Persia and Byzantium had ended, the Monophysites enjoyed comparative peace and found opportunity to strengthen their position by showing to King Kawad that their faith, which was opposed by the Nestorians, was the true one, because it was held equally by the Greeks, Armenians, Georgians, and Albanians. The year 506 was a time when the Armenians also had to take an official attitude towards the growing danger of Nestorianism. They could not wait very long, since the issues were

[1] See Chabot, *Synodicon Orientale*, p. 312; cf Scher, *Histoire Nestorienne*, vol. ii, pp. 128-30.

[2] See Christensen, *Iran Sassanide*, p. 347; cf Labourt, *Christ. Perse*, p. 155.

[3] He had been a student of the great Monophysite polemist, Philoxenos of Mabboug. (See Labourt, *Christ. Perse*, p. 157; cf Tisserant, *Nestorienne*, col. 178.)

[4] See Chabot, *Synodicon Orientale*, p. 314.

[5] See Charanis, *Anastasius*, p. 29.

becoming more and more acute. With peace restored between their two neighbours, they found a favourable time for such an action.

In the context of this general situation the first letter of the Armenians can be better understood. Thus, when we read the complaints which the Syro-Persian delegates put before the Armenians at the council of Babgēn, we see in them a direct connection with the situation which we have just outlined. For example, the delegates say that "the evil leaven appeared in the twenty-seventh year of Peroz's reign" and that the leaders of their opponents "held councils in various places". Again, they say that in these councils the teaching of Nestorius, Diodore, and Theodore was confirmed. They even give the names of Barsauma, Acacius, Babaï, and other bishops. All these point directly to the situation described above.

It is very reasonable to think that Simon of Beit-Aršam and his companions already knew that the Armenians, Georgians, and Albanians were assembled in council. It was not by sheer accident that their mission coincided with the convention of a council in Armenia. And as there are no canons left by that council,[1] it becomes more difficult to think that this was one of the supposed periodical councils of the Armenian Church. It must have been convened, then, for doctrinal reasons. The cause or the reason was, with all probability, the conflict between Monophysitism and Nestorianism. The peaceful time which followed the settlement of the war between Persia and Byzantium provided them with the conditions necessary for such an important council. As the Armenians since the Council of Ephesus were bitterly opposed to Nestorianism amd favoured the Monophysite (Cyrilline) christology, at the same time adhering tacitly to the position of the *Henoticon*, it was not difficult for a Simon of Beit-Aršam—a man devoted to the cause of Monophysitism—or for the Monophysite Syro-Persian Christians in general, to be aware of such a council and to ask its intervention in the disputes of their own Church.

[1] See Melik't'angean, *Canon Law*, pp. 356–65, particularly p. 358.

It is highly significant to note that these delegates informed the council that they had received permission from Kawad to come to Armenia. Secondly, we read in the closing paragraph of the first letter that Babgēn wrote this letter in Armenian and in Persian and sealed it. Now, as the ecclesiastical language of these Christians was Syriac, it seems that the letter was written also in Persian for the purpose of presenting it to Kawad as a proof of their orthodoxy.[1]

We conclude from these observations that in this letter we have the first official, more precisely, conciliar act of the Armenian Church concerning the doctrine of Christ's person seen in the post-Chalcedonian polemical context of its exposition. The position of the Armenian Church is clear: *It is anti-dyophysite in its basic principle and anti-Nestorian in its outward expression.*

There is no difficulty at all in understanding and estimating this position. The christological milieu of the time explains it straightforwardly. As we said, at this council the Armenians faced a conflict between Monophysitism and Dyophysitism. The latter came to their consideration under the form of Nestorianism. They had already opposed it in its Chalcedonian expression as the analysis of the treatises of Xorenaçi and Mandakuni has shown. The Council of Chalcedon as such was not yet brought into the arena. Now it appears in the second letter. The position expressed in this letter was, in fact, the natural consequence or the reasonable extension of the attitude expressed in the first.

What do we learn from it? First, we are told that Simon of Beit-Aršam came a second time and told Babgēn, the Armenian Catholicos, that the opponents of the orthodox faith (i.e. the Nestorians) did not accept his letter. On the contrary, they renewed their attacks, this time "*being strengthened by the Council of Chalcedon*".

What does this expression exactly mean? The immediate answer would be that the Nestorians continued their fight against the Monophysites by claiming that the Council of Chalcedon

---

[1] The accounts of Simon's work as given by Barhébraeus and Michael Syrus support this supposition very firmly indeed. See Additional Note 12.

approved their own teaching. In connection with this letter, we must add that this claim of the Nestorians had a particular reason. As the Armenian Catholicos in his letter was saying that the Greeks, the Armenians, the Georgians, and the Albanians had the same faith, presumably these Nestorians challenged that argument by saying that the Greeks had their own faith and therefore brought forth the Council of Chalcedon as a proof. However, it is clear that for one reason or another, according to the evidence of this second letter, Nestorians also regarded the Council of Chalcedon as having approved their doctrine and strengthened their position.

Now, when this case was made known to Babgēn by the official representative, Simon of Beit-Aršam, he then clarified the position of his Church as expressed in the first letter by adding in this one the following words: "We flee from and deny the false teaching of Nestorius and of others like him [which doctrine was confirmed] in Chalcedon." Secondly, he added the name of Eutyches to the list of the heretics. We must note that this is very important for understanding the theological attitude of the Armenian Church. It is clear that right from the beginning the repudiation of the Council of Chalcedon did not mean the acceptance of the teaching of Eutyches. We may remember that P'arpeçi also had anathematized Eutyches towards the end of the fifth century.[1]

Here we have, then, the first instance in which the Armenian Catholicos together with his bishops and the secular heads of his country, rejected the Council of Chalcedon.

For us there is no difficulty in understanding this action in its full meaning. From what we have said in the previous chapters it follows that such a decision would be only natural. The way of Armenian ecclesiastical life and theological tradition was already leading to this end, which would have been reached sooner or later. The second delegation of Simon of Beit-Aršam only provided the occasion for making that decision. It was not the cause, as some scholars have contended.[2]

[1] See above, p. 156.   [2] See Additional Note 14.

However, it is important to note that purely on theological grounds we have in this second letter no adequate or complete exposition of the christological doctrine of the Armenian Church. There is not much said in the first letter either. Therefore, it is not possible to expound the purely theological attitude of the Armenian Church in a systematic form or to represent its christology in more detail. We think that the christology of the two treatises which we studied in the previous chapter is quite representative of the theological attitude of Babgēn's council as well. Perhaps we may point out certain aspects of the contents of these two documents which provide us with some clear indications for an adequate understanding of that theological attitude. These points are:

(*a*) A strong emphasis on the sufficiency of the Council of Nicaea, which had a supreme authority for all Monophysites.

(*b*) Acceptance of *three* Ecumenical councils,

(*c*) An unyielding opposition to the Antiochene or the Nestorian theologians.

(*d*) Above all, appropriation of Cyril's christological teaching as embodied in the *Twelve Anathematisms,* accompanied by an adherence to Zeno's *Henoticon.*

(*e*) An explicit rejection of the Council of Chalcedon.

Surely we must suppose that some time elapsed between the first and the second delegations of Simon of Beit-Aršam. Therefore the second letter must have been written one or two years after the Council of Dowin (506). Was there a second council for this letter? We do not know. However, it is obvious that the decision was made as a sequel to the first letter. In this second letter appear the names of the senior bishop, Meršapuh of Taron, and of the Marzban, Vard Mamikonean. Both of them had been prominent figures in the Council of Dowin. Therefore this decision must be considered as an integral part of the work of the Council of Dowin. In fact, in this second letter we have an extension of the doctrinal position as expressed in the first letter.

This time the Council of Chalcedon was openly condemned, because it had become directly involved in the controversy. Therefore we conclude that in the Council of Dowin (506/8) there is the first official and formal rejection of the Council of Chalcedon by the Armenian Church.

LOOKING FORWARD
Some Conclusions and
Considerations

The decision that was taken in the Council of Dowin in 506/8 under the circumstances which were described in the last chapter, was a beginning and not an end. It was the first step which engaged the Armenian Church in a continuous and strenuous process of doctrinal disputes, ecclesiastical quarrels, and political entanglements of the most difficult and complicated nature. As I have already shown in the Introduction, the Chalcedonian problem became a decisive factor in the whole course of the subsequent history of the Church of Armenia.

Several councils held in Dowin and elsewhere dealt with the same problem in different conditions. The problem itself underwent considerable changes as a result of the development of christological doctrine in the sixth century. New aspects and new ideas emerged and deeply affected theological tradition and ecclesiastical relationships in the sixth, seventh, and eighth centuries.

Thus, in the middle of the sixth century, just at the time when the Chalcedonian problem was still occupying the mind of the Byzantine Empire, particularly under the reign of Justinian (527–65), the Armenians once more rejected the Council of Chalcedon, again in relation to Nestorianism.

In fact, Nersēs of Bagrevand (548–57), while answering an official letter addressed to him by the Syrian Christians in the Persian Empire, and after having consecrated their bishop in the person of Abdišoy, tells them that their faith is in accord with the faith of the Church of Armenia and that his Church also anathe-matizes Nestorius, Diodore (of Tarsus), Theodore (of Mopsuestia), Barsauma, Theodoret (of Cyrus), the Council of Chalcedon, the Tome of Leo, Apollinarius, Eutyches, and Severus (of Antioch) and his corrupt writings.[1]

If the mention of Chalcedon and the Tome of Leo marks a mere reaffirmation of the position of the Armenian Church as adopted in the Council of Dowin (506/8), the inclusion of the name of Severus in the list of heretics brings a new element of great significance for the history of the relationship between the Armenian and Syrian Churches and, particularly, for the under-standing of the doctrinal developments of the christological posi-tion of the Armenian Church.

This new element assumes a greater significance when we realize that the condemnation of Severus is frequently mentioned throughout the sixth century. Even in the beginning of the seventh century, at the time of the controversy between the Armenian and Georgian Churches, we find the name of Severus mentioned again in the list of heretics.[2] As late as in 616 we find him again condemned in the famous doctrinal treatise of Catholi-cos Komitas (615–28).[3]

What are the implications for the Armenian Church of such historical events and doctrinal attitudes or dispositions in relation to doctrinal disputes in the sphere of the internal conflicts of the "Monophysite" section of Eastern Christendom?

E. Ter-Minassiantz and K. Ter-Mkkrtschian have rendered most valuable services in this field by opening new paths of in-vestigation;[4] but their work has not been taken up and con-tinued on the same scholarly lines.

---

[1] See *Book of Letters*, p. 56. It is interesting to note the textual identity between this part of the text (pp. 55–6) and a section of the letter written by the Syrians (p. 53).

[2] *Book of Letters*, p. 138; cf p. 146.

[3] *Book of Letters*, p. 216.

[4] See Ter-Minaseanç, *Armen. Kirche* (Armenian text) pp. 84–135. Ter-Mkrt'-cean, *Seal of Faith*, Introduction, pp. lvii–cvii; cf ibid., *History of the Armenian Church*, Part I, pp. 200–5. Their interpretations of the doctrinal attitude of the

The doctrinal developments of anti-Chalcedonian theological thinking have already drawn the attention of high-ranking scholars—theologians and historians—such as J. Lebon and R. Draguet.[1] But the attention that has been given to the post-Chalcedonian period of history and theology on the Chalcedonian side has been far deeper and greater than the study of the anti-Chalcedonian side. The study of the controversy over the *Three Chapters* and, later, of the Monothelite controversy has revealed interesting aspects in the christological field of Christian theology. Charles Moeller's exhaustive study, *"Le Chalcédonisme et le néo-Chalcédonisme en Orient de 451 à la fin du VIe siècle"*[2] has indicated in a poignant way the importance of post-Chalcedonian theology in the Byzantine tradition. On the other side, J. Lebon and R. Draguet have opened new perspectives in the understanding of the "Monophysite" tradition taken in its Syrian context with the two opposite positions of Severus of Antioch and Julian of Halicarnassus.

But the Armenian tradition has not been subjected to a deep-searching investigation, which would indeed be a task well worth undertaking. There is no doubt that it will be rewarding if it is seriously attempted. Draguet is fully justified when he says in his concluding remarks:

> L'histoire littéraire et doctrinale de la diffusion du Julianisme en Orient ferait à elle seule l'objet d'un nouveau travail; les sources grecques et syriaques y contribueraient beaucoup; la doctrine julianiste intéressant d'une façon toute spéciale l'histoire de l'Église d'Arménie, il faudrait accorder une attention particulière aux productions de la littérature théologique arménienne.[3]

Indeed, the purely theological parts of the Armenian literature of the sixth, seventh, and eighth centuries include most interesting

---

Armenian Church with regard to Severian and Julianist christological doctrines vary and even clash at a certain point. Whereas for Ter-Minassiantz the Armenians have been completely inclined towards Julianism, for Ter-Mkkrtschian that interpretation is an exaggeration which needs to be balanced.

[1] See *Bibliography*.   [2] See *Bibliography*.

[3] Draguet, *Julien d'Halicarnasse*, p. 260, Louvain, 1924.

pages concerning the later developments of the christological doctrines held by the "Monophysites". I have already mentioned some authors in the Introduction. And, in fact, what I have attempted to do in this present study is to take a first step which may lead to a series of studies dealing with the subsequent history and theology of the Armenian Church, a subject that has a value extending beyond the limits of a national Church to reach an ecumenical dimension worthy of special consideration both for historical reasons and for present-day needs.

At this juncture, I touch upon a most delicate point: the actual significance of this study and related investigations in the literature and history of the post-Chalcedonian period.

At present, thanks to the spirit of open-mindedness, sincere and fresh scholarly inquiries, and common studies aiming at a mutual understanding as fostered by the Ecumenical Movement, the prospect of a *rapprochement* between the Chalcedonian and non-Chalcedonian Churches is returning to the minds of theologians and Church leaders. The post-Chalcedonian centuries have shown most convincingly that orthodoxy, as a living faith being witnessed by the life of the Church, was maintained equally in both the Chalcedonian and the non-Chalcedonian Churches. In other words, the Christian faith was truly made manifest through such life and work which never impaired nor eclipsed the teachings of Christ. On the contrary, we realize more and more clearly how the integrity and purity of the Christian faith was constantly expressed through the whole sacramental life of the Church on both sides, in the Churches which accept Chalcedon and its formulations and in the Churches which reject the Council of Chalcedon but have other ways of expressing the same incarnational faith.

I have already indicated the significance of the Chalcedonian problem for our actual ecumenical encounter in an article which deals with the post-Chalcedonian interpretations of Chalcedon and with the various attempts at reconsideration and revaluation of the Chalcedonian problem in an ecumenical perspective.[1] There is no doubt that studies of this nature and scope will contribute towards the *rapprochement* of the two groups of Churches of the Eastern Orthodox tradition.

History tells us most eloquently how disastrous have been the consequences of the division of Eastern Churches because of the Council of Chalcedon and other related factors of a non-theological nature. Isolation has resulted in hard, staunch, exclusive, unyielding attitudes which have led to the dislocation and the decomposition of the Eastern Christian world and have impaired its integrity and solidarity. Generally speaking in the past, polemics have dominated the relationship between the two groups of Churches. The self-defensive, self-justifying tendency and method, with the natural implication of mutual condemnation, have prevailed in the conversations that have taken place. Fresh attempts at a deeper understanding of each other's positions as expressed in the post-Chalcedonian theological tradition may greatly help us in our search for the recovery of the unity of the Eastern Churches.

That vision constitutes one of the major factors in this study, and that same vision must be, I believe, a driving force in all studies which may follow along the same lines.

[1] Vardapet K. Sarkissian, "The Ecumenical Problem in Eastern Christendom", See *Ecumenical Review*, vol. xii, no. 4, July 1960, pp. 436–54.

ADDITIONAL NOTES

1

As it appears from the Acts themselves, one of the most significant aspects of the Council was the continuously and repeatedly emphasized association of Leo with Cyril. There are several places where this constant tendency can clearly be seen, namely to identify the christological views of Cyril with those set forth in the Tome.

Not only did the letters of Cyril to Nestorius and to John of Antioch precede the reading of the Tome, but also—and especially—in any case of ambiguity in expression, unfamiliarity of formulation, or suspicion of unorthdoxy in the Tome, the only authority brought for approval of the passages concerned was always Cyril.

Thus, for example, for the three main passages in the Tome which seemed to the bishops of Palestine and Illyricum unorthodox, the assurance of orthodoxy came from parallel citations from Cyril. Those passages were:

(a) "Et ad resolvendum conditionis nostrae debitum natura inviolabilis naturae est unita passibili, ut, quod nostris remediis congruebat, unus atque idem mediator Dei et hominum, homo Iesus Christus, et mori posset ex uno et mori non posset ex altero" (*Tome*, sect. iii; Bindly, *Ecum. Docum.*, p. 169).

The assurance of the orthodoxy of this passage was found in a citation from Cyril's letter to Nestorius: "Since his own body did, as Paul says, by the grace of God taste death for every man (Heb. 2.9), he himself is said to have suffered death in his own nature since it would be madness to say or think this, but because, as I have just said, it was his flesh that tasted death" (see Sellers, *Chalcedon*, p. 246).

(b) "Agit enim utraque forma cum alterius communione quod proprium est; Verbo scilicet operante quod Verbi est, et carne exsequente quod carnis est. Unum horum coruscat miraculis, aliud succumbit iniuriis" (*Tome*, sect. iv; Bindley, p. 170).

The parallel quotation from Cyril was brought again by Aëtius,

219

the archdeacon of Constantinople, from the letter of Cyril to Acacius of Melitene: "There are some sayings which are in the highest degree God-befitting; others befit manhood; and others there are which, as it were, hold a middle rank, demonstrating that the Son of God is at once God and man" (Sellers, p. 247).

(c) "Quamvis enim in Domino Iesu Christo Dei et hominis una persona sit, aliud tamen est unde in utroque communis est contumelia, aliud unde communis est gloria. De nostro enim illi est minor Patre humanitas; de Patre illi est aequalis cum Patre divinitas" (*Tome*, sect. iv; Bindley, p. 171).

The answer to the objection to this passage was taken again from Cyril—from his *Scolia de Incarnatione*—brought by Theodoret, the staunch opponent of Cyril: "He became man and did not change his properties, for he remained what he was; for it is assuredly understood that it is one thing which is dwelling in another thing, that is the divine nature in manhood" (see Sellers, p. 248).

The question now arises: Why was Cyril thus being taken as the reliable authority in matters of orthodox christology? The straightforward answer would be that Cyril was the dominant figure in Christian thought for Eastern Orthodox Christians of the time, and his teaching had become somewhat the standard christology by which any statement on christology had to be judged in order to meet their understanding and find approval. Therefore, no one could disregard him if he had to be intelligible to the Eastern theologians. In fact, Cyril had become the highest authority, the most difficult to refute for his opponents, and the most venerated to rely on for his supporters (see Duchesne, *Sep. Churches*, pp. 23 ff; Idem, *Hist. Church*, vol. iii, pp. 302–3, 308–9; Prestige, *Fathers and Heretics*, pp. 150 ff; Bardy, *Chalcédoine*, pp. 272 ff).

What is singularly important here and which is so often overlooked is that in the Council of Chalcedon the authority of Cyril was used as a shield. His name was reverently mentioned, expressions from his letters were quoted, but all that did not in fact coincide with a real, full recognition of the ethos of his christological doctrine. In fact, the passages extracted from his letters in support of Leo's Tome were totally cut off from the general context of his thought. The leaders of the Council of Chalcedon used his name and his reputation only to allay minds disturbed or disquietened by the new language of the Tome or

to assure others of the preservation of their loyalty to the traditional
Cyrilline christology. The homage paid to Cyril at Chalcedon never
went deep enough to meet the true essence of his christology. Rather it
was a purely formal act necessitated by the circumstances, unavoidable
as they were at the time of Chalcedon; a time when, in the words
of Evagrius, Cyril was "lauded and proclaimed to the world as the
sonorous herald and mighty champion of true doctrine" (i, 7, Eng.
tr., p. 14).

The post-Chalcedonian history shows this more clearly. In fact, the
later attempts made towards the reconciliation of the opponents of the
Council of Chalcedon had Cyril's thought at the centre of the things
that were taken into consideration. It was strongly felt that Chalcedon
had to be understood in terms of Cyrilline christology if it was to survive the criticisms of its opponents and secure its place in the orthodox
doctrinal formulations of the Church. The second council of Constantinople is the culmination of this process. "Aux alentours de 553, sous
peine de crime et d'apostasie, on devra admettre toute l'œuvre de
Cyrille, *y compris sa partie la plus personnelle et la plus discutée*, les *Anathématismes.* Rome ignora ceux-ci jusqu'en 519; l'union de 433 n'en
soufflait mot; le concile de Chalcédoine approuva le Cyrille de l'union
de 433, en gardant un silence prudent sur l'autre aspect de la termin-
ologie du patriarche. En 533, la situation est renversée. Si la christologie s'allégea peut-être ainsi de certaines richesses de la tradition, il
ne faut pas oublier cependant que ces *Anathématismes* entreront peu à
peu dans l'usage du magistère ordinaire de l'Église, tel qu'il se reflète
dans l'usage commun des théologiens" (Moeller, *Néo-Chalcédonisme*,
pp. 644–5; cf p. 647; see also Richard, *Néo-Chalcédonisme*, p. 158).

This is by no means a minor detail in pointing to the defective side
of the attitude of Chalcedon to the real Cyril. As Kidd has said: "It
(Chalcedon) ignored the real Cyril" (*Hist. Church,* vol. iii, p. 395). Or,
as Mgr Duchesne had already remarked in more explicit terms: "In
fine, Cyril, the true Cyril had been sacrificed to Leo" (*Hist. Church,*
p. 317). In Duchesne's view there is no case of synthesis in Chalcedon.
Thus, after outlining the central feature of Cyril's thought as compared
with the Dyophysite teaching of a Theodore of Mopsuestia, he concludes: "À Chalcédoine on avait fait la police de la théologie; on n'avait
pas fait l'union des cœurs; car les cœurs, les vrais cœurs, ne sont contents que quand ils sont assouvis" (*Autonomies,* p. 40). Then, commenting on the Roman side of the question, he adds: "Rome est le lieu du

gouvernement, non la patrie de la théologie ou le paradis de la mystique. ... L'instrument diplomatique de Chalcédoine, lequel n'était d'ailleurs qu'une version grecque d'une lettre latine de saint Léon, fut élevé à la situation de *regula fidei*" (ibid., p. 40). In order to complete the presentation of Duchesne's view we must quote him also for the later history of Chalcedon: "Trente ans après le concile de Chalcédoine il lui fallut songer à faire retraite en bon ordre, à sauver sa face, comme disent les Chinois. À cet effet fut inventé l'Hénotique, édit impérial adressé aux Égyptiens, en 482; on y canonisait les formules les plus aisées de saint Cyrille et l'on déclarait répudier tout ce qui avait pu se dire ou se faire en sens contraire, à Chalcédoine ou ailleurs.

"C'était au fond l'abandon du concile et du 'tome' de saint Léon, abandon dissimulé, enveloppé dans un silence habile, que l'on pouvait, avec quelque bonne volonté, qualifier de respectueux" (ibid., p. 41. See also pp. 42, 43–7).

Recent attempts to reassert the identity of views between Cyril and Leo usually miss the point: to see the thought of Cyril in its integrity. They dwell on particular passages, isolated from the general context of his thought. These passages—how different they are often in their general tone!—cannot reveal the true Cyril (see for example, the article of Galtier, *Cyrille et Léon à Chalcédoine*). Moeller sees different Cyrils in one Cyril, such as "the Cyril of the *Twelve Anathematisms*", "the Cyril of the Reunion Act", etc. The Cyril recognized in Chalcedon is for him the Cyril of the Reunion Act of 433 and not the Cyril of the Anathematisms (see *Néo-Chalcédonisme*, pp. 659–60). This in itself is a genuine way of solving the problem; but I doubt whether the Church Fathers themselves made such distinctions in their understanding of Cyril's thought. Secondly, this way leads us to think that Cyril was not able to maintain a unity of thought in his christological system. We think that the core of Cyril's christology was that which was sanctioned in the Council of Ephesus and was embodied in the Anathematisms and exposed in various ways in his writings. The variety of formulas in his terminology or differences of emphasis point to the richness of his thought and to the wisdom of his use of language in avoiding clashes or securing peace. In fact, he never compromised on the basic principles of his teaching. It is not, therefore, legitimate to show in him such distinct aspects. The unity and consistency of his thought cannot allow such an approach to him as a theologian.

We still think that the Council of Chalcedon disregarded the real

Cyril by giving full recognition to the Tome of Leo which revealed such close associations with Antiochene christology, as we shall see later. What was said by J. Labourt, the first great historian of the Nestorian Church, more than fifty years ago remains true for us, even being confirmed by the results of new researches. Having related the story of the second council of Ephesus (449) and the subsequent troubles, he says: "Le concile de Chalcédoine remit toutes choses en ordre. C'est une question longuement controversée de savoir en quel sens furent prises les décisions dogmatiques de cette assemblée. M. Harnack (Dogmengeschichte, p. 368) a pensé que la majorité avait entendu se prononcer dans le sens de saint Cyrille et du premier concile d'Éphèse. Nous ne pouvons souscrire à ce jugement. Que la majorité fût attaché à l'opinion cyrillienne et même au monophysisme, nous n'y contredirons pas. L'évènement le montra bien. Mais qu'elle se soit déclarée en faveur des opinions qu'elle professait, c'est ce que nous ne saurions admettre" (Christ. Perse, pp. 257–8). On the contrary "La majorité a adhéré au 'tome' de Léon sur l'invitation des commissaires impériaux, quoi qu'aient pu penser et dire Anatolius de Constantinople et ses partisans. Or, le 'tome' de Léon condamne Nestorius au même titre qu'Eutychès et prescrit l'adhésion au θεοτόκος; mais sa christologie est aussi nettement dyophysite que la christologie antiochienne: elle l'est presque d'avantage" (ibid., p. 258).

In a word, Cyril was not accepted officially by the Council of Chalcedon through a genuine recognition of his christology as a whole.

2

There are some other people also who are involved in this story of Maštoc's journey to East Syria.

The one whose name is not mentioned by Koriwn and whom Maštoc met was the bishop of Samosata. Koriwn writes: "[Maštoc] leaving the holy bishop [of Edessa] came with his assistants to the city of Samosata, where he was honoured by the most honourable bishop himself and by the Church" (p. 48). As Peeters has tried to show (See Origines, pp. 209–10; cf Idem, Jérémie, p. 18), the bishop of Samosata at the beginning of the fifth century was none other than Andrew, who later played a prominent part in the Nestorian controversy. He was one of the most ardent and uncompromising supporters of Nestorius' cause after his condemnation at Ephesus and even after the reconciliation of Cyril of Alexandria and John of Antioch by the Reunion Act of 433.

If, indeed, he was the bishop of Samosata when Maštoç visited the city then this may provide us with another hint to the relation of Maštoç with the Antiochene Christian tradition.

The other persons whom Maštoç met during his journey and whose names are mentioned by Koriwn were Acacius of Amida, Babilas of Edessa, and Rufinus in Samosata.

Acacius was most probably the bishop of Amid who played a considerable rôle in the life of the Persian Church. (See Labourt, *Christ. Perse*, pp. 89, 93, 101, 122; cf Nau, *Acace*, col. 244). We do not know anything about his doctrinal position but presumably he was under the influence of the theological tradition of Antioch (see Peeters, *Jérémie*, pp. 17–18).

Babilas is a problematic name. There is no person by this name to be found on the episcopal throne of Edessa. Therefore the great majority of scholars agree in identifying him with the famous Rabboula of Edessa, suggesting that the Armenian word *Babilas* is a wrong transcription of *Rabulas* which must have been in the original text of Koriwn.

But here is a stumbling-block which has not been noticed by some of these scholars. If Rabboula is the person referred to, then Maštoç's journey cannot have taken place before 412, because Rabboula became the bishop of Edessa only after 412 and remained in his episcopal see until 436 (see Peeters, *Rabboula*, p. 202; cf Hayes, *École d'Édesse*, pp. 173–8). On the other hand, the chronological data given by Koriwn (see pp. 44–50, also pp. 98–100), in itself a very confused chronology, puts the journey earlier than 412 and according to various interpretations and calculations by scholars it is fixed as 404/5 (Ormanean, *Azgapatum*, col. 272, 276–7), 406/8 (Akinean, *Armenian Alphabet*, col. 512), 392/3 (Manandean, *Crit. Hist.*, pp. 265–6). Thus, seeing the chronological difficulty in the identification of Babilas as Rabboulas, Akinean suggests that *Babilas* is not a wrong transcription of *Rabulas* but of *Bakidas*. And indeed, there is a bishop by the name of Pakïda or Pēquidā in the episcopal see of Edessa in the period between 398 and 409 (see Duval, *Histoire d'Édesse*, pp. 138, 150; cf Labourt, *Christ. Perse*, p. 93). This suggestion, made for the first time by H. Thorossian as Akinean says (I have not seen the articles of Thorossian which have been published in *Bazmavēp*), is more likely. But if we take the date as fixed by Manandean, 392/3, then this identification also becomes untenable. And, indeed, there are good reasons for taking seriously the dating of Manandean (see his article *Armenian Alphabet*; cf Tallon, *Livre des Lettres*, pp. 21–2). Again, the hypothesis of Maštoc's meeting and friendship with Ibas during this journey and other identifications and conclusions referred to have to be taken cautiously.

Here we cannot embark on the most complicated problem of the date of Maštoc's journey. It would take us far from our immediate purpose. It is a theme to be dealt with independently and at some considerable length. But it seems to us that Maštoc might have made more than one journey to East Syria, and the present confusion in Koriwn's and other historians' accounts might have arisen out of confounding or combining those journeys.

Thus, having shown how unsettled the problem is, it seems to us that the cautious approach to the interpretation of the significance of Maštoc's journey is the safest way of not falling into sheer speculation or into exaggerated conclusions.

3

On the one hand, Movsēs Xorenaci says that Sahak was not received by the local authorities with due respect. Therefore, he sent Maštoc and Vardan to the Emperor. Here (iii, 57) Xorenaci produces copies of letters exchanged between Sahak, the Emperor Theodosius II, Atticus, Patriarch of Constantinople, and Anatolius, Governor of the eastern provinces of the Byzantine Empire. The authenticity of these letters has been rightly suspected and almost unanimously rejected by scholars. But the correspondence itself reflects the difficulties and bears witness to the general atmosphere of the ecclesiastical affairs of the time.

In these letters, Theodosius and Atticus let Sahak know their discontent at his having betrayed the tradition of his fathers by turning to the side of the Syrians for help in the invention of the Armenian alphabet. But now that relations have been restored they tell him that they were satisfied by knowing that it was by the help of God that the Armenian alphabet was invented (they refer to the episode of miracle in the invention of the Armenian alphabet which is related in Koriwn and Xorenaci)—and not by that of the Syrians!

Here we have a clear reflection of the internal conflict between the two elements in Armenian Christianity. The tide was now turning, for a short time, as we shall see, in favour of the Hellenophile section.

On the other hand, Koriwn relates the story of Maštoc's visit to Byzantine Armenia and to Constantinople without reference to any difficulty or any oppsiotion from the authorities in the Byzantine section. It is more than probable that Koriwn in his hagiographical representation of Maštoc̣'s life, shows his hero always and everywhere hailed with praise, admiration, and devotion, and consequently discards any reference to opposition or antagonism. This must be the reason why he tells us that Maštoc̣ was received with honour by the bishops, princes, and especially by Anatolius the Governor. One would tend to question Koriwn's sincerity on this point. If, indeed, Maštoc̣ was hailed with such sympathy and honour, as Koriwn wants us to believe, why then did he go to Constantinople when his work in the Byzantine section was so urgently needed? We must remember that Koriwn writes as a hagiographer rather than as a historian, this term being understood in the sense in which it can be applied to characterize Xorenac̣i as a writer. For Koriwn, Maštoc̣ is the hero, the saint.

4

Again, P. Peeters exaggerates in his interpretation of the situation in the Armenian Church. First, speaking of the Church in Persia, he says: "Non seulement l'épiscopat de Perse n'a pris aucune part active aux controverses d'Éphèse, mais sur le moment il n'y a prêté aucune attention. Le bruit de ces batailles théologiques n'a guère dépassé l'Euphrate, et les derniers échos s'en sont perdus dans le désert de Syrie. Une année, sinon d'avantage, après le concile, Ibas d'Édesse juge nécessaire d'alerter ses amis de Perse. Sa fameuse lettre à Mari de Beit-Ardašir entre dans un exposé rétrospectif, qui remonte au déluge. Tout ce détail était complètement oiseux pour un lecteur, instruit de la querelle dont l'Église grecque retentissait depuis trois ans." Then, turning to the Armenians, he adds: "En Arménie l'ignorance ne pouvait être plus complète; mais elle a duré plus longtemps. Plusieurs années (sic) après 431, on n'y connaissait même pas les canons d'Éphèse. Ce fut un détachement de 'traducteurs' qui les y rapporta de Constantinople, au retour de la troisième expédition organisée par le patriarche S. Sahak. Koriwn l'affirme expressément dans la Vie de S. Mesrop, et il en parle de bon escient puisqu'il avait lui-même été attaché à cette mission. On verra plus loin, par d'autres témoignages et par celui de Koriwn lui-même, que les condamnations prononcées à Éphèse furent d'abord accueillies chez les Arméniens avec une indifférence qui ressemble à de l'incompréhension" (Jérémie, pp. 15-16).

If the canons were not received by the leaders of the Armenian

Church that does not necessarily mean that the news of the Council of Ephesus had not reached them. Otherwise, the whole correspondence between Acacius and Sahak—here the Council is explicitly mentioned and its decisions discussed—remains unexplained. Secondly, now we have a document which is a fragment of a letter written by Eznik from Constantinople and addressed to his teacher, Maštoç, in Armenia immediately after the Council of Ephesus, in which the disciple of Maštoç gives a brief account of the christological disputes which had taken place in the imperial city and elsewhere in the Empire. The fragment has been preserved in the *Seal of Faith* (see p. 130). Here I quote it in French translation by Tallon: "Pour ce qui est de la stabilité des Églises qu'un vent d'erreur levé à l'improviste a cru ébranlée, grâce aux prières que tu as adressées au Dieu de sainteté, le calme s'est fait. Tous les évêques des Romains se sont mis d'accord pour tenir fermement la foi primitive, celle des trois cents Pères, et par anathème ils ont interdit qu'on osât proposer je ne sais quelle foi d'origine étrangère et de fraîche date; mais ils ont ordonné, sur cette même foi, de bâtir, et à la même fois, de l'enseigner. Ils se sont mis d'accord pour confesser le Christ comme vrai Dieu, Fils de Dieu, Monogène, né du Père avant toutes les créatures, et Seigneur créateur de toutes choses; et pour confesser que ce même Dieu Verbe, à la fin des temps, à chair revêtue, s'est fait homme pour nous sans subir, à partir de son identité divine, ni conversion, ni déchéance, ni destruction; et que, Dieu, en sa naissance de la Vierge, il est homme parfait selon la naissance charnelle; que la Vierge est nommée et est réellement Mère du Seigneur et Mère de Dieu; que celui qui est Dieu parfait est dit homme parfait parcequ'il est parfait en ses membres et (comme Dieu parfait) il a doté d'une âme sa chair sainte, et non comme homme . . ." (*Livre des Lettres*, pp. 52–3).

In view of this evidence (cf Xorenaçi, bk. iii, ch. 61) which has escaped the attention of Peeters, it is more reasonable to think that after the Council of Ephesus when both Nestorius and Cyril were condemned, and the Emperor was trying to find a way out of the dilemma in which he was put by this bitter conflict of two strong sections in the Church in Constantinople, responsible people in the Church were much more occupied in trying to secure a unity first among themselves or to establish their respective positions than to send copies of the canons to individual Churches.

This fluid and unsettled state could have been the only reason for the delay in sending the canons or informing the Armenian Church officially. But for the news of the Council there was no reason why they should not have reached Armenia. The students were not late in coming back to Armenia and bringing the canons.

5

Tallon sees here a later interpolation. He says that in the original text Nestorius must have been meant here and not Theodore (see *Livre des Lettres*, p. 31, n. 1). But I think there is no need to imagine an interpolation to understand Nestorius as being referred to. This passage in which special reference is made to, and a characteristic emphasis is put on, "the writing on the Incarnation" is quite revealing. Obviously, this is a reference to Theodore's *De Incarnatione* which became such a controversial document in the later disputes of the Three Chapters. As Richard says: "Des ouvrages de Théodore de Mopsueste, celui qui a valu le plus de reproches est sans contredit son traité sur l'Incarnation" (*Fragments*, p. 55; cf Devreesse, *Essai*, pp. 44–8).

The only difficulty in understanding the reference of Acacius to Theodore and not to Nestorius is his second assertion in the passage where he says that the bishops at Ephesus decreed that the books should be destroyed. Certainly that was a measure taken against Nestorius' writings. The difficulty can be removed only if we understand this reference as being Acacius' own interpretation of the Council's decision. Thus he, on his own responsibility, must have extended the decision to be applied, legitimately in his own view, to the writings of Nestorius' teacher. That was very natural. What difference could there be between Theodore and Nestorius? And as the problem here was concerned with the writings of Theodore so the decisions of the Council of Ephesus on Nestorius' writings could be applied to those of Theodore as well.

Richard also has reached this conclusion: "Voilà donc comment notre évêque (i.e. Acacius) apprit que Théodore et Nestorius étaient à mettre dans le même panier et que le concile d'Éphèse, en condemnant au feu les écrits du second, avait implicitement voué au même sort ceux de son maître en hérésie. C'est, somme toute, ce qui ressort, quoique un peu confusément, de sa lettre à son collègue arménien" (*Acace*, p. 405).

6

In fact, Dom B. Mercier and Tallon translate it *Diodore* and Richard comments on this translation. But I think there are good reasons to substantiate my translation.

(*a*) The words *Tʻēodor* and *Diodor* are so similar in writing that the change from one to another is very easy. For example, in Koriwn's text we have *Tʻēodios* (Theodius) for *Tʻēodor* (Theodore). In the *Book of Letters* itself, in Sahak's answer to Proclus' letter Theodore's name is mentioned as *Diodor* (Diodore)—see *Erratum*. Of course this is a mistake of the copyist of the manuscript and proves that the similarity of the two names in Armenian is an open danger for such confusion.

(*b*) As all these letters are closely interrelated and have the writings of Theodore at the centre as the common subject, Diodore's case is not likely to find its proper place in them. It is a discordant note.

(*c*) In all the other sources on the same problem, namely the treatise of Innocentius Maroniae and the letter of the two Armenian priests, there is no allusion at all to Diodore. All speak of Theodore alone, as we shall see. Moreover, the Armenian sources—Koriwn and Xorenaçi —are completely silent over the name of Diodore and have instead Theodore. The whole controversy was about Theodore and Nestorius.

(*d*) We have also internal evidence in the letter itself. The association of Nestorius and Theodore, expressed very characteristically, is much more relevant and is in complete accordance with the other sources than the association of Nestorius and Diodore.

With all these considerations we think that we are justified in translating *Diodor* as Theodore.

7

M. Richard argues categorically against the sincerity of the presentation of the facts by Innocentius. He says: "Le récit d'Innocent ne mérite d'ailleurs que peu de confiance. À l'en croire il faudrait rejeter après le décret impérial du 3 août 435 contre Nestorius la diffusion des écrits de Théodore qui aurait provoqué l'intervention de Rabboula et d'Acace en Arménie. Nos documents contredisent absolument cette tentative de justifier par une manœuvre déloyale des Nestoriens le déclenchement de la campagne contre Théodore. Les écrits de ce dernier étaient tout de même autre chose qu'un succédané des homélies de Nestorius" (*Acace*, p. 409, n. 1).

That Innocentius' account is not completely accurate is not doubted. At least, there is a striking chronological anachronism between the condemnation of Nestorius' writings by an imperial decree (435) and the beginning of the anti-Theodorean campaign in 432. But this can be easily understood if we take into account the fact that Innocentius had no intention of presenting an historical event as such, but rather a theological issue. In other words, Innocentius was not concerned with the details of the chronological order. Therefore, he did not care about the dates or other minor details. He presented the story in its broad lines. However questionable may be the details of his historical account, there can be no doubt about the basic fact he reported: the anti-Theodorean campaign started because the Nestorians took and used Theodore's writings as a vehicle of propaganda. Whether Theodore's works are not really a substitute for Nestorius' homilies, that problem has to be distinguished from the interpretation of Theodore's doctrine by both the Nestorians and the anti-Nestorians of the time. To both sides he was the "Teacher of Nestorius". Otherwise Rabboula and Acacius would have had no reason, not even any pretext, to attack Theodore. If personal feelings had something to do with their theological attitude to Theodore's writings, they would not have had the chance of opposing them if these latter had not been taken as a shelter for Nestorian teaching. Therefore on this basic point Innocentius is not wrong.

Furthermore, Innocentius' account is supported by the letter of the two Armenian priests. Again, it is significant to note that the Armenian sources—Koriwn and Xorenaçi—present the beginning of the controversy in the same way as Innocentius. I suppose that Richard has not seen the testimonies of the Armenian historiographers.

8

One might even think that Rabboula might have thought that Acacius was in a better position than himself to carry on this task since at that time Armenia's relations with Melitene were very friendly and could give Acacius the opportunity of an intervention with hopeful prospects.

That Rabboula is not disassociated from this intervention may be accepted on the ground that the two Armenian priests in their letter to Proclus mention his name together with that of Acacius. Innocentius also confirms this.

What had been his own part in this intervention? We do not know precisely. Did he himself write to the Armenians as the letter of the two

Armenian priests suggests? We do not think so, because if he had written, his letter would have been preserved together with those of Acacius. He might have taken part in the intervention through the directives he gave to Acacius, as Richard also tends to think. Perhaps Koriwn's rather vague expression—"bishops assembled in synod"—implies a reference to Rabboula as well.

There is a third person who is said to have written to St Sahak and St Maštoc. He was the famous Cyril of Alexandria (see Xorenaci, bk. iii, ch. 61). If, indeed, Cyril had written directly to Sahak and Maštoc his letter would have been preserved and held in higher esteem than those of Acacius. We think that Xorenaci's reference to Cyril may be understood as a reference to his correspondence with Rabboula and Acacius and, at the same time, to the part he played in the story of Proclus' Tome to the Armenians. At any rate, it could be interpreted only as a very general reference to Cyril's part rather than a direct correspondence with Sahak and Maštoc.

9

The identity of these three priests is difficult to establish. Their mission is again obscure. Tallon suggests that they were three Syrian priests. He deduces their nationality from their names: Hon, Koth, and Anjn, without, making it clear who or why these names are only they were Syriac. He goes as far as to say "à titre d'hypothèse", that they were three Syrian priests sent by Rabboula to inspect the situation in Armenia (see *Livre des Lettres*, pp. 25–6).

There is no evidence whatsoever to support this hypothesis. On the contrary, there are many objections to it. Thus, why did they come to report to Acacius if they were sent by Rabboula? If Rabboula was so directly involved in the problems of the Armenian Church he would have dealt with it personally. Secondly, if these priests came into contact with the Iranophile princes and Syrophile bishops, as Tallon suggests, then, again, it is unlikely that these people would follow the advice of a Rabboula or an Acacius, because these princes sympathized with the Persian policy, which favoured Nestorian expansion in the Persian Empire. Thirdly, from Acacius' letter itself it is clear that these three people were connected with him personally. He calls them "our beloved priests".

10

N. Adontz has seen in the answer-letter of Sahak to Proclus a later fabrication. The person who did it must have taken Sahak's letter addressed to Acacius, reproduced it with only slight elaborations, and represented it as the answer of Sahak and Maštoc̣ to Proclus (see *Maštoc̣*, pp. 25–7).

There is no doubt that textual alterations were made in Proclus' Tome, as we shall see and try to explain. But we have no grounds to suppose that the letter of Sahak to Proclus is anything more than purely a later invention. Why would people think of an answer if there had been no answer? Adontz ignores this question altogether. It seems to us more likely that Sahak himself wrote this letter, and since the theme of Proclus' letter was the same as that of Acacius' he did not deem it wrong to give the same answer with some additions made for the clarification of the doctrine of the Armenian Church.

M. Richard, in his turn, has imagined for Sahak a very complicated way of answering Proclus' letter. He thinks that Sahak was not a good Hellenist and, therefore, having no one in his entourage who knew Greek better than himself, took up his letter to Acacius and answered Proclus in similar if not identical terms (see *Acace*, pp. 407–9). His argument is very weak indeed. In fact, we know from the testimonies of the Armenian historians of the fifth century that Sahak was the greatest Hellenist of his time, and only with that mastery of Greek was he able to direct the translations of the Holy Scriptures and the Church Fathers so successfully. Therefore for Sahak to write a letter in Greek was not as difficult a task as Richard supposes.

11

The case of the authorship of these homilies is a complicated problem. Traditionally they have been recognized as the homilies of John Mandakuni. They were published in Venice under the name of Mandakuni. B. Sargisean made a detailed study of them without raising any doubt concerning the authenticity of the authorship (see *Mandakuni*, Venice, 1895).

For the first time, K. Tēr-Mkrtč'ean noticed that in many manuscripts of the Collection of Ejmiacin they had been copied under the name of John Mayragomec̣i, a seventh-century Armenian author and an ardent controversialist engaged in the controversy over the corruptibility or incorruptibility of Christ's human body. Having studied the manuscript tradition of these homilies and having carefully investigated the historical evidence on Mayragomeçi's life and work, Tēr-Mkrtč'ean came to the definite conclusion that the author of these homilies was not Mandakuni but Mayragomeçi. The transference of the authorship from the latter to the former must be explained by the doctrinal position of Mayragomeçi and the dislike which surrounded his memory (see *Mandakuni*, pp. 94–5, 99–100).

Tēr-Mkrtč'ean's arguments seem to be well founded. But still many historians of Armenian literature place this work under the name of Mandakuni. They all mention that the authorship has been questioned by Tēr-Mkrtč'ean but they do not take the step of replacing the name of Mandakuni with that of Mayragomeçi.

However, this is not our justification for including this work in our survey. The homily that we take into account has not been found under the name of Mayragomeçi (see Tēr-Mkrtč'ean, *Mandakuni*, p. 94). It is impossible to think that a man like Mayragomeçi who was so zealously and violently engaged in the most complicated problems of christology could have written this homily, which has nothing in it to reveal his mind and to reflect the theological milieu in which he lived. Therefore it is most likely that this homily was the work of Mandakuni as it stands in the printed edition. Its authorship has not been challenged in any manuscript.

12

Barhébraeus gives the following information about Simon of Beit-Aršam which is worth quoting, because his coming to Armenia is mentioned explicitly: "Erat autem per id tempus presbyter quidam, Simeon nomine, ex Beth-Aršam, pago juxta Seleuciam sito, vir orthodoxus. Hic cum regis Cavadis consilium comperisset, erum adiit, jussionemque ab eo obtinuit ut totam terram Sennaar et Persidem universam perlustraret, atque orthodoxos animaret ad libere conventus suos congregandos, impetumque Nestorianorum a se retundendum. Haec ita ille peregit. Quacunque autem transibat, chirographa accepit a Graecis, Armenis Syrisque, se nempe a Nestorii dogmate esse alienos. Porro haec scripta detulit ad regem, qui eadem sigillis suis regiis confirmavit. Et appellata sunt codices confessionis et reposita Tagriti, quae urbs sola Barsumae corruptionem evaserat". (*Chronicon Ecclesiasticon*, vol. iii, col. 86).

Michael Syrus in his turn confirms this testimony. He says: "À cet époque vivait Siméon le Perse surnommé le Disputateur, évêque de Beit Aršam, solide dans la foi, versé dans les Écritures, et adonné aux controverses même avant son épiscopat. C'est pourquoi les Nestoriens, les Manichéens et les Marcionites de Perse tremblaient même devant son nom. Il circulait et visitait les Chrétiens" (Chronique, vol. ii, p. 165; cf pp. 166 ff.)

See also Labourt, Christ. Perse, p. 158, n. 1; cf Duval, Litt. Syr., pp. 148–52; Chabot, Litt. Syr., p. 69; Duchesne, Eglise VIe. siecle, pp. 311–12.

13

These two names are most problematic. Whom are we to see behind them?

N. Adontz has suggested that Ampelis was Timothy Aelurus and Anatolis, who is mentioned next to him, was none other than Timothy's brother, who accompanied him in his exile to Cherson.

K. Tēr-Mkrtč'ean after refuting Adontz's view (Adontz's view was made available to me through Tēr-Mkrtč'ean's criticism. I have not seen his article in Christ. Vostok, 1913, pp. 175–86) suggests on his part that Amphilochius of Side could have been the person to whom this reference is made. In fact, he was one of those bishops who in 457 wrote to Emperor Leo I saying that they did not approve of the Council of Chalcedon (see Lightfoot, Amphilochius; Janin, Amphiloque). Only a few lines have survived of his letter (see P.G., t. 77, col. 1515–16). Tēr-Mkrtč'ean's suggestion is that it could be this letter which is mentioned here, in our document.

Inglizean agrees with Tēr-Mkrtč'ean in identifying Ampelis with Amphilochius (see Arm. Kirche, pp. 367–8, n. 27).

There are real objections to both views. First of all, a common objection to both of them is that neither Timothy, nor Anatolis, nor Amphilochius could have added Zeno's Henoticon to the letter mentioned in our document. All three had already died before the publication of the Henoticon.

The identification with Timothy, although an attractive view, raises this problem: why do the two names Ampelis = Timothy differ so much?

On the other hand, the identification with Amphilochius raises more than one problem. Thus, the mention of the city of Cherson

makes it very difficult to accept that identification. In fact, Amphilochius was the bishop of Side in Pamphylia, whereas Cherson is in the
Crimea. In our document Cherson is mentioned twice and leaves no
room for false transliteration. Secondly, the name Ampelis is not necessarily Amphilochius, because this latter has been translated into Armenian as *Amp'iłok'ēs* (see Timothy, *Refutation*, p. 32, referring to
Amphilochius of Iconium). Thirdly, Amphilochius of Side never had
such a great reputation or enjoyed such a high authority among the
Monophysites. To make his letter a document for proving the orthodoxy of the christological doctrine of the Armenian or Syrian Church is
not natural, or, to be more precise, does not sound very reasonable.
For Timothy Aelurus this objection cannot be raised. Moreover, the
list of the Church Fathers quoted in this document shows clearly some
direct connection with Timothy's work. Again, another hint which
makes the identification of Ampelis with Timothy more likely is that
the priest mentioned here as "Anatolis the priest" is exactly the expression used for his brother by Timothy himself in his *Refutation*.
Thus, referring to the second Council of Ephesus (449), Timothy says
that he was present there together with his blessed brother "Anatolius
the priest" (see p. 35). But how are we to explain then the expression
"Anatolis *of Constantinople*"?

It seems that this identification, if at all possible, must be made after
deeper investigation and further study. The scope of our study does not
permit us to enter into it. In fact, what is more important for us here is
the mention of the *Twelve Chapters* or *Anathematisms of Cyril* and the
Henoticon in connection with the case of Ampelis and Anatolis. We
must note here that the mention of the *Twelve Anathematisms* is very
important because it gives us a hint to the understanding of the theological implications of this document and that of the *Henoticon* for the
understanding of the ecclesiastical policy.

14

It was indeed with a feeling of surprise that I became aware of the way
in which Fr V. Inglizean has tackled this problem.

He assumes that even in the time of the Council of Dowin (506), the
Armenians were still unaware of the Council of Chalcedon. So they
could not have taken any decision about it either before 506 or at the
Council of Dowin itself (see *Arm. Kirche*, p. 366). It was only after the
Council of Dowin and in the time of the writing of this second letter

that they became aware of these Monophysite troubles and acted along the directives of Simon of Beit-Aršam, who himself dictated the letter and made available to the Armenians the Monophysite writings (see *Arm. Kirche*, p. 367).

Is it at all possible to imagine Babgēn and his bishops being as ignorant as Inglizean thinks and wants us to believe? How would the leader of the Armenian Church and the heads of the Georgian and Albanian Churches together with their bishops allow a certain Syrian priest to dictate his view to a whole Church or to a body of Churches? Was the Armenian Church, which so strenuously opposed Nestorianism, left in the hands of Simon of Beit-Aršam? Is it not more reasonable to think that Simon already knew the attitude of the Armenian Church and on the basis of that knowledge and in the perfect hope and assurance of obtaining its support, came to Armenia?

There is no need to argue against Inglizean's view, which seems to be no more than the sheer repetition of an old-fashioned idea that the Armenians must not be blamed for their rejection of the Council of Chalcedon, because they were misled by the Syrian Monophysites! In other words, the Armenians were only victims of misguidance! I think that fifth century history and theology are quite eloquent to tell us that the Armenian Church was not theologically as poor as to be unable to make its own decisions in such matters of Christian doctrine.

The earlier chapters of our study contain the full answer to Inglizean's view.

TRANSLITERATION
SYSTEM

ա = a		**բ** = b	
գ = g		**դ** = d	
ե = e		**զ** = z	
** է** = ē		**ը** = ə	
թ = t'		**ժ** = ž	
ի = i		**լ** = l	
խ = x		**ծ** = c	
կ = k		**հ** = h	
ձ – ǰ		**ղ** = ł	
ճ = č		**մ** = m	
յ = y		**ն** = n	
շ = š		**ո** = o	
չ = č'		**պ** = p	
ջ = ǰ		**ռ** = r̄	
ս = s		**վ** = v	
տ = t		**ր** = r	
ց = ç		**ւ** = w	
փ = p'		**ք** = k'	
	ու = u		

237

BIBLIOGRAPHICAL
ABBREVIATIONS

Books or articles marked with an asterisk are written in the Armenian language.

*Abełean, *Literature*——M. Abełean, *History of the Ancient Arm. Literature*, vol. i (from the beginning to the tenth century), 2nd impression, Beirut, 1955.

*Abełean, *Koriwn*——M. Abełean, *Koriwn: "The Life of Maštoc"* (the text, critical edition based on various manuscripts, translation, introduction, and notes), Erevan, 1941; reprinted in Cairo, 1954. I have used this reprinted edition.

*Ačařean, *Mesrop*——H. Ačařean, *Mesrop Maštoc*, Antelias, 1953 (not complete. Originally published as a series of articles in Ejmiacin review. Reprinted in Hask).

A.C.O.——*Acta Conciliorum Oecumenicorum*, ed. by E. Schwartz, 1914 ff.

Adeney, *Eastern Churches*——W. F. Adeney, *The Greek and Eastern Churches*, Edinburgh, 1908.

*Adontz, *Maštoc*——N. Adontz, *Maštoc and his disciples according to foreign sources*, Vienna, 1925. (Originally published in *HA*, 1925, col. 193–202, 321–8, 435–41, 531–9.)

*Agat'angełos——*History of St Gregory and of the Conversion of Armenia*, Venice, 1862. (The critical edition, Tiflis, 1909, has not been available to me.)

*Akinean, *Kiwrion*——N. Akinean, *Kiwrion, Catholicos of the Georgians*, Vienna, 1910 (National Library, No. 60).

*Akinean, *Timothy*——N. Akinean, *Timothy Aelurus in Armenian Literature*, Vienna (National Library, No. 58).

*Akinean, *Maštoc*——N. Akinean, *Maštoc Vardapet Hacekaci*, art. in *HA*, t. 49 (1935), col. 505–50.

*Akinean, *Sahak*——N. Akinean, *Sahak the Great, Catholicos of the Armenians*, art. in *HA*, t. 49 (1935), col. 470–504.

*Akinean, *Armenian Alphabet*——N. Akinean, *The Invention of the Armenian Alphabet*, art. in *HA*, t. 52 (1938), col. 289–333.

*Akinean, *Šahapivan*——N. Akinean, *The Canons of the Council of Šahapivan*, Vienna, 1953 (reprinted from *HA*, 1949).

*Akinean, *Koriwn*——N. Akinean, *Koriwn: "The Life of St Maštoc"*, Vienna, 1952 (reprinted from *HA*, 1949).

Amadouni, *Hiéromoines Arméniens*——G. Amadouni, *Le Rôle historique des Hiéromoines Arméniens*, art. in *Il Monachismo Orientale*, pp. 279–305. See *Orientalia Christiana Analecta*, No. 153 (1958), Rome.

Amann, *Théodore*——E. Amann, *Théodore de Mopsueste*, art. in *D.T.C.*, t. xv, col. 235–79.

Amann, *Théopaschite (Controverse)*——E. Amann, art. in *D.T.C.*, t. xv, col. 505–12.

Amann, *Trois Chapitres*——E. Amann, *Trois Chapitres (Affaire de)*, art. in *D.T.C.*, t. xv, col. 1868–1924.

*Ananean, *Dowin Document*——P. Ananean, *A historical document on the second Council of Dowin*, in *Bazmavēp*, 1957, pp. 111–21, 1958, pp. 64–72, 117–31.

Appleyard, *Eastern Churches*——E. S. Appleyard, *Eastern Churches*, Containing sketches of the Nestorian, Armenian, Jacobite, Coptic, and Abyssinian Communities, London, 1850.

*Ararat——Religious and philological review of the Catholicosate of Ejmiacin, 1868–1916. It has been replaced since 1943 by *Ejmiacin*.

Arpee, *Armenian Christianity*——L. Arpee, *A History of Armenian Christianity*, New York, 1946.

Arsēn Saparaci——See Melik'set'-Bek.

Asdourian, *Armenian und Rom*——P. Asdourian, *Die politischen Beziehungen zwischen Armenien und Rom v. 190 v. Chr. bis 428*, Venice, 1911. (I have used the Armenian edition, Venice, 1912.)

Aslan, *Études historiques*——K. Aslan, *Études historiques sur le peuple arménien*, Paris, 1909.

Balgy, *Doctr. Cath. inter Arm.*——A. Balgy, *Historia doctrina catholica inter Armenos unionisque eorum cum Ecclesia romana in concilio Florentino*, Vienna, 1878.

Bardy, *Brigandage*——G. Bardy, *Le "Brigandage d'Éphèse" et le Concile de Chalcédoine*, in Fliche et Martin, *Histoire de l'Église*, vol. iv, pp. 211–40.

Bardy, *Chalcédoine*——G. Bardy, *Du Concile de Chalcédoine à l'avenement de Justin Ier.* (451–518), in Fliche et Martin, vol. iv, pp. 271–336.

Bardy, *Églises de Perse et d'Arménie*——G. Bardy, *Les Églises de Perse et d'Arménie au Ve. et au VIe. siècles*, in Fliche et Martin, vol. iv, pp. 321–36, 497–512.

Bardy, *Barsauma*——G. Bardy, *Barsauma*, art. in *D.H.G.E.*, t. vi, col. 948–50.

Bardy, *Théodoret*——G. Bardy, *Théodoret*, art. in *D.T.C.*, t. xv, col. 299–325.

Bardy, *Question des Langues*——G. Bardy, *La question des langues dans l'Église ancienne*, vol. i, Paris, 1948.

Barhébraeus, *Chronicon Ecclesiasticon*——G. Barhébraeus, *Chronicon Ecclesiasticon*, 3 volumes, ed. by J. B. Abbelos and T. J. Lamy, with a Latin translation, 1872–4.

Batiffol, *Siège Apostolique*——P. Batiffol, *Le Catholicisme des origines à Saint Léon*, t. iii: *Le Siège Apostolique* (359–451), Paris, 1924.

Baynes, *Rome and Armenia*——N. H. Baynes, *Rome and Armenia in the fourth century*, in *English Historical Review*, t. xxv (1910), pp. 625–43.

Bedjan, *Héraclide*——P. Bedjan, *Le Livre d'Héraclide de Damas* (the Syriac text of Nestorius' *Heraclides*—see the Introduction and the Appendixes), Paris, 1910.

Bidez, *Evagrius*——J. Bidez and L. Parmentier, *The Ecclesiastical History of Evagrius* (the Greek text with introduction, critical notes, and indexes), London, 1898.

B.L.——*Book of Letters—Girk T'lt'oc*—in the "Sahak-Mesropean Library", vol. v, Tiflis, 1901.

Bréhier, *Justinien*——L. Bréhier, *La politique religieuse de Justinien*, in Fliche et Martin, t. iv, pp. 437–82.

Bréhier, *Successeurs de Justinien*——L. Bréhier, *Les successeurs de Justinien*, in Fliche et Martin, pp. 483–93.

Bréhier, *Anastase*——L. Bréhier, *Anastase*, art. in *D.H.G.E.*, t. ii, col. 1447–57.

Brière, *Légende de Nestorius*——M. Brière, *La Légende Syriaque de Nestorius*, in *R.O.C.*, t. v (15), (1910), pp. 1–25. (Syriac text with French translation.)

Burkitt, *Eastern Christianity*——F. C. Burkitt, *Early Eastern Christianity*, London, 1904.

Bury, *Lat. Rom. Emp.*——J. B. Bury, *History of the Later Roman Empire*, 2 volumes, London, 1923.

*Č'amč'ean, History——Fr M. Č'amč'ean, *History of the Armenians from the beginning to* A.D. *1784*, in six books, 3 volumes, Venice, 1784–86.

Camelot, *Théologies*——P. Th. Camelot, *Théologies Grecques et Théologie Latine à Chalcédoine*, in *R.S.Ph.Th.*, t. xxxv (1951), pp. 401–02.

Cavallera, *Timothée*——F. Cavallera, *Le Dossier Patristique de Timothée Aelure*, in *Bulletin de Littérature Ecclésiastique*, 1909, pp. 342–59.

Chabot, *École de Nisibe*——J. B. Chabot, *L'École de Nisibe, son histoire, ses statuts* (extrait du *Journal Asiatique*—9ème. série, t. viii, Juillet-Août, 1896), Paris, 1896.

Chabot, *Synodicon Orientale*——J. B. Chabot, *Synodicon Orientale ou Recueil de Synodes Nestoriens* (Syriac text with French translation), Paris, 1902.

Chabot, *Michel le Syrien*——J. B. Chabot, *Chronique de Michel le Syrien, Patriarche Jacobite d'Antioche* (3 volumes: French translation), Paris, 1901–5.

Chabot, *Litt. Syriaque*——J. B. Chabot, *Littérature Syriaque*, Paris, 1935.

Chadwick, *Eucharist and Christology*——H. Chadwick, *Eucharist and Christology in the Nestorian controversy*, in *J.T.S.*, New Series, vol. ii (1951), pp. 145–64.

Charanis, *Anastasius*——P. Charanis, *Church and State in the Later Roman Empire. The religious policy of Anastasius I* (Univ. of Wisconsin Studies in the Social Sciences and History, 26), Madison, U.S.A., 1939.

Christensen, *Iran Sassanide*——A. Christensen, *L'Iran sous les Sassanides* (deuxième édition revue et augmentée), Copenhagen, 1944.

D'Alès, *Symbole de 433*——A. d'Alès, *Le Symbole de l'année 433 et la première école Nestorienne*, in *Rech.S.R.*, t. xxi (1931), pp. 257–68.

D'Alès, *Lettre d'Ibas*——A. d'Alès, *Lettre d'Ibas à Marès le Persan* in *Rech. S.R.*, t. xxii (1932), pp. 5–25.

Demougeot, *Empire Romain*——E. Demougeot, *De l'unité à la division de l'Empire Romain (395–410)*, Paris, 1951.

Der-Nersessian, *Arm. Byz. Emp.*——S. Der-Nersessian, *Armenia and the Byzantine Empire*: A brief study of Armenian Art and Civilization, Preface by H. Grégoire, Cambridge, Mass., 1947.

Devreesse, *Après Éphèse*——R. Devreesse, *Après le concile d'Éphèse le retour des Orientaux à l'unité (433-7)*, in *E.O.*, t. xxx (1931), pp. 271–92.

Devreesse, *Trois Chapitres*——R. Devreesse, *Le début de la querelle des Trois Chapitres*, in *Rev S. R.*, t. xi (1931), pp. 543–65.

Devreesse, *Antioche*——R. Devreesse, *Le Patriarchat d'Antioche depuis la paix de l'Église jusqu'à la conquête arabe*, Paris, 1945.

Devreesse, *Ve. Concile*——R. Devreesse, *Le Cinquième Concile et l'œcuménicité byzantine*, in *Studi e Testi*, No. 123 (Miscellanea Giovanni Mercati, iii, pp. 1–15, Vatican, 1946.

Devreesse, *Essai*——R. Devreesse, *Essai su Théodore de Mopsueste* in *Studi e Testi*, No. 141, Roma, 1948.

Diepen, *Assumptus Homo*——H. Diepen, *L'Assumptus Homo à Chalcédoine*, in *Revue Thomiste*, 1951, p. 573–608.

Diepen, *Trois Chapitres*——H. M. Diepen, *Les Trois Chapitres au concile de Chalcédoine: une étude de la Christologie de l'Anatolie Ancienne*, Oosterhout, 1953.

Dombalis, *1500th Anniversary*——C. N. Dombalis, *A Symposium on the Occasion of the 1500th Anniversary of the Council of Chalcedon*, in *Ecumenical Review*, vol. iv (1952), No. 4, pp. 393–404. See the articles of G. Florovsky and A. Schmemann.

Doucin, *Hist. Nest.*——P. L. Doucin, *Histoire du Nestorianisme*, Paris, 1698.

Dowling, *Armenian Church*——T. E. Dowling, *The Armenian Church*, London, 1910.

Draguet, *Julien d'Halicarnasse*——R. Draguet, *Julien d'Halicarnasse*, Louvain, 1924.

Duchesne, *Autonomies*——L. Duchesne, *Autonomies Ecclésiastiques—Églises Séparées*, 2me. édition, Paris, 1905.

Duchesne, *Separated Churches*——L. Duchesne, *The Churches Separated from Rome*, tr. by A. H. Matthew, London, 1907.

Duchesne, *Church History*——L. Duchesne, *Early History of the Christian Church*, tr. by C. Jenkins, London, 1914–24.

Duchesne, *Église VIe. siècle*——L. Duchesne, *L'Église au VIe. siècle*, Paris, 1935.

Dulaurier, *Église Arménienne*——E. Dulaurier, *Histoire, Dogmes, Traditions, et Liturgie de l'Église Arménienne Orientale*, Paris, 1855.

Dulaurier, *Chronologie Arménienne*——E. Dulaurier, *Recherches sur la Chronologie Arménienne*, Paris, 1859.

Duval, *Histoire d'Édesse*——R. Duval, *Histoire politique, religieuse et littéraire d'Édesse jusqu'à la première Croisade*, Paris, 1892.

Duval, *Litt. Syriaque*——R. Duval, *La Littérature Syriaque*, Paris, 1899.

Dyer, *Armenian Church*——S. A. Dyer, *The Armenian Church—NOT Eutychian*. A latter article in *The Guardian*, 12 December 1888, p. 1899.

*Ełišē, *History*——Ełišē, *History of Vardan*, critical edition by E. Tēr-Minaseanç, Erevan, 1957. A recent English translation by S. Boyadjian, New York, 1952; French translation in Langlois, *Historiens Arméniens*, vol. ii, pp. 183–251.

Evagrius——*Ecclesiastical History*, in six Books, tr. from the Greek text, London, 1846. See also Bidez.

Every, *Byzantine Patriarchate*——G. Every, *The Byzantine Patriarchate 451–1204*, London, 1947.

*Eznik——*Ełc Ałandoç* (*Adversus Haereses*), Venice, 1862. A recent critical edition has just been published in *P.O.*, prepared by P. L. Mariès. I have not seen it.

*Fenteglean, *Koriwn*——G. Fenteglean, *Koriwn: The Life of Maštoç*. Text established and commented by G. F. with an Introduction, Jerusalem, 1930.

Festugière, *Antioche*——A. J. Festugière, *Antioche Paienne et Chrétienne*, Paris, 1959.

Fortescue, *Eastern Churches*——A. Fortescue, *The Lesser Eastern Churches*, London, 1913.

Fortescue, *Armenian Church*——E. F. K. Fortescue, *The Armenian Church: A sketch of the History, Liturgy, Doctrine, and ceremonies of this ancient national Church*. With an appendix on the Confession of Faith and Baptism by S. C. Malan, London, 1872.

*Gabrielean, *Armenian Philosophy*——H. Gabrielean, *History of Armenian Philosophical Thought*, vol. i, Erevan, 1956.

Galanus, *Conciliationis*——C. Galanus, *Conciliationis Ecclesiae Armeniae cum Romana, ex ipsis Armenorum Patrum et Doctorum testimoniis, in duas partes, historialem et controversialem divisae*, Rome, 1650, 1658, 1661 (three volumes).

Galtier, *Cyrille et Léon*——P. Galtier, *St Cyrille d'Alexandrie et St Léon le Grand à Chalcédoine*, in *Das Konzil von Chalkedon*, vol. i, pp. 345–87.

Garitte, *Narratio*——G. Garitte, *La Narratio de Rebus Armeniae*—Édition critique et Commentaire, in the series "*C.S.C.O.*", vol. cxxxii, Subsidia, t. 4, Louvain, 1952.

Gibbon, *Roman Empire*——E. Gibbon, *The History of the Decline and Fall of the Roman Empire*, ed. by J. B. Bury, 7 volumes, London, 1909–14.

Goubert, *Byzance*——P. Goubert, *Byzance avant l'Islam*, Tome I: *Byzance et l'Orient sous les successeurs de Justinien, l'Empereur Maurice*, Paris, 1951.

Goubert, *Pulchérie*——P. Goubert, *Le rôle de sainte Pulchérie et de l'eunuque Chrysaphios*, in *Das Konzil von Chalkedon*, vol. i, pp. 303–21.

Goubert, *Successeurs de Justinien*——P. Goubert, *Les successeurs de Justinien et le Monophysisme* in *Das Konzil von Chalkedon*, vol. ii, pp. 179–92.

Goubert *Géorgie*——P. Goubert, *Évolution politique et religieuse de la Géorgie à la fin du VIe. siècle*, in *Mémorial Louis Petit*, Bucarest, 1948.

Greenslade, *Schism*——S. L. Greenslade, *Schism in the Early Church*, London, 1953.

Grégoire, *Peuple de CP*——H. Grégoire, *Le peuple de Constantinople ou les Bleus et les Verts*, in *Comptes Rendus de l'Académie des Inscriptions et Belles Lettres*, pp. 568–78, Paris, 1946.

Grousset, *Histoire d'Arménie*——R. Grousset, *Histoire de l'Arménie*, Paris, 1947.

*Haçuni, *Important Problems*——V. Haçuni, *Important Problems of Armenian Church History*, Venice, 1927.

Hamilton and Brooks, *Zachariah*——F. I. Hamilton and E. W. Brooks, *The Syriac Chronicle known as that of Zachariah of Mitylene*, Engl. tr., London, 1899.

Hayes, *École d'Édesse*——E. R. Hayes, *L'École d'Édesse (Thèse de doctorat)*, Paris, 1930.

HA——*Handēs Amsorya*, Armenian philological review, published by the Armenian Mekhitarist Community in Vienna, 1887- .

Hannestad, *Relations*——*Les Relations de Byzance avec la Transcaucasie et l'Asie centrale aux 5e et 6e siècles* in *Byzantion*, t. xxv, xxvi, xxvii (1955-56-57), pp. 421–56, Bruxelles, 1957.

Hefele, *Conciles*——C. J. Hefele, *Histoire des Conciles d'apres les documents originaux*, tr. and ed. by H. Leclercq, Paris, 1907- .

Hefele, *Councils*——C. J. Hefele, *A History of the Councils of the Church from the original sources*, Eng. tr., vol. iii, A.D. 431 to A.D. 451, Edinburgh, 1883.

Honigmann, *Original Lists*——E. Honigmann, *The Original Lists of the members of the Council of Nicaea, the Robber-Synod and the Council of Chalcedon*, in *Byzantion*, t. xvi (1942/43), pp. 20–80.

Honigmann, *Juvenal*——E. Honigmann, *Juvenal of Jerusalem*, in *Dumbarton Oaks Papers*, 5 (1950), pp. 209–79.

Honigmann, *Évêques*——E. Honigmann, *Évêques et évêchés monophysites d'Asie Antérieure au VIe. siècle*, in the series *"C.S.C.O."*, vol. cxxvii, Subsidia, t. ii, Louvain, 1951.

Hore, *Orthodox Church*——A. H. Hore, *Eighteen centuries of the Orthodox Greek Church*, London, 1899.

*Inglizean, *Three Chapters*——V. Inglizean, *Armenia in the midst of the early quarrels over the Three Chapters*, National Library, vol. clxxxi, Vienna, 1957.

Inglizean, *Arm. Kirche*——V. Inglizean, *Chalkedon und die armenische Kirche* in *Das Konzil von Chalkedon*, vol. ii, pp. 361–416.

Innocentius Maroniae——*Innocentii Episcopi Maroniae de his qui unum ex Trinitate Iesum Christum dubitant confiteri*, in *A.C.O.*, t. iv, vol. ii, pp. 68–74.

Issaverdens, *Armenia*——J. Issaverdens, *Armenia and the Armenians*, vol. ii: *Ecclesiastical History*, Venice, 1877.

Jalland, *Leo the Great*——T. G. Jalland, *The Life and Times of St Leo the Great*, London, 1941.

Jalland, *Church and Papacy*——T. G. Jalland, *The Church and the Papacy: A Historical Study*, London, 1949.

Janin, *Églises Orientales*——R. Janin, *Les Églises Orientales et les Rites Orientaux*, Paris, 1955.

Janin, *Amphiloque*——R. Janin, *Amphiloque*, art. in *D.H.G.E.*, t. ii, col. 1348.

Jugie, *Nestorius*——M. Jugie, *Nestorius et la controverse nestorienne*, Paris, 1912.

Jugie, *Eutychès*——M. Jugie, *Eutychès et Eutychianisme*, art. in *D.T.C.*, t. v, col. 1582–1609.

Jugie, *Monophysisme*——M. Jugie, *Monophysisme*, art. in *D.T.C.*, t. x, col. 2216–51.

Jugie, *Theologia Monophysitarum*——M. Jugie, *Theologia Dogmatica Christianorum Orientalium ab ecclesia Catholica Dissidentum*, vol. v: *De Theologia Dogmatica Nestorianorum et Monophysitarum*, Paris, 1935.

Kelly, *Creeds*——J. N. D. Kelly, *Early Christian Creeds*, London, 1950.

Kelly, *Doctrines*——J. N. D. Kelly, *Early Christian Doctrines*, London, 1958.

Kidd, *Documents*——J. B. Kidd, *Documents illustrative of the History of the Church*, vol. ii: A.D. 313–461, London, 1923.

Kidd, *Church History*——J. B. Kidd, *A History of the Church*, vol. iii: A.D. 408–61, Oxford, 1922.

Kidd, *Eastern Christendom*——J. B. Kidd, *The Churches of Eastern Christendom* (from 451 to the present time), London, 1927.

King, *Rites Eastern Christianity*——A. A. King, *The Rites of Eastern Christendom*, 2 volumes, Rome, 1947.

*K'iparean, *Literature*——K. K'iparean, *History of Armenian Literature*, pt. i: from the beginning to A.D. 1700, Venice, 1944.

*Kiwlēsērean, *Armenian Church*——B. Kiwlēsērean, *The Armenian Church*, Jerusalem, 1930.

Koriwn, *The Life of St Maštoç*——See Abelean, Akinean, Fenteglean.

Labourt, *Christ. Perse*——J. Labourt, *Le Christianisme dans l'Empire Perse sous la dynastie Sassanide* (224–632), Paris, 1904.

Langlois, *Historiens Arméniens*——V. Langlois, *Collection des Historiens anciens et modernes d'Arménie*, 2 volumes, Paris, 1867.

Lantscoot, *Bêth Lapat*——A. van Lantscoot, *Bêth Lapat*, art. in *D.H.G.E.*, col. 1233–5.

Laurent, *Arm. Byz. Isl.*——J. Laurent, *L'Arménie entre Byzance et l'Islam, depuis la conquête arabe jusqu'en 886*, Paris, 1919.

*Łazarean, *Armenian Language*——S. Łazarean, *A Concise History of the Armenian Language*, Erevan, 1954.

Lebon, *Monophysisme Sévérien*——J. Lebon, *Le Monophysisme sévérien*: Étude historique, littéraire et théologique sur la résistance monophysite au Concile de Chalcédoine jusqu'à la constitution de l'église Jacobite, Louvain, 1909.

Lebon, *Citations patristiques*——J. Lebon, *Les Citations patristiques Grecques du " Sceau de la Foi"*, in *R.H.E.*, t. xxx (1929), pp. 5–32.

Lebon, *Les Symboles*——J. Lebon, *Les Anciens Symboles dans la Définition de Chalcédoine*, in *R.H.E.*, t. xxxii (1936), pp. 809–76.

Lebon, *Monophysisme Syrien*——J. Lebon, *Monophysisme Syrien*, in *Das Konzil von Chalkedon*, vol. i.

Leclercq, *Litt. Arm.*——H. Leclercq, *Littérature Arménienne*, art. in *D.A.C.L.*, t. ix, col. 1576–99.

Le Quien, *Oriens Christianus*——M. le Quien, *Oriens Christianus*, in *Quatuor Patriarchatus Digestis*, Parisiis, 1740.

Levenq, *Bêth Garmai*——G. Levenq, *Bêth Garmai*, in *D.H.G.E.*, col. 1230–3.

Liberatus——*Breviarum Causae Nestorianorum et Eutychianorum*, in *P.L.*, t. lxviii.

Lightfoot, *Amphilochius*——J. R. Lightfoot, *Amphilochius*, art. in *D.C.B.*, vol. i, p. 107.

Lightfoot, *Acacius*——J. R. Lightfoot, *Acacius*, art. in *D.C.B.*, vol. i, p. 14.

Loofs, *Nestorius*——F. Loofs, *Nestorius and his place in the history of Christian Doctrine*, Cambridge, 1919.

Macler, *Armenia*——F. Macler, *Armenia (Christian)*, art. in Hastings *E.R.E.*, vol. i, pp. 802–7.

Malan, *Gregory*——S. C. Malan, *The Life and Times of S. Gregory the Illuminator*, the founder and Patron saint of the Armenian Church, tr. from the Armenian, London, 1868.

★Malxaseanc̣, *Xorenac̣i-Introduction*——S. Malxaseanc̣, *Movses Xorenac̣i: History of Armenia*, translation, introduction and critical notes, 2nd impression, Cairo, 1953. (I have used the *Introduction*.)

★Malxaseanc̣, *Xorenac̣i-Riddle*——S. Malxaseanc̣, *On the Riddle of Xorenac̣i* (see Appendix III, pp. 130–44), Erevan, 1940.

★Malxaseanc̣, *Dictionary*——Malxaseanc̣, *Expository Dictionary of the Armenian Language*, 4 volumes, 2nd impression, Beirut, 1955.

★Manandean, *Hellenizing School*——H. Manandean, *The Hellenizing School and the periods of its development* in *Handēs Amsorya*, t. xxxix (1925), 225–32, 347–54, 539–48; t. xl (1926), 15–23, 121–9, 209–16, 305–13, 437–45, 525–33; t. xli (1927), 16–23, 109–16, 289–301, 417–425, 559–69; t. xlii (1928), 25–30, 109–20, 205–13, 303–10, 401–7.

★Manandean, *Critical History*——H. Manandean, *A Critical Survey of the History of the Armenian people*, vol ii, pt. i: From the foundation of the Arsacid Kingdom in Armenia to the period of the Marzbans (I–V centuries), Erevan, 1957.

★Manandean, *Armenian Alphabet*——H. Manandean, *On the problem of the date of the invention of the Armenian Alphabet*, in *Bulletin of the Academy of Sciences of the Armenian S.S.R.*, No. 7 (1952), pp. 41–57.

Mandakuni, *Homilies*——Y. Mandakuni, *Homilies* (*Čaṙkʻ*), 2nd edition, Venice, 1860.

Mandakuni, *Demonstration*——Y. Mandakuni, *Demonstration of why to confess the Saviour "Of Two Natures" or "One Nature"*, B.L., pp. 29–40.

Mariès, *De Deo d'Eznik*——L. Mariès, *Le De Deo d'Eznik de Kolb, connu sous le nom de Contre les Sectes, Étude de critique littéraire et textuelle*, Paris, 1924.

Martin, *Église d'Édesse*——J. P. Martin, *Les origines de l'Église d'Édesse et des Églises syriennes*, Paris, 1889.

Mécérian, *Bulletin Arménologique*——J. Mécérian, *Bulletin Arménologique*, in *Mélanges de l'Université St Joseph*, pp. 177–312, t. xxvii (1947). Beirut.

Mécérian, *Bilan*——J. Mécérian, *Bilan des relations Arméno-Iraniennes au Ve. siècle*, in *Bulletin Arménologique*, 2me. cahier. See *Mélanges de l'Université St Joseph*, t. xxx (1953), Beirut.

*Melikʻ-Bašxean, *Paulician Movement*——S. Melikʻ-Bašxean, *The Paulician Movement in Armenia*, University publication, Erevan, 1953.

*Melikʻsetʻ-Bek, *Georgian Sources*——L. Melikʻsetʻ-Bek, *The Georgian Sources on Armenia and the Armenians* (translations of Georgian documents concerning the history of Armenia—3 volumes), vol. i: V–XII centuries, Erevan, 1934.

*Melikʻtʻangean, *Canon Law*——N. Melikʻtʻangean, *The Canon Law of the Armenian Church*, Introduction and Sources, Shoushi, 1903.

Michael Syrus——See Chabot.

Moeller, *Ve. Concile*——C. Moeller, *Le Ve. concile œcuménique et le magistère ordinaire au VIe. siècle*, in *Rev. S. Ph.Th.*, t. xxxv (1951), pp. 413–32.

Moeller, *Néo-Chalcédonisme*——C. Moeller, *Le Chalcédonisme et le Néo-Chalcédonisme en Orient de 451 à la fin du VIe. siècle*, in *Das Konzil von Chalkedon*, vol. i, p. 637–720.

Mozley, *Libanius*——J. R. Mozley, *Libanius*, art. in *D.C.B.*, vol. iii, pp. 709–12.

Murphy, *Peter speaks through Leo*——F. X. Murphy, *Peter Speaks Through Leo: The Council of Chalcedon*, Washington, 1952.

Narsès, *Trois Docteurs*——Narsès, *Homélie de Narsès sur les Trois Docteurs Nestoriens*, ed. and tr. by Abbé F. Martin, in *Journal Asiatique*, 9me. série, t. xiv (1899), pp. 446–92 (intr. and text), t. xv (1900), pp. 469–525 (translation).

Nau, *Héraclide*——F. Nau, *Nestorius: "Le Livre d'Héraclide de Damas"* (French translation), Paris, 1910.

Nau, *Acace*——F. Nau, *Acace*, art. in *D.H.G.E.*, t. i, col. 244.

Neale, *Eastern Church*——J. M. Neale, *A History of the Holy Eastern Church*, pt. i: *General Introduction* (2 volumes), London, 1850.

Nersoyan, *Doctrinal Position*——T. Nersoyan, *The Doctrinal position of the Armenian Church* (a paper), New York.

Nève, *Arménie Chrétienne*——F. Nève, *L'Arménie Chrétienne et sa Littérature*, Louvain, 1888.

Nicolas, *Christologie de St Léon*——M.-J. Nicolas, *La Doctrine christologique de saint Léon*, in *Revue Thomiste*, 1951, pp. 609–60.

*Ormanean, *Azgapatum*——M. Ormanean, *Azgapatum: History of the Armenian Nation* (3 volumes), vol. i, Constantinople, 1913.

Ormanean, *Armenian Church*——M. Ormanean, *The Church of Armenia*, tr. by M. Gregory, 2nd edition by T. Poladian, London, 1954.

Pargoire, *Église Byzantine*——P. J. Pargoire, *L'Église Byzantine de 527 à 847*, Paris, 1905.

*P'arpeci——Łazar P'arpeci (Lazar of Pharbi), *History of Armenia and the letter to Vahan Mamikonean*, crit. edition by G. Tēr-Mkrtč'ean and S. Malxaseanc in the series "Armenian Historiographers", Tiflis, 1904. (I have used also the Venice edition.)

Peeters, *Origines*——P. Peeters, *Pour l'histoire des origines de l'alphabet arménien*, in *Revue des Études arméniennes*, t. ix (1929), pp. 203–38. Reprinted in *Recherches d'histoire et de philologie orientales* (2 volumes) in the series "Subsidia Hagiographica" (No. 27), vol. i, pp. 171–207, Bruxelles, 1951.

Peeters, *Jérémie*——P. Peeters, *Jérémie évêque de l'Ibérie Perse*, in *Analecta Bollandiana*, vol. li (1933), pp. 5–25.

Peeters, *Rabboula*——P. Peeters, *La vie de Rabboula, évêque d'Édesse*, in *Rech. S.R.*, t. xviii (1928), pp. 170–204.

Peeters, *Jacques*——P. Peeters, *La légende de saint Jacques de Nisibe*, in *Analecta Bollandiana*, t. xxxviii (1920), pp. 285–373.

Petit, *Arménie*——L. Petit, *Arménie*, in *D.T.C.*, t. i, col. 1888–1968.

Photius, *Letter to Zachariah*, in Papadopoulos-Kerameus, *Fotija*, St Petersbourg, 1892. I have not seen the book. The extract of the letter is reproduced in Garitte, *Narratio*.

Photius, *Bibliotheca*——See Migne, *P.G.*, t. ciii.

Prestige, *Fathers and Heretics*——G. L. Prestige, *Fathers and Heretics*: six studies in Dogmatic Faith with prologue and epilogue (Bampton Lectures, 1940), London, 1954.

Ramsay, *Asia Minor*——W. M. Ramsay, *The Historical Geography of Asia Minor*, London, 1890.

Ramsay, *Church Rom. Emp.*——W. M. Ramsay, *The Church in the Roman Empire before* A.D. 170, 9th ed., London, 1907.

Richard, *Proclus*——M. Richard, *Proclus de Constantinople et le Théopaschisme* in *R.H.E.*, t. xxxviii (1942), pp. 303–31.

Richard, *Fragments*——M. Richard, *La tradition des fragments du traité* περὶ τῆς ἐνανθρωπήσεως *de Théodore de Mopsueste*, in *Le Muséon*, t. lvi (1943), pp. 55–75.

Richard, *Néo-Chalcédonisme*——M. Richard, *Le Néo-Chalcédonisme*, in *Mél. S.R.*, t. iii (1946), pp. 156–61.

Richard, *Acace*——M. Richard, *Acace de Mélitène, Proclus de Constantinople et la Grande Arménie*, in *Mémorial Louis Petit—Mélanges d'histoire et d'archéologie Byzantines* (Archives de l'Orient Chrétien), Bucarest, 1948.

Rouziès, *Acace*——U. Rouziès, *Acace*, art. in *D.H.G.E.*, t. i, col. 242–3.

Rycaut, *Greek, Arm. Churches*——P. Rycaut, *The present state of the Greek and Armenian Churches*, London, 1679.

Salaville, *Hénotique*——S. Salaville, *L'Affaire de l'Hénotique ou le premier schisme byzantin au Ve. siècle*, in *Echos d'Orient*, t. xviii (1918), pp. 255–66, 389–97, t. xix (1920), pp. 49–68.

*Sargisean, *Mandakuni*——B. Sargisean, *Critical study on John Mandakuni and his writings*, Venice, 1895.

Scher, *Histoire Nestorienne*——*Histoire Nestorienne (Chronique de Séert)*, tr. from the Arabic text by Mgr A. Scher, in *P.O.*, t. iv (1906–8), pp. 215–312, t. vii (1911), pp. 97–203.

Sellers, *Chalcedon*——R. V. Sellers, *The Council of Chalcedon*; A historical and doctrinal survey, London, 1953.

Simeon Beth-Aršam, *Epistola*——*Epistola Beth-Arsamensis de Barsauma espiscopo Nisibeno, deque heresi Nestorianorum* in *Assemani, Bibl. Orient.*, vol. i, pp. 346–58.

Simon, *Chrétiens Orientaux*——R. Simon, *Histoire critique des dogmes, des coutumes et des cérémonies des Chrétiens Orientaux*, Trevoux, 1711.

Stanley, *Eastern Church*——A. P. Stanley, *Lectures on the history of the Eastern Church*, London, 1889.

Stein, *Bas-Empire*——E. Stein, *Histoire du Bas-Empire. De la disparition de l'Empire d'Occident à la mort de Justinien, 476-565*, t. ii, Belgium, 1949.

Sullivan, *Christology*——F. Sullivan, *The Christology of Theodore of Mopsuestia*, in the series of *Analecta Gregoriana*, vol. lxxxii, Rome, 1956.

Tallon, *Livre des Lettres*——M. Tallon, *Livre des Lettres (Girkʻ Tʻłtʻoc)*, Ier. groupe: Documents concernant les relations avec les Grecs, extract from *Mélanges de l'Université St Joseph*, t. xxxii (1955), Fasc. i, pp. 1–146, Beyrouth, 1955.

Tamarati, *Église Géorgienne*——M. Tamarati, *L'Église Géorgienne des origines jusqu'à nos jours*, Rome, 1910.

Tchéraz, *Égl. Arm.*——M. Tchéraz, *L'Église arménienne, son histoire, ses croyances*, in *Le Muséon*, 1897, pp. 232–42, 324–9.

Tékéyan, *Controverses Christologiques*——P. Tékéyan, *Controverses Christologiques en Arméno-Cilicie dans la seconde moitié du XII siècle (1165–1198)*, in the series *Analecta Christiana Orientalia*, vol. cxxiv, Rome, 1939.

Tēr-Mikelean, *Arm. Kirche*——A. Tēr-Mikelean, *Die Armenische Kirche in ihren Beziehungen zur byzantinischen, vom IV. bis zum XIII. Jahrhundert*, Jena, 1892. (I have used the Armenian version published in the same year in Moscow.)

Tēr-Minaseanç, *Arm. Kirche*——E. Tēr-Minassiantz, *Die armenische Kirche in ihren Beziehungen zu den syrischen Kirchen bis zum ende des 13. Jahrhunderts*, in the series *Texte und Untersuchungen*, vol. xxvi, Leipzig, 1904. (I have used the Armenian edition made by the author himself and enriched with further additions, Ejmiacin, 1908.)

*Tēr-Minaseanç, *Nestorianism*——E. Tēr-Minaseanç, *Nestorianism in Armenia*, in *Literary and Philological Researches*, vol. i, pp. 175–242, Erevan, 1946.

*Tēr-Mkrtčʻean, *Timothy*——G. Tēr-Mkrtčʻean, *The date of the Armenian translation of Timothy Aelurus' Refutation and the third Armenian translation of the Holy Scriptures*, in *Ararat*, 1908, pp. 564–89.

*Tēr-Mkrtčʻean, *Paulikianer*——K. Tēr-Mkrttschian, *Die Paulikianer im byzantinischen Kaiserreiche und verwandte Ketzerische Erscheinungen in Armenien*, Leipzig, 1893. (I have used the Armenian translation made by A. Abełean and published in Jerusalem, 1938.)

*Tēr-Mkrtč'ean, *Christ's Nature*——K. Tēr-Mkrtč'ean, *Our view and the view of Mekhitarist Fathers concerning the problem of Christ's Nature*, in *Ararat*, 1896, pp. 155–64.

*Ter-Mkrtč'ean, *Participation*——K. Tēr-Mkrtč'ean, *Babgēn Catholicos and the first participation of the Armenian Church in the doctrinal controversies*, in *Ararat*, 1898, pp. 431–46.

Tēr-Mkrtč'ean, *Misunderstandings*——K. Tēr-Mkrtč'ean, *Misunderstandings about the past history of the Armenian Church*, in *Ararat*, 1902, pp. 807–34.

*Tēr-Mkrtč'ean, *Mandakuni*——K. Tēr-Mkrtč'ean, *John Mandakuni and John Mayragomeçi* (extract from *Solakat'*) Ejmiacin, 1913.

*Tēr-Mkrtč'ean, *Seal of Faith, Introduction*——K. Tēr-Mkrtč'ean, *The "Seal of Faith"*, edition of the text, with a remarkable Introduction, Ejmiacin, 1914.

*Thomas Arcruni——*History of the House of Arcrunik'*, Constantinople, 1852.

Thorossian, *Littérature*——H. Thorossian, *Histoire de la Littérature arménienne, des origines jusqu'à nos jours*, Paris, 1951.

*Timothy Aelurus——*Refutation of the Definitions of the Council of Chalcedon*, ed. by Tēr-Mkrtč'ean and E. Tēr-Minaseanc, Ejmiacin, 1908.

Tisserant, *Jacques*——E. Tisserant, *Jacques de Nisibe*, art. in *D.T.C.*, t. viii, col. 292–5.

Tisserant, *Narsai*——E. Tisserant, *Narsai, Fundateur de l'École de Nisibe*, art. in *D.T.C.*, t. xi, col. 26–30.

Tisserant, *Nestorienne*——E. Tisserant, *Nestorienne (l'Église)*, art. in *D.T.C.*, t. xi, col. 157–263.

Tixeront, *Dogmes*——J. Tixeront, *Histoire des Dogmes dans l'Antiquité Chrétienne*, vol. iii: *La Fin de l'âge Patristique* (430–800), Paris, 1928.

Tixeront, *Église d'Édesse*——J. Tixeront, *Les origines de l'Église d'Édesse et la légende d'Abgar*, Paris, 1888.

T'op'čean, *Arm. Monchtum*——*Die Anfänge des armenischen Monchtums*. (I have seen the Armenian translation in Luys, Nos. 15, 19, 22.

Tournebize, *Histoire*——F. Tournebize, *Histoire politique et religieuse de l'Arménie*, Paris, 1900.

Tournebize, *Arménie*——F. Tournebize, *Arménie*, art. in *D.H.G.E.*, vol. iv.

Vailhé, *Église Arménienne*——S. Vailhé, *Formation de l'Église Arménienne*, in *Echos d'Orient*, t. xvi (1913), pp. 109–22, 193–211.

*Vardanean, *Proclus*——A. Vardanean, *The Letter of Bishop Proclus to St Sahak the Armenian Catholicos and to St Maštoc̣*, in *HA*, t. xxxv (1921), col. 1–25.

Vasiliev, *Byzantine Empire*——A. A. Vasiliev, *History of the Byzantine Empire*, 2 volumes, Madison, 1958.

Vasiliev, *Justin*——A. A. Vasiliev, *Justin the First. An introduction to the epoch of Justinian the Great* (Dumbarton Oaks Studies, i), Cambridge, Mass., 1950.

Venables, *Ibas*——E. Venables, *Ibas*, art. in *D.C.B.*, vol. ii, pp. 192–6.

Vine, *Nestorian Churches*——A. R. Vine, *The Nestorian Churches*: A concise history of Nestorian Christianity in Asia from the Persian Schism to the modern Assyrians, London, 1937.

Vööbus, *Syrian Asceticism*——A. Vööbus, *History of Asceticism in the Syrian Orient*, vol. i: *The origin of Asceticism; Early Monasticism in Persia*, in the series *C.S.C.O.*, vol. clxxxiv, Subsidia, t. 4, Louvain, 1958.

Weber, *Arm. Kirche*——S. Weber, *Die katholische Kirche in Armenien*, Freiburg im Breisgau, 1903.

Weber, *Hatschachapatum*——S. Weber u. E. Sommer, *Ausgewählte Reden aus dem Hatschachapatum* (5. Jahrhundert) hl. Mesrop, in the *Ausgewählte Schriften der armenischen Kirchenväter*, ed. by S. Weber, vol. i, pp. 233–318. See Introduction. Published in the series *Bibliothek der Kirchenväter*, Bd. 57, Munchen, 1927.

Wigram, *Doctrinal Position*——W. A. Wigram, *The Doctrinal Position of the Assyrian or East Syrian Church*, London, 1908.

Wigram, *Assyr. Church*——W. A. Wigram, *An Introduction to the History of the Assyrian Church or the Church of the Sassanid Persian Empire*, London, 1910.

Wigram, *Separation*——W. A. Wigram, *The Separation of the Monophysites*, London, 1923.

Williams, *Armenians*——G. Williams, *Armenians*, art. in *D.C.B.*, vol. i, pp. 163–6.

*Xorenac̣i, *History*——M. Xorenac̣i, *The Writings of Movsēs Xorenac̣i,* Venice, 1865.

*Xorenac̣i——(*Treatise*) of the Blessed Bishop Movsēs Xorenac̣i, the great Rhetor, see *B.L.*, pp. 22–8.

*Yač̣axapatum——*The Homilies of St Gregory*, Venice, 1830.

Zachariah, *Chronicle*——See Hamilton and Brooks.

INDEX OF PROPER NAMES

INDEX OF SUBJECTS